Inhospitable World

INHOSPITABLE WORLD
Cinema in the Time of the Anthropocene

Jennifer Fay

Oxford University Press is a department of the University of Oxford. It furthers the University's objective of excellence in research, scholarship, and education by publishing worldwide. Oxford is a registered trade mark of Oxford University Press in the UK and certain other countries.

Published in the United States of America by Oxford University Press
198 Madison Avenue, New York, NY 10016, United States of America.

© Oxford University Press 2018

All rights reserved. No part of this publication may be reproduced, stored in a retrieval system, or transmitted, in any form or by any means, without the prior permission in writing of Oxford University Press, or as expressly permitted by law, by license, or under terms agreed with the appropriate reproduction rights organization. Inquiries concerning reproduction outside the scope of the above should be sent to the Rights Department, Oxford University Press, at the address above.

You must not circulate this work in any other form
and you must impose this same condition on any acquirer.

CIP data is on file at the Library of Congress
ISBN 978–0–19–069678–8 (pbk.)
ISBN 978–0–19–069677–1 (hbk.)

Hardback printed by Bridgeport National Bindery, Inc., United States of America

For Abby Wells

Außer diesem Stern, dachte ich, ist nichts und er
Ist so verwüstet.
Er allein ist unsere Zuflucht und die
Sieht so aus.

[There's nothing but this star, I thought, and it's
So devastated.
It alone is our refuge and it
Looks that way]
                Bertolt Brecht, translation by James McFarland[1]

CONTENTS

Acknowledgments   ix

Introduction   1

PART I: On Location . . .   21
1. Buster Keaton's Climate Change   23
2. Nuclear Conditioning   59
3. The Ecologies of Film Noir   97

PART II: . . . at the End of the World   127
4. Still Life   129
5. Antarctica and Siegfried Kracauer's Extraterrestrial Film Theory   162
Conclusion: The Epoch and the Archive   201

Notes   209
Bibliography   229
Index   243

ACKNOWLEDGMENTS

I discovered the philosophical vocabulary for this book in Kelly Oliver's graduate seminar here at Vanderbilt, which she graciously allowed me to participate in. The conversations, guest speakers, and Kelly's own brilliant conceptualizations of the earthly and worldly domains in Kant, Hegel, Arendt, Heidegger, and Derrida, which she then formulated in her book *Earth & World: Philosophy after the Apollo Mission*, have been essential to my thinking and writing over the last few years. Indeed, my colleagues at Vanderbilt have been a constant source of inspiration, support, and lively exchange. In addition to Kelly, I thank Colin Dayan, Celia Applegate, Meike Warner, Mark Schoenfield, Dana Nelson, Teresa Goddu, Alex Dubilet, Jessie Hock, Jesse Montgomery, Lutz Koepnick, Vanessa Beasley, Rick Hilles, Jay Clayton, Candice Amich, Leah Lowe, Yoshi Igarashi, Barbara Hahn, Anand Taneja, Jonathan Waters, Se Young Kim, Jonathan Rattner, and Lynn Enterline. I give special thanks to the "Wild Reading Group": Ben Tran, Allison Schachter, Thomas Wild, Scott Juengel, and James McFarland. I am indebted to James (Jim) for translating the Brecht verse that opens this book, and for his always sharp and enthusiastic engagement with challenging material. Alex Dubilet and Jessie Hock have asked some of the best questions and provided many welcomed diversions. How lucky I am to live and work in close proximity to such great minds and good friends. Adam Miller (Vanderbilt PhD in English) helped me to prepare the manuscript for publication, and he read carefully and commented astutely on all of its features. He worked some of his magic into this project.

I am also indebted to the intellectual community that congregates around Vanderbilt's Robert Penn Warren Center for the Humanities and Mona Frederick's warm hospitality. The Film Theory and Visual Culture Seminar and the Contemporary in Theory Seminar have been among my favorite gatherings and conversations over the years. Thanks also to the Faculty-Staff Connections Reading Group (especially Jeana Poindexter,

Emma Furman, and Cindy Martinez) for inviting me to share work related to this project. The Vanderbilt Research Scholar Grant provided me with the funds to extend my research leave and write most of this manuscript while keeping close contact with my Nashville community. A few blocks from campus is the Belcourt Theatre, a hub for cinephilia and the center of my social world. Stephanie Silverman and Allison Inman have made Belcourt a home for cinema and a welcoming place for the conversations it stimulates. I am indebted to Allison and Toby Leonard for the sneak preview of *Dawson City: Frozen Time*. That film helped me to write the conclusion and thus to think my way out of this project.

Beyond Nashville, I am grateful for the invitations from friends and colleagues to share work in progress at other institutions. I thank Neill Matheson at the University of Texas, Arlington; Jill Smith, Aviva Briefel, and David Collings at Bowdoin College; Timothy Bewes and Jacques Khalip at Brown University's Pembrook Center for the Humanities; Christopher Sieving and Richard Neupert at the University of Georgia; Aaron Jafee for organizing the great Paleo-Futurism Conference at the University of Kentucky; Jeff Menne and Graig Uhlin at Oklahoma State University; Caetlin Benson-Allott at the University of Oklahoma; and Ian Whittington, who invited me to participate in a plenary panel for the Space Between Conference at the University of Mississippi.

For their feedback on this project and general expressions of enthusiasm for this work (and ideas in general), I also thank David Clarke, Daniel Morgan, Gerd Gemünden, Karl Schoonover, Paul K. Saint-Amour, Scott Curtis, Barbara Klinger, Mark Goble, Jennifer Peterson, Daniel Nasset, Georges Toles, Johannes von Moltke, Erica Carter, Sarah Keller, Brian Jacobson, Paul Young, Jacques Khalip, Akira Lippit, Sara Blair, James Cahill, Jeff Menne, Leslie Stern, Eric Rentschler, and Bonnie Honig. Davide Panagia read most of this manuscript and provided invaluable direction at a crucial stage. Ackbar Abbas, who has taught me so much about Hong Kong and Chinese cinema, generously offered detailed feedback on chapter 4. Justus Nieland and Scott Juengel, my inner circle and trusted insiders, read everything a few times even as they were up against their own impending deadlines. Scott, especially, pushed me to think harder, to linger in contradiction, and to appreciate the time needed for reflection. My friends and former colleagues at Michigan State University, including Justus, Zarena Aslami, my former chair Patrick O'Donnell, and my buddy Sarah Wohlford continually remind me of how good I had it back in East Lansing. Whoever else may read this book, whatever conversations it may or may not inspire, the process of writing it has been truly joyous in the company (sometimes only virtually or in spirit) of these people.

At Oxford University Press, Angela Chnapko has been a model editor and I am grateful to her for contracting this project on film for lists in political theory and environmental studies. Above all, I thank her for finding two amazing outside readers whose generous and incisive reports have guided the manuscript's completion. Tom Conley, one of the readers, has offered especially detailed commentary (twice!), and his enthusiasm for the project has buoyed my confidence. I hope I have fulfilled the promise both readers found in the earlier draft. I also thank Yang Yi for permission to reproduce two astounding images from his *Uprooted* series and Hélène Lacharmoise of Galerie Dix6 for providing the images and facilitating the permission. Liu Xiaodong has graciously allowed me to reproduce his devastating painting *Out of Beichuan*. Thanks to him and to Lisson Gallery for this permission.

Family members have been supportive and so patient with me as I have hunkered down with this long-term and rather melancholic book. Sonja Fay, Kathleen Fossan, Chris Fossan, Paula Page, Joan Squires, Walt Sell, and Loie Galza have encouraged me with their kindness and understanding. Sonja helped with a German translation at a key moment. Fellow professor Brendan Fay has been a most sympathetic ear and interlocutor on matters both intellectual and emotional, especially around the difficult events of the passing of my mother, Gae Galza, and our father, Tom Fay. I thank my parents *in absentia* and invoke them in memoriam.

Scott Juengel, my partner in life and favorite human being, fills me with love for the world and hope for the future in whatever form it (and we) may take. He is my best reader and my most beloved distraction. To repurpose a 1980s love song for the Anthropocene: "I'll stop the world and melt with you." I dedicate this book to another good one. Abby Wells is the remarkable woman, family friend, and surrogate parent who put me through college and helped me through graduate school. Through her own example, Abby has taught me about the forms generosity takes and what it means, in all senses, to invest in the people we love.

Chapter 1 draws on material published as "Buster Keaton's Climate Change" in *Modernism/modernity* 21:1 (2016). Chapter 2 is a significantly revised and expanded version of the essay "Atomic Screen Tests," also in *Modernism/modernity* 23:3 (2016). I thank Johns Hopkins University Press for permission to republish this material. Chapter 5 is based on the essay "Antarctica and Siegfried Kracauer's Cold Love," which appeared in *Discourse* 33:3 (2011, published in 2012). I thank Wayne State University Press for permission to republish this material.

Nashville
Summer 2017

Inhospitable World

Introduction

Bertolt Brecht's 1949 poem fragment, "Außer diesem Stern," offers in its precise and offhanded style a vision of our planet in the time of the Anthropocene (see the epigraph).[1] Hovering in a place beyond earth from where the damaged star and the unnerving nothingness that surrounds it may be apprehended, the speaker remarks that this star, our only refuge, is "devastated" and "it looks that way." Brecht, the exile, eschews the cozy associations of home or *Heimat* and fixates on the star as a temporary place of retreat, asylum, or sanctuary against its alternative: nothing. And, thus, the refuge is frighteningly precarious. With the poem's final line—"it looks that way"—Brecht produces a chilling ambiguity. On one hand, we apprehend the terror of beholding a refuge that has been destroyed but, that despite its ruinous state, still looks like a refuge, one that appears to the speaker to be our only shelter. On the other, Brecht intimates that our refuge is devastating to this star, and that our only refuge itself looks like devastation. Referring to earth as a star and not a planet, moreover, Brecht channels something of the etymology of the English word disaster—the pejorative *dis* (bad) *astro* (star)—and the catastrophe that results from planetary misalignment. Earth is an ill-fated star and our refuge is both devastated and devastating.

What I mean to signal through Brecht's wordplay is the difficulty of disentangling the state of the planet from the status of the refuge, and also the challenge of ordering a casual chronology. Is the star devastated and *therefore* our refuge imperiled? Or, is the star devastated *because* it is our refuge, outside of which there is nothing? Brecht captures what I take to be the central conundrum of the Anthropocene and the epiphenomenon of climate change: namely, that our collective efforts to make the planet more welcoming, secure, and productive for human flourishing, especially in the twentieth and twenty-first centuries, are precisely the measures that have made this a less hospitable earth, transforming it from something given into a disaster we have made. Humans have altered more than 50 percent of the earth's landmass, depositing "anthropogenically modified materials" (plastics, concrete, bricks, and so-called technofossils but also crops, animals, and food production) everywhere we have settled. And even where humans have not put down roots, our chemical imprint is airborne due to such phenomena as carbon emissions, pesticide residues, and radionuclides.[2] The effect is that Homo sapiens have cast the planet out of the temperate norms of the Holocene epoch that were so congenial to human evolution. We are now living in what a working group of geologists has proposed as the Anthropocene, or the "Human Epoch." Humanity, they argue, is acting on the planet like a force of nature, a nature that seems to be turning against organic life, as it has been known to us.[3] This new geological designation is a radical orientation to the deep geological past that is, from the vantage of now, entangled with recent narratives of human socioeconomic development, even as the scale of earth history renders the human into a brief, unthinking, physical force. We must now contend simultaneously with our species-being (vulnerability for extinction we share with all living things) and our apparently exceptional, suprahistorical status as a geophysical entity that rises above biology, sociality, and politics.[4] Anthropocene humanity and its world-building activities *are* the new nature that appears to us in the form of weather events and extreme environmental conditions that are more violent, erratic, and threatening than anything in our collective history. "We," a so-presumed universal humanity, are plagued by the geological force that *is* humanity. In the attempts to master nature (including a human biological nature), we are now more than ever subject to a new nature we cannot master.[5] This star called Earth, then, may be only a temporary refuge, a planet of last resort.

Environmentalist Bill McKibben has proposed that we rename not the current epoch *on* earth, but the planet itself: *Eaarth*. The repetition of the letter "a" signals, as if by typographical error, the *Unheimlichkeit* of a planet that appears to be our home, but with a difference. Though McKibben does not name the uncanny, he evokes it in his description. "It looks familiar enough—we're still the third rock out from the sun, still three-quarters water. Gravity still pertains: we're still earth*like*."[6] What nature we encounter is not a gift (or punishment) from the gods, nor is it a contemporary state of natural history. On planet Eaarth, trees, streams, rain, storms, and even rocks should be apprehended, writes McKibben, as "a subset of human activity."[7] Eaarth is anthropogenic, supernatural (perhaps full of literal valleys that are uncanny). McKibben's coinage, intended to shock the reader with the degree of human-caused damage, is also an aesthetic or sensory response to this doppelgänger planet. Eaarth raises to a new level of disorientation what the uncanny for Freud summons forth: the feeling that home, homeliness, and all that is familiar have been transformed into their dreadful opposites, that the home has been replaced with an artificial substitute that resembles it. A feeling that leads to a disintegrated psyche and perhaps also to death (at least in the literary examples from which Freud draws), the uncanny is a dread that emerges from a brush with (and even self-canceling preference for) the mechanical or the mystical.[8] That the extensive definitions of *heimlich* quoted by Freud make reference to "cheerful" weather, to *heimlich* waves and ocean currents, and to *heimlich* woods and shady paths suggests how nature may be absorbed into this aesthetic regime when we encounter its artificial double.[9]

The Anthropocene is to natural science what cinema, especially early cinema, has been to human culture. It makes the familiar world strange to us by transcribing the dimensionalities of experience into celluloid, transforming and temporally transporting humans and the natural world into an unhomely image. Maxim Gorky's oft-quoted reflection on the program of Lumière films exhibited in 1896 begins more like a gothic novel than a report on the evening's entertainment. The first motion pictures, black and white, silent except for the sound of the projector, are short snatches of everyday life, and they deeply unsettle Gorky as ghostly animations:

> Yesterday I was in the Kingdom of Shadows.... Everything there—the earth, the trees, the people, the water and the air—is tinted in a grey monotone: in a grey sky there are grey rays of sunlight; in grey faces, grey eyes, and the leaves of the trees are grey like ashes. This is not life but the shadow of life and this is not movement but the soundless shadow of movement.[10]

For Gorky cinema is a new instrument of the industrial revolution that revives supernatural experience: "It is terrifying to watch but it is the movement of shadows, mere shadows."[11] Or, perhaps the cinematograph forecasts the grim fate of the human and the natural world in the industrial age to come. Reducing all matter to deadening grayscale, this new technological marvel creates the uncanny as a diminished aesthetic experience. Like the effects of the Anthropocene in many accounts, cinema is also a product of the Industrial Revolution and arises out of a desire for the preservation of life, a sense of mastery over time and space, and what Marshall McLuhan called "the extensions of man."[12] The names of the precinematic and early film devices attest to the inventors' biogenetic aspirations: Zoopraxiscope, Zoetrope, Kinetoscope, Mutoscope, Vitagraph, Vitascope—the list could go on. Gorky comments on cinema's proliferative strangeness, its capacity to turn the familiar world into a "grotesque creation." *L'Arrivée d'un train en gare de La Ciotat* (1895), one of the films in this short program, features a train that appears to be headed right for the theatrical audience sitting in this convivial café. "Watch out!" cries Gorky. The cinematic train might jump out of the screen and crash into the world where it would "mangle," "destroy," and turn "to dust" the very reality it animates.[13]

Cinema is not simply uncanny like *Eaarth*, as we see in the previous example; it is a technology of the Anthropocene that helps to produce *Eaarth*, as such. And this brings me to the book's argument. Filmmaking occasions the creation of artificial worlds, unnatural and inclement weather, and deadly environments produced as much for the sake of entertainment as for scientific study and military strategy. Cinema's dominant mode of aesthetic world-making is often at odds with the very real human world it is meant to simulate. The chapters in this book take the reader to a scene—the mise-en-scène—where human world-making is undone by the force of human activity, whether it is explicitly for the sake of making a film, or for practicing war and nuclear science, or for the purpose of addressing climate change in ways that exacerbate its already inhospitable effects. Whereas eco-criticism often attends to our planetary emergency as a corruption of a presumed natural place or a crisis that demands sustainable models so that the status quo may persist or be restored, the episodes in this book emphasize our always unnatural and unwelcoming environment as a matter of production, a willed and wanted milieu, however harmful, that is inseparable from but also made perceivable through film. This anthropogenic environment is an expansion of what Hannah Arendt described as the necessary "unnaturalness of human existence" on a planet that sustains our biological life.[14] What is new in the Anthropocene is that the environment, which supports but is supposed to be distinct from the human world according to long-held Enlightenment presumptions, is now also largely human made. While no one film or set of films adds up to a totalizing explanation of climate change, cinema enables us to glimpse anthropogenic environments as both an accidental effect of human activity and a matter of design. Thus, not only is cinema like the Anthropocene in its uncanny aesthetic effects, but also, insofar as cinema has encouraged the production of artificial worlds and simulated, wholly anthropogenic weather, it is the aesthetic practice of the Anthropocene. Or, to put it more forcefully, cinema helps us to see and experience the Anthropocene as an aesthetic practice.

To write about cinema in the epoch of the Anthropocene is to bring out new connections between these two terms or practices that change how we think about both of them. This book explores the connection between film theory and aesthetics, on one hand, and the production of artificial worlds, weather, climates, and even planets, on the other, in or on which hospitality and survival in the world are at stake. Specifically, I posit a philosophical relationship between the histories, temporalities, and aesthetics of human-driven climate change and the politics, environmentalism, and ethics of cinema. While films are the primary objects of analysis, the chapters focus on the historical materiality of film production and the environmental design of on-location shooting. As I explain in the balance of this introduction, film enjoys a rather unique relationship to the material, elemental world through which we may appreciate both the artificiality of human world-making and the ambitions to design an artificial, unhomely planet.

THE ARTIFICIAL WORLD; OR, THE WORLDLINESS OF FILM

The scene of filmmaking reveals an acute connection between anthropogenic environments and cinematic practices because of this medium's materiality and its interface with what is often a physically existing object-world. Consider this extended example. The dark film studio that arose in the 1920s as the paradigmatic space for feature film production eliminated the natural world as a backdrop or context for narrative cinema. Rather than film on location, the major producers built monumental indoor studios in which nature could be simulated on the set for the sake of creating predictable, repeatable, and, above all, realistic effects. In 1927, Siegfried Kracauer toured the studio complex UFA, the quintessence of a modern dream factory where the masterpieces of Weimar cinema, including Lang's *Metropolis* (1927), Lubitsch's *The Last Laugh* (1924), and Murnau's *Faust* (1926), had been shot or were in production. These are films all notable for their immersive diegetic worlds in which rain and floods, sunrises and sunsets, futuristic cities, modern hotels, and dilapidated proletarian quarters had been built on set.

UFA's film city, on the outskirts of Berlin, is "a desert within an oasis."[15] As Kracauer walks through the multiacre, studio fortress, gated and locked off from verdant suburbia, he discovers not a simulacrum of the outside world but its fabricated, disaggregated inventory. In the backlot on a hillside, a church-front for one film stands next to the facade of a pleasure resort for another. For filming purposes, the base of a cathedral sits several yards away from its ornate roof. Seemingly real from a distance, up close these structures are uninhabitable shells built for speedy dismantling or radical repurposing: "they are just empty nothingness" fashioned according to the script.[16] A medieval castle, already in a state of disrepair ("the materials of its construction are peeking through"), will not be allowed to age naturally "because ruins have to be made to order. Here all objects are only what they are supposed to represent at the moment: they know no development over time."[17] In warehouses, props for any number of historical periods and national styles are stored side by side in vast warehouses. "Ripped out of time and jumbled together," these objects have clear usefulness (chairs, stairs, lamps) but no narrative meaning or unique history until they appear on film. Elsewhere in the complex, flora is kept in greenhouses, while animal trainers tend to the fauna in cages. Costumed actors stand by the film sets waiting "endlessly" for their scenes. When it comes time to shoot the film, these elements are taken out of storage and assembled on the set, "where things human unfold." In the process, the scattered world becomes the foundation of a total fictional cosmos. "The objects that have been liberated from the larger context are now reinserted into it, their isolation effaced and their grimace smoothed over." These embarrassed things are thus twice alienated, first from the jumble of the real world they are meant to replicate and then from their compartmentalized existence in the studio warehouse: "Out of graves not meant to be taken seriously, these objects wake to an illusion of life."[18]

These objects or inventory do not strike Kracauer as uncanny (even graves in the studio are just props), and no one would mistake a film set for the real world and thus suffer *unheimlich* uncertainty. It is rather that the dominant mode of film production is governed by a simulationist aesthetic, a preference for the artificial, the mechanical, the temporary, and the made over any location or object that is "naturally" or historically given. "Nature, body and soul, is put out to pasture," while in the studio "the world's elements are produced on the spot in immense laboratories."[19] It is as if realism in cinema can be achieved only through high-tech replication. On one hand, "the natural things outside—trees made out of wood, lakes with water, villas that are habitable—have no place within [the studio's] confines." And on the other, he writes, "the world does reappear there.... But the things that rendezvous [in the studio] do not belong to reality."[20] There are, for example, fake trees made out of wood and artificial rain made with water. The film studio inverts the codes of defamiliarization, as theorized by Russian formalist Victor Shklovsky. According to Shklovsky, something familiar is made unfamiliar "by both description and by the proposal to change [a thing or action's] form without changing its nature."[21]

In contrast, the studio retains the object's original form and utterly changes the nature. "Glass clouds brew and then scatter." Nothing is natural, and yet when projected, "Everything guaranteed nature."[22]

Set designers even simulate, and thus subject to finely calibrated predictability, entire landscapes and the weather itself. On the set of *Faust*, microclimates erupt and dissipate according to the script's program:

> Fog made of water vapor produced by a steam engine envelops the range of appropriately sculpted mountain peaks from which Faust emerges. For the horrible crash of the foaming deluge, some water is sprayed through the side canyon. The wild urges subside when the wheat covering the fields and meadows beneath the jagged, pine-covered summits rustles in the wind of a propeller. Cloud upon cloud wafts eastward, masses of spun glass in dense succession.... Huts surrounded by greenery will most likely shimmer in the blazing, high-wattage glow of the evening sun.[23]

What will appear to be fortuitous or tragic weather on screen is not left to chance in the studio. Sunsets are exactly repeatable and wind rustles carefully placed greenery with the flip of a switch. At UFA, all "natural" elements are under the power of a director, and "the planet Earth now expands *en miniature*" as if controlled from without. For cinema's special-effects technicians, "the cosmos is a little ball to be batted around at will."[24]

It is a cliché to observe that cinema is a window onto the world, or even a window onto our environmentally degraded world. What Kracauer helps us to fathom is that cinema mirrors the practice of human worlding, inclusive of its natural environment and thus, in a sense, he theorizes a world concept through a production design that is unique to cinema. The sets, he observes, are constructed with the same materials used in actual cities to build actual, durable houses in which humans could live out their historical lives. As Kracauer notes of UFA's construction: "One could also make real things out of them."[25] The UFA city, however, is not at all congenial to human dwelling. The houses, mere facades, are vulnerable—by design—to human-made catastrophes. The workers' quarters in *Metropolis*, for example, are fabricated to succumb to the spectacular flood, also crafted within the studio, that is unleashed by the film's robotic pretender. Film producers "build cultures and then destroy them as they see fit. They sit in judgment over entire cities and let fire and brimstone rain down upon them if the film calls for it. For them, nothing is meant to last: the most grandiose creation is built with an eye to its demolition."[26] But one *could* build a home in this artificial world.[27]

INTRODUCTION [7]

Eric Hayot has recently explored the history and theory of aesthetic worlds in literary fiction that, he argues, are produced and interpreted in relation to an extradiegetic context—what he calls "the lived world." The aesthetic world of literature is conceptual: it indexes a "history of the idea of the world as such."[28] From the history of literature we learn about the intellectual history of the world as a concept through novelistic/poetic details of everyday life, geographical extension, and narratively engrossing effects. Yet even when analyzed as a physical book and paper form, literature has nothing of the materiality of the film studio or the temporality of film production; nor does it share with cinema the ambitions of environmental design, even if literature describes the phenomena we now associate with the Anthropocene, and even though the production of books disappears trees. The production of the world in literature leads to "totality as a function of the human imagination."[29] The world of the film studio is first concrete (sometimes literally) and fragmentary (parts of buildings, fragments of towns, disaggregated inventory stored in warehouses) before it becomes a cinematic projection of an immersive diegesis. Kracauer alerts us to the chronotope of the *pro-filmic* world that is temporally *before* and spatially *in front* of the camera. If the projected image appears to us as nature, we need only glimpse behind the scenes to learn how this artificial nature comes into being and meaning. For this reason, the studio is politically important because, writes Kracauer, it exemplifies "the regime of arbitrariness." On its stages all kinds of worlds are possible. But this is not really fiction. "The real world," he insists, "is only one of the many possibilities that can be moved back and forth: the game would remain incomplete if one were to accept reality as a finished product."[30] Worlds are always in the process of their making and unmaking, and totality and completion, in film as in reality, are illusions. As Miriam Hansen writes, Kracauer's essay "links the paradoxical relation between fragmentation and diegetic unity to the historical dialectics of nature, arrested in the appearance of the social order as natural."[31]

Film studios strive to create a projected image of nature entirely human made, and this sleight of hand in the dark studio carries over into on-location shooting, as chapters in this book explain. At a certain point, however, roughly at midcentury, the distinction between a human-made world and a natural, given environment starts to disappear. Even leaving the studio confines, there are simply no locations on Earth that are not in some way already a product of or contaminated by human design. To rephrase Hansen, there is little in the Anthropocene world that strikes us as natural. But that does not mean we apprehend our state of affairs as accidental or even as designed. In fact, climate change may well catapult us into a bare condition of arbitrariness. This book traces a movement from the artificial studio, in which simulated nature may be totally controlled before and on film, to the anthropogenic planet that is predicted to *defy all prediction*.

I take the ambition of film production as a fitting (if only partial and certainly perverse) description of how the Anthropocene answers a wish for a human-made and manipulated planet. Hannah Arendt, writing a few decades later (and not about film), sees foreboding signs that the studio's artificiality is more than just a cinematic dream. At the height of the Cold War and boom time of the nuclear arms race, it appeared that modern science and industry would deliver humanity from the contingencies of the natural world altogether. With alarm, Arendt begins *The Human Condition* with a meditation on the meaning of *Sputnik*, the Soviet satellite launched in 1957. This 184-pound metal sphere represented the possibility not just of fleeing Earth for the moon or some other planet in the universe. During its roughly four-month sojourn in orbit around Earth, *Sputnik* was a prototype for an anthropogenic planet. Looking up at the heavens, people could see among the stars and moon an "earth-born object made by man," and, she argues, these spectators began to project themselves onto a future planet of human design.[32] The fancy for flight is a "fateful repudiation" of an earthbound human ontology. It marks a "rebellion against human existence as it has been given, a free gift from nowhere," on Earth, which the modern human wishes "to exchange, as it were, for something he has made himself," a fabricated planet.[33] (*Eaarth* orbits Earth.) For Arendt, a man-made planet and forms of test tube procreation promised to eliminate the contingencies of evolution and connections to "nature" beyond our control. To be buffered from the unforeseen stresses of terrestrial dwelling, this is a dream for a wholly self-conditioned being and it marks a willingness, if not yearning, to live in a controlled, synthetic world. As Benjamin Lazier comments, *Sputnik*, as an "artful substitute for the living Earth," was for Arendt nothing short of a totalitarian ambition to replace the real world with a total "artful fiction."[34] If humans were ever to succeed in making their own planet, scientists and engineers would replace politicians, and, as Arendt worries, we would need machines to do our thinking for us because technological feats of producing and sustaining such a world would be beyond the comprehension of most people living in it. "Such an event, no longer totally impossible, would imply that man would have to live under man-made conditions, radically different from those the earth offers him. Neither labor nor work nor action nor, indeed, thought as we know it would then make sense any longer." In contrast to humans who have been naturally conditioned by Earth's environment, these "hypothetical wanderers" would be "self-made to a considerable extent."[35] Modern, especially nuclear, scientists, she declares in the book's penultimate page, have expanded "the realm of human affairs to the point of extinguishing the time-honored dividing line between nature and the human world."[36] Today, of course, we have not yet fled the earth for space, nor have we abandoned the fantasy of transplanetary migration or evaded the threat of nuclear annihilation, but we have turned Earth into something we have largely made ourselves and thus have become increasingly self-conditioned.

Important to Arendt's account, and to my own project in this book, is the theoretical-political differentiation between Earth and world. The world, writes Arendt, is "related to the human artifact, the fabrication of human hands, as well as to affairs which go on among those who inhabit the man-made world together."[37] The world is a product of anthropogenic design and has a thingly character to it. In and through it, humans encounter their shared past and future, their durable things, and create spaces for political action. The earth, by contrast, is given and is the realm in which human existence is closest to nonhuman animals. Humans are constituted equally through these two realms that exist in overlapping (and not opposing) geographical and temporal domains. And while the human world is artificial (in that it is not "naturally" given), it is only on Earth that the world may exist and be meaningful, as such. As Kelly Oliver explains of Arendt's taxonomy, "the earth corresponds to being whereas the world corresponds to meaning."[38] What Arendt diagnoses in *The Human Condition* is that human world-making at midcentury had started to overtake and potentially threaten the earth, as if the human world could survive anywhere else but here. The dream of planetary flight found a rejoinder in nuclear testing that had by 1957 already transformed the entire planet into a disposable laboratory (and as I will discuss, a film studio). It was as if we had already left this earth behind. Or we were treating it, in Kracauer's parlance, as "a little ball to be batted around at will."[39]

I raise Arendt's earth/world distinction (as well as her sense that something fundamentally changes in the 1950s) because it roughly correlates with the account of the Anthropocene from earth system scientists. To demonstrate the geophysical uniqueness of the Anthropocene epoch, working groups at the International Geosphere-Biosphere Programme differentiate between the human socioeconomic system and the earth system. The first is represented by such big data sets as population growth, international tourism, telecommunications, transportation, paper production, real gross domestic product, large dam construction, fertilizer use, and paper production, metrics that capture both resource use and the circulation of people, money, and products. The earth system is represented by trends in "atmospheric composition, stratospheric ozone, the climate system, the water and nitrogen cycles, marine ecosystem, land systems, tropical forests and terrestrial biosphere degradation."[40] Granted, these categories are not exhaustive of what people do or the range of systems that compose the earth's intricate workings, nor do they perfectly map onto Arendt's sense of world and earth. Instead, they are trackable metrics that, when compared, show a surprising correlation starting in the early 1950s between the rise of human activity on the planet and changes to the earth system that cast it out of the variability of Holocene norms. Starting in midcentury, human activity has become "a planetary-scale geological force." This sudden spike in human activity marks what is now referred to as the Great Acceleration.[41] The point, however, is not to announce that humans have changed the planet ("humans have always altered their environments, sometimes on a large scale").[42] The Great Acceleration captures the new speed and magnitude of human enterprise since midcentury, resulting in a "coupling" of the socioeconomic system with the biophysical earth system that shows few signs of returning to natural variation. This means that human culture has become deadly nature, or that "nature" is a product of industrial design. Because this "planetary-scale coupling" of the earth and socio-economic systems is without precedent in geological history, scientists warn: "We are now living in a no-analogue world." Having left the Holocene for the absolutely unpredictable Anthropocene, they wonder if the next fifty years will bring about "the Great Decoupling" of these systems, or "the Great Collapse" of both.[43] Our geological past offers no precedent through which we may predict our ecological future, and various models of climate change seem downright apocalyptic.

In the shorter term, the human imprint on Earth, especially with the onset of the Great Acceleration, means that the planet's capacity to sustain human life is no longer assured. Will Steffen, Paul J. Crutzen, and John R. McNeill write of the "human-driven changes to the environment": "the consequences of this unintended experiment of humankind on its own life support system are hotly debated, but worst-case scenarios paint a gloomy picture for the future of contemporary societies."[44] This certainly dooms many species, but it also, in Arendt's prognosis, endangers politics. With fewer places on the planet that humans will be able to call home, climate change requires us to think about new strategies of accommodation—a different kind of geo-politics and geo-aesthetics for a new geological epoch. In short, the Anthropocene confronts us with the fact that we need to learn how to live and die in an unpredictable and increasingly inhospitable world.

Cinema has something to teach us about how and why we got here and how we envision our unthinkable future, as such.

But we would do well to briefly turn to the past to understand how hospitality, in its Enlightenment origins, is both the problem and potential solution to our current environmental crisis.

HOSPITALITY AND THE ENDS OF THE WORLD

One of the more enduring models of international rights and earthly dwelling comes from Immanuel Kant and his 1795 essay "Perpetual Peace."[45] I turn briefly to Kant because, in many respects, our current international law has its origins in his political writing, as Seyla Benhabib argues, insofar as he presumes republican states, sovereign governance, and the conditional rights of the foreigner.[46] Writing during both the French and the Industrial Revolutions, at the end of a century during which the empires of Europe had been in near-continual conflict (despite various declarations of peace), Kant raises doubts that the Enlightenment will lead humankind into a state of perpetual, nonviolent equilibrium. His "philosophical sketch," as he calls it, is an urgent elaboration of a cosmopolitan order to come that is grounded in the principles of hospitality. A neighborly term for host–guest relations, hospitality also captures for Kant the relationship between individual subjects and modern nations, as well as between modern humanity and the planet. Kant offers a curious account of natural history as the origins for a global political order. It is striking that he endows the planet or nature with the capacity to be hospitable.[47] Indeed, before humans may welcome each other, the planet first accommodates us. Kant reasons that nature both cares for humans even as it uses war to disperse populations to the earth's most "inhospitable regions." Nature provides people with the raw materials that may be harvested initially for the sake of survival and then traded with other communities and nations. Even the "cold wastes around the Arctic Ocean" are host to fur-bearing animals and whales that become food and clothing for native inhabitants before they may be traded for other provisions. Though the arctic has no trees, nature furnished driftwood through ocean currents so that people may craft houses, boats, and weapons. "Nature's care," Kant writes, "arouses . . . admiration."[48] Kant imagines that in his own lifetime populations in the temperate regions will begin to retain native resources for themselves as they build their cities and industries, putting an end to nature's driftwood. At this point trade between nations performs and resumes the task of nature's thoughtful distribution. He hastens to add that this may only occur when nations learn to live in peace with one another,[49] "for the *spirit of commerce* sooner or later takes hold of every people, and it cannot exist side by side with war."[50] Thus, he writes of his globalized vision: "seeing to it that men *could* live everywhere on earth, nature has at the same time despotically willed that they *should* live everywhere, even against their own inclinations."[51] In Kant's progressive narrative, war disperses, nature cares, trade incentivizes, and humans are compelled to form states, make international laws, and maintain peaceful relations. Over time, the human inclination for war will give way to the human interest in association, bringing about a worldwide cosmopolitan constitution.

According to Kant, the endurance of this global order rests on "universal hospitality," or "the right of a stranger not to be treated with hostility when he arrives on someone else's territory."[52] In an odd turn, Kant revives an archaic sociability between visiting and hosting neighbors as a model for relations between individuals and states, which may sustain the end of war. Not to be confused with the right of a guest to impose him- or herself in the home, Kant's "right of resort" is conditional and presumes humankind's "common possession of the earth's surface. Since the earth is a globe, they cannot disperse over an infinite area, but must necessarily tolerate one another's company."[53] Humans collectively own the earth before individuals lay claim to property, and we therefore must allow one another to pass through, or stop over, a given territory, especially when refusal could lead to death. Hospitality is not a charitable offering, nor does it come with the right of permanent residence (this would require contracts between governments); it is a universal human right of temporary resort that maintains a nonviolent tension between the sovereignty of the state, which the guest must not violate, and the rights of visitors, who must be allowed to traverse the planet because they are bound, as we all are, to the earth's spatial limitations.[54] In Kant's view a life-sustaining planet, bountiful in raw materials and minimally sustaining to human habitation, is the ecological basis of—indeed, the fundamental condition for—universal hospitality among people. By exchanging the free gifts of nature, humankind stabilizes the economic, political, and, above all, moral basis of cosmopolitan right. In an earlier draft of "Perpetual Peace," Kant worries that as a result of naval wars between European powers, "entire peoples" would "slowly starv[e] to death as a result of restrictions in the circulation of foodstuffs."[55] What he could not have anticipated is that the very overharvesting and manipulation of the planet's resources, traded in times of peace, would threaten the very nature of Earth's resourceful terrain and thus foment conditions of war.

Though Kant attributes a certain agency to nature as the system of natural relations and inclinations that humans must master and overcome to realize the promise of universal history, his narrative is resolutely focused on the human subject of reason and the industriousness of humans to use nature to build worlds and global trade. He espouses the very practices that lead to the Anthropocene epoch, which, according to Will Steffen and colleagues, intensifies "in the footsteps of the Enlightenment." Among the material and social factors are the shortages in wood and a turn to coal power and to "political structures that rewarded risk-taking and innovation, materials connected to legal regimes, a nascent banking system, and a market culture." The Great Acceleration, starting in 1945, amplifies the Enlightenment presumption of human world domination, emerging out of an "intellectual, cultural, political and legal context in which the growing impact upon the Earth System counted for very little in the calculations and decisions made in the world's ministries, boardrooms, laboratories, farmhouses, village huts, and for that matter, bedrooms."[56] The human activities contributing most to climate change emanate from the OECD (Organisation for Economic Cooperation and Development) member countries, the largest economies that have prospered most in the post–World War II period of globalization.[57]

Given that this geological epoch is a product largely of *peacetime* trade and consumerist prosperity, that it is the partial fulfillment of Enlightenment conceptions of world history, the Anthropocene is the end of the Enlightenment world and its conception of hospitality in two ways. First, as cities and low-laying island nations are submerged in rising sea levels and the planet becomes intolerable to Holocene life, the Anthropocene is the most recent but all-encompassing planetary catastrophe. As the summation of the history of rapacious capitalist, mostly first-world, middle and upper class, Western human culture, the Anthropocene is the conclusion of the world and may forecast the end of the species. In the second sense, however, the Anthropocene is the triumph of worlding and the realization of humanity's complete self-conditioning and liberation from nature. It marks the end of history as the *telos* of the world. Pheng Cheah characterizes Marxist materialist historiography and universal proletarian revolution in ways that might illuminate the Anthropocene as a human accomplishment: "It is the highest achievement of historical progress, the fullest development of history's rational purpose, and also its terminal horizon, the point at which history concludes because there is nothing else to be achieved."[58] As the human-built world overtakes the planet and reshapes what were once stable and seemingly immutable climate patterns, humans have succeeded in making the earth a human world, even at the likely and unintended expense of most life on the planet. Human progress and world-building threaten to deliver us not to a state of enlightened global prosperity, but to a fragile earth order. The Anthropocene confronts us with the unsustainability of Kant's model. It may also spell the end, in theory if not in fact, of the Enlightenment subject of history, along with the earth as humankind's hospitable home.

Writ large in the present, hospitality in the epoch of the Anthropocene is already one of the most pressing emergencies as the earth's livable areas shrink, food security diminishes, and we await the even more violent climate to come. The United Nations Human Rights Council reports that 250 million people will be displaced by climate change by the year 2050, creating the need for a new legal category: the climate change refugee.[59] Fleeing not war but weather events and an unlivable terrain, citizens need refuge from a human-caused environmental disaster. The language of climate mingles easily with the vocabulary of war despite the fact that international law does not yet accommodate this new state of affairs. There is currently no multilateral provision for climate change refugees, who often find themselves in the more volatile political places, or in countries least responsible for greenhouse gas emissions.[60] The fate of the refugee in a less hospitable planet only amplifies hostilities. Indeed, in 2014, the United Nations reported that 51.2 million "persons of concern . . . (refugees, asylum-seekers, returned, internally displaced and stateless persons)" are "concentrated in 'climate-change hot spots' around the world," demonstrating the geographical coincidence of environmental and political instability.[61] The Anthropocene means that the subject, the home, and the planet at the heart of hospitality (and the Enlightenment subject it once placed at its center) are already past, if they ever existed in the first place. Living now on a less hospitable and less sustaining planet, we may have to resort to the extralegal, prelegal, perhaps also pre-Enlightenment forms of hospitality and the generosity of hosts, and learn how to dwell in a diminished world. The films at the center of this book all deal with scenarios of eviction, homelessness, estrangement, dispossession, and alienation. A few of them stage outright the dismantling of a house, the ejection of the human from her world, or the obliteration of the world itself, and the minimal hospitality that may arise in its wake.

CINEMA IN THE TIME OF THE ANTHROPOCENE

The pivotal term "hospitality" speaks to one of the book's projects, namely, to reconnect "eco-cinema" to its etymological roots of *eco* (from *oikos*, meaning home or dwelling). Each chapter focuses on rather exceptional filming locations in which earth and world, hospitality and its negation are in acute and destructive tension, places that bring to the fore cinema's world-making powers and its denatured, unhomely optics. Though there is a latent chronology in the book's organization, I do not posit a causal relationship between the chapters, however much they rhyme in terms of design. My aim is to theorize the Anthropocene of our contemporary moment as a kind of accidental present that may be connected to unlikely times and seemingly disconnected spaces of the film studio, the outdoor laboratory, and an array of aesthetic and narrative responses to unnatural weather and environments. Each chapter, in a sense, unfolds a microhistory that runs parallel to the histories in the other chapters. Likewise, the locations all are part of the same modern human world, even if they are separated by distance and time. Read together, these chapters may help us to contemplate a few pressing questions: if hospitality presumes a life-sustaining environment and self-sustaining world, what are the implications of ecological inhospitality? How might hospitality be understood as concerning not only human rights but also a regard and even a right that humans extend to the earth and the earth back to humans? And how may we apprehend the earth outside of our worldly use and need for it? Is there any hospitality to be found in the image?

Part I: "On Location . . ." is composed of three chapters that take place in American locations during the so-called American century when the United States rose as the global economic and military power, becoming in the process the "most polluting nation in history" and the nation most responsible for spearheading many of the geo-engineering projects associated with the Great Acceleration.[62] Chapter 1 begins in the interwar period with Buster Keaton's slapstick comedy and his elaborate outdoor sets (entire towns built to scale) and the crafty weather design (hurricanes, made on the spot) that destroys them. Splitting the difference between D. W. Griffith, who insisted on naturally occurring weather for his cinematic realism, and the Hollywood norm of fabricating weather in the controlled space of the studio, Keaton opted to fabricate weather on location. His elaborately choreographed gags with their storm surges and collapsing buildings required precise control of manufactured rain and wind, along with detailed knowledge of the weather conditions and climatological norms on site. He creates reflexive gags around weather simulation combined with purposeful errors in continuity, such that the storms are fragmentary, discontinuous, and obviously artificial. *Steamboat Bill, Jr.* (1928) is one of many examples of Keaton's weather design in which characters find themselves victims of elements that originate with the off-screen director. Through his cinema, I argue, we apprehend eruptive weather not as a natural act of God or Mother Nature, but as a matter of pointedly manipulated mise-en-scène reflective of the interwar era's weather-mindedness. Thus, Keaton's weather comedy is an early aesthetic paradigm of the Anthropocene.

Keaton builds towns to scale on location, which he then destroys with his weather, all for the sake of entertainment. Chapter 2 moves to another location in which worlds and catastrophic environments are manufactured for the sake of rehearsing war, practicing science, testing bombs, and producing films. Nevada's Atomic Testing Site, which hosted mock nuclear war with live ammunition from the late 1940s to the early 1960s, doubled as both an outdoor laboratory and a film studio. Here, worlds meant to resemble small American towns in every detail were built and obliterated by nuclear explosions, giving rise to thousands of nuclear test films. Whereas Keaton wants to maintain the appearance of contingent and unpredictable weather (which is clearly planned and human produced), the atomic films strive to produce predictability and repeatability against (and with the effect of effacing) the unpredictability of nuclear materials and the consequences of the planetary radioactive fallout. Cinema does not merely record these detonations. It transforms explosions into aesthetic experiences, turns the chaos of fallout into comprehensible narratives, and trains viewers to survive or endure the culture of nuclearism. By domesticating this other-earthly force (most nuclear elements do not exist naturally on the planet), cinema naturalizes this regime that leaves a stratigraphic signature in the planet's geological record, a signal so pronounced and so clearly anthropogenic that the prominent geologist Jan Zalasiewicz has proposed that the Anthropocene began in 1945 at the instant of the first atomic test.[63] It is thus fitting that the very technology that marks the exact onset of the Anthropocene would be marshalled explicitly as an instrument of planetary renovation and large-scale terra-forming projects. The chapter concludes with consideration of "Operation Plowshare," the U.S. Atomic Energy Commission's proposed program in development from 1958 to 1975 to use atomic bombs for geological engineering, to create harbors, deep canals, roadways, and megadams, but also to unearth oil, minerals, and other materials needed for industry. Plowshare targets the earth's "unfriendly terrain" to make it useful and welcoming to human development and global commerce. Though this plan was never implemented beyond the test range, the vision of planetary transformation is clear enough on film. *Plowshare* (circa 1964/65) reveals cinema's unique role in transforming what counts as welcoming nature and what looks like a planet designed as humankind's home.

From the nuclear backlot made to look like an American town, chapter 3 takes us to the American city and the genre of film noir. Situated in the built environment and urban blight that its characters call home, noir explores an artificial world that does not foster human happiness and growth, but leads to a kind of human incapacity to act and respond. Beyond merely depicting these negative environments, noir lays bare the attachments to bad living and unsustainable striving that underwrite the accumulating culture of the Anthropocene at midcentury. Noir gives us the characters, places, and scripts for human, specifically white, first-world, mostly hetero, masculine expiration as the counter to both nuclear survivalism and middle-brow consumer capitalism. The hospitality of film noir is rental property. Indeed, impermanent dwelling of the individual and first-world humanity as a whole is one of noir's lessons for the Anthropocene. That these films are typically shot in actual urban habitats on the cusp of erasure means that film noir may be read as a kind of extinction narrative. Subsisting in the slums and shabby neighborhoods of America's postwar cities, these characters give up and resign themselves to their mortality in a disappearing artificial world that was always unfit for them. It preaches the pleasures of death as an alternative to the normative and accumulating life. I celebrate American noir as an ecological genre that, in the spirit of Roy Scranton's book, teaches Americans, especially, how to die in the Anthropocene.[64]

Part II: ". . . At the End of the World" is composed of two chapters, one on China's Three Gorges Dam and the second on Antarctica. These chapters are paired because both consider the end of celluloid and the world (temporally and geographically). Climate scientists remark that we have entered a "no-analog" age—an age without parallel or analogy in geological history, and thus an age whose future defies prediction. The final two chapters consider what this statement means for cinema and specifically for celluloid, the twentieth century's dominant analog medium. Are we in a no-analog age, an age without or beyond cinema? Does cinema have a future on this planet that defies all prediction?

Jia Zhangke's digital film *Still Life* (2006) and other nonanalog artworks including Liu Xiaodong's oil paintings and Yang Yi's digital photographs are the subjects of the fourth chapter, which takes us to China just as that country surpasses the United States in greenhouse gas emissions and colossal geo-engineering projects.[65] I tarry on the location of the Three Gorges Dam, the largest hydroelectric megadam in world history and the subject of *Still Life*. Built, in part, to address the problems of global warming, the dam has had a number of surprising effects on the environment and has led to massive displacement of people to make way for the water. Jia offers a compelling portrait of the costs of contemporary dwelling and the price some people must pay (with their homes and livelihoods) for the sake of national development. Populating his film with migrant workers, refugees, tourists, visitors, and even aliens from outer space, none of whom are at home in this world, Jia captures the city at the moment of its undoing, a place that is changing, he remarks, too fast for film. Reading Jia's film together with Liu's and Yang's artwork and through the genre of still-life painting, I argue that Jia's film envisions a kind of minimal hospitality that emerges when the world, this particular world of now-submerged cities and towns, is past. The hospitality we find in this work is an invitation to an unknowable future, one that may also be without analogical media.

In the face of unpredictability (an epoch without analog) or only horrific forecasts (Will Steffen's "gloomy picture"), climate change may put us in the thrall of end times and apocalyptic fantasies of collapse. This future-orientation is what Srinivas Aravamudan has critiqued as "the catachronism of climate change," which borrows predictions from science in the service of a quasi-messianic projection that "re-characterizes the past and present in terms of a future proclaimed as determined but that is of course not fully realized."[66] In the spirit of his essay, this book also argues against scenarios of religious or redemptive prediction, and it steers clear of apocalyptic cinema, especially futuristic eco-disaster narratives. As Aravamudan writes: "The Anthropocene is never simply what you predict it will be; otherwise the future would just be an extension of the present. The future still holds some secrets from us; otherwise it would not be the future except in a trivial sense."[67] This book seeks to rescue the future from this trivialization and to challenge any notion that our present environmental crisis is the *telos* of history or an unavoidable product of human nature. In the final chapter, I return to Siegfried Kracauer's film and photographic theory along with cinematic records of early Antarctic exploration to understand how this utterly inhospitable continent and this media theory advance an alternative and denaturalized history of the present. Cinema has the capacity to reveal an earth outside of human feeling and utility without sacrificing the particularity that gets lost in scientific abstraction. Antarctica, for so long outside of human history altogether, simply numbs feeling and refuses to yield to human purpose. It is also a continent on which celluloid encounters its signifying limits. In Kracauer's late writing, cinema and photography are antihumanist technologies that, by defamiliarizing the world, enable us to experience it outside of ourselves. Writing after the catastrophe of World War II, moreover, Kracauer, himself a German Jewish exile, provides us with a postapocalyptic theory of film. Rather than write about the Anthropocene as an apocalypse to come, this chapter orients us to the ecologies and numbing aesthetics of Antarctica through a theory of the image and of history written after the worst has already occurred. After the apocalypse of war, we find that time persists and that there are no divine revelations. But if master narratives predicting the *telos* of history are canceled by the facts of war, it also means that human experience is no longer tethered to the limits of its historical or religious imagination. Channeling Kracauer's theory of film and theory of history through his own sense of being homeless in and even extraterrestrial to the world, I argue that Kracauer helps us to imagine an estranged and selfless relationship to an inhospitable or even posthospitable earth that may not accommodate us. This final chapter, however alienating, ends on a note of open futurity.

PART I
On Location . . .

CHAPTER 1

Buster Keaton's Climate Change

In the spectacular climax of Buster Keaton's *Steamboat Bill, Jr.* (1928), a small Mississippi River town is besieged by a ferocious cyclone. The unrelenting storm brings down piers, boats, and buildings as hapless residents scramble to find shelter. Eventually the camera settles on the local hospital where the hurricane-strength winds collapse all four of the structure's walls to reveal Will Canfield Jr. (Keaton), sitting upright in bed, startled awake by his sudden exposure to the elements. Buffeted by airborne debris and witness to destruction in every direction, a frightened and confused Will pulls the sheet over his head, only to have the intensifying winds blow his bed across town, discarding our bewildered hero in front of a rickety house. What follows is perhaps the most famous sequence in Keaton's oeuvre. Framed in long shot, Will stands facing the camera with his back to the house when the entire two-story facade breaks free from its structural moorings and falls right on top of him (Figures 1.1 and 1.2). Will survives unscathed only because he happens to be standing at the exact position of an open, second-story window through which his body passes in an application of providential geometry. Despite the show-stopping virtuosity of the stunt, Will's survival burlesque continues apace: the storm tosses his body like a ragdoll, heaps detritus on top of him, and drags him through the mud of this all-but-disappeared town. When he regains his footing, he leans so far into the brutalizing wind that he seems to defy gravity, a body suspended midpratfall (Figure 1.3). Gradually Will turns dimwitted survival into ingenious engineering and brute physical strength. He eventually boards his father's old paddle steamer, the town's sole place of refuge. Utilizing ropes and eccentric nautical savvy, he rescues the film's three other main characters, including, of course, his soon-to-be bride.

Figure 1.1 Will (Keaton) stands with his back to the house facade that is about to fall over him. *Steamboat Bill, Jr.* (1928).

Figure 1.2 Will (Keaton) is now standing over the house facade. *Steamboat Bill, Jr.* (1928).

Figure 1.3 Will (Keaton) is suspended in Keaton's artificial windstorm. *Steamboat Bill, Jr.* (1928).

Will Jr. proves himself worthy of modern love when he transforms his bumbling incapacity into a form of accidental aptitude in the face of natural disaster. In the end, Will improbably brings order to people, things, and the environment they traverse. In fact, beyond merely weathering the storm, he turns its destruction to his romantic advantage. Eric Bullot and Molly Stevens explain that the Keatonian transformation "from obvious incompetence to extreme capability" is typically the result of "urgency, necessity, and the virtues of pragmatism that force him to observe, calculate, and predict" unforeseen outcomes under duress.[1] Failures in the social world, Keaton's heroes manage to thrive in extreme and exceptionally dangerous circumstances, despite that his success is often inadvertent and could just as easily lead to failure.[2] Instead, these heroes discover that destruction is the engine of narrative reconciliation. This is the catastrophic aesthetic of what Bullot and Stevens refer to as Keaton's singularly "devastating humor."[3]

This chapter reads *Steamboat Bill, Jr.* as not simply a trajectory of devastation, but a study in environmental design that always anticipates its future ruination: in other words, the storm scene described previously exposes a manufactured world and a simulated environment that is most virtuosic in its unworking. Creating the most expensive comedy to date, Keaton's company built to scale three full blocks of the fictional River Junction town along the banks of the Sacramento River not far from the state capital.[4] According to the studio press book, thousands of people gathered on the day of Keaton's storm "to witness the synthetic holocaust" that reduced the entire set to rubble.[5] The spectacle of weather design was the central attraction, and the press book explains the engineering behind Keaton's cyclone to his adoring public. Several hoses, cranes, cables, and six wind machines powered by Liberty airplane motors created the fierce drafts and pelting rain.[6] The wind current generated from just one engine was strong enough, recalls Keaton, "to lift a truck right off the road."[7] The *Los Angeles Times* declared in its review that the "wind machines and other storm-producing devices . . . must have been numerous and effective during the making" of *Steamboat*. "There is no end of a hullaballoo when a tornado breaks loose in this comedy. . . . The cyclonic finish of this film is the best part of its entertainment."[8]

Steamboat Bill, Jr. is only the most obvious example of Keaton's climatography. We could also refer to the raging river in *Our Hospitality* (1923), the avalanche of primordial boulders in *Seven Chances* (1925), the abrupt, evicting California storm in *One Week* (1920), and the monsoon-like rains in *The Boat* (1921), to name just a few. Repeatedly, his characters are confronted with erratic and treacherous environments whose unpredictability is incorporated into the gags. Critics rightly discuss Keaton—and slapstick more generally—within the context of urban modernity, machine culture, and the dizzyingly generative and comical features of mechanical reproducibility.[9] But in the examples listed previously it is striking that weather is itself unnatural. Alan Bilton remarks that the "natural world" in Keaton's southern-themed work is "another enormous machine, a vast organic engine prone to both overheating and breaking down. . . . Nature is simply another primed and waiting booby trap . . . deserving respect for its lethal ingenuity and explosive power."[10] Keaton's films fascinate not just because they depict calamitous weather; his shooting itself occasions the *production* of this weather, the direction of its force, and accurate prediction of its effects on real locations, north and south, and this artificiality, moreover, is part of his films' allure as is clear in the publicity and reviews.

These experiments in manufactured weather were not produced with a consciousness of global warming or the planetary force of human enterprise. Yet they tap into an interwar awareness that "natural" disasters were often attributable to industry and war, that "nature" was already a product of "culture." In the American South, for example, coal mining, logging, cash-crop cotton agriculture, and hydrological management had severely disrupted the fragile ecosystem of the Mississippi Delta. In the aftermath of the Great Mississippi Flood of 1927, the most devastating in US history to that time, Americans could not deny that their geo-engineering was a force like nature but one whose long-term consequences were increasingly difficult to calculate. In his 1927 account of the disaster, noted New Orleans journalist Lyle Saxon lambasts the "levees only" policy for flood control that functionally disabled the river's natural spillways, many of which were already destroyed by riverbank settlements.[11] Saxon appears to endorse an editorial from *The Outlook*, reproduced in the book's appendix: "The great floods now ravaging the Mississippi Valley are considered by many to be an 'act of God.' They are, on the contrary, most distinctly the work of man."[12] Though the history of the Mississippi is a history of its flooding, Saxon's account describes the catastrophe as a distinctly modern, anthropogenic event.[13] Indeed, many compared its violence to World War I. The *New Republic* reported that it was the "gravest problem" the nation had faced "since the Great War," and that "the stench from the corpses of drowned animals" decomposing in the floodplain "completes an impression of desolate misery like that of the French devastated regions in the War."[14] In attempting to control the river through the levee system, engineers instead amplified the river's lethal energy. In his own Mississippi River comedy, Keaton plays with cinema's capacity to structure and thus make legible environmental contingency in the age of such "natural" disasters, and he is attuned to the resolutely modern notion, as Ian Hacking explains with reference to Charles Sanders Pierce, that the universe is "irreducibly stochastic."[15]

That Keaton actually designs violent weather (rather than inadvertently unleashing its destructiveness) suggests that the mere comparison between wars and floods does not go far enough. *Steamboat's* "synthetic holocaust" is an entertaining artifice analogous to the militarization of climate science during World War I. Specifically, it is an answer to the creation of lethal environments, or what Peter Sloterdijk calls the paradigm of "ecologized war" inaugurated when Germans released poison gas onto the battlefield at Ypres in 1915.[16] With the enemy entrenched and inaccessible to conventional weapons, Germany's new military strategy targeted not the soldier's body but his life-sustaining environment through a slow-drifting chlorinated "microclimate." Ecological warfare intoxicates the enemy's breathable habitat while keeping one's own airspace clear. From this point forward, writes Sloterdijk, "atmoterrorist warfare" ushered in a wholly new horizon of environmental partition and manipulation, and the concomitant vulnerability of life in times of war and peace. Contra

Walter Benjamin, who asserted that after World War I "nothing remained unchanged but the clouds," Sloterdijk's study tells us that the clouds, above all, changed everything.[17]

Keaton himself knew a thing or two about the risks and slapstick potential of violent storms and war. His early childhood in Piqua, Kansas, gives *Steamboat* a decidedly autobiographical touch. In his memoir, Keaton tells us that shortly after his birth, the town was "blown away during a cyclone" in 1895. As a toddler, a few years later, he awoke to "the noise of a Kansas twister. Getting up I went to the open window to investigate the swishing noise. I didn't fall out of the window, I was sucked out by the circling winds of the cyclone and whirled away down the road." It was, he deadpans, "a pretty strenuous day . . . But superb conditioning for my career as 'The Human Mop.'"[18] Honing his survival skills in tornado alley also prepared him for his service as a foot soldier in France during World War I. Where he expected to encounter bombs and enemy fire, "in that war, we saw little but rain and mud."[19] In this respect, Keaton's war was a bit like his childhood in inclement Kansas; conversely, we may productively think of *Steamboat Bill, Jr.* with its rain, mud, and shelterless town as Keaton's combat film, his "World War I along the Mississippi."

Creating microclimates for his film-aesthetic practice, Keaton reprises his childhood brush with tornados in Kansas, but he also reflects the weather-mindedness of World War I, even as he anticipates the unnatural weather of our contemporary moment. From the unwitting, reactive calamity along the Mississippi to the witting and strategic production of atmospheric weaponry in Europe, Keaton's cinema foregrounds anthropogenic environmental change and modern—at times tragic—modes of inhospitable world-making. Thus, his environmental comedy enables us to glimpse both modern meteorology and what I will describe as modernist weather in the making.

WAITING FOR THE STORM: HOLLYWOOD NORMS AND GRIFFITH'S EXCEPTION

Simulated weather effects were common practice in Hollywood and had coevolved with the creation of climate-controlled film studios and the immense back lots where entire villages and towns could be erected and recorded under natural light and an open sky. Yet open-air filmmaking became something of an exception by 1928. The migration of film companies from the East Coast to Los Angeles during the 1910s is a move typically understood as a search for better weather and more diverse natural locations. Brian R. Jacobson explains that, contrary to this narrative, West Coast production consolidated around the efficiency and artificiality of the enclosed studio and its ability to fabricate any locale. Indeed, Los Angeles weather, he notes, was not as uniformly sunny as its promoters promised. Spring rains, the almost daily clouds, and morning fog meant that even the studio back lot was beholden to California's seasons.[20] Balancing the need to make films on a reliable basis and to satisfy the demand of exhibitors and audiences for interesting and realistic landscapes, the studio heads overcame Southern California's weather system with a "studio system" of their own: "A flexible pro-filmic space comprised of interior studio stages lit by electrical lights, sun-lit backlots built on the principles of studio interior, and 'natural' locations that, like manufactured sets, could serve as repeated shooting sites," as Jacobson explains.[21] As companies expanded their real estate and invested in décor and special effects, "sunlight and natural settings [were] useful but often either inessential or reproducible."[22] With the coming of sound in 1927, the soundstage, insulated from the outside world and infinitely malleable to reproduce the world's appearance, became the dominant space of production. In 1929, the *Los Angeles Times* remarked that "outside locations, while still used more or less effectively, seem to be gradually relegated to the background, and the magnificently constructed settings are becoming more and more prevalent."[23] The author describes the dimensions of an enclosed studio that is 240 feet long, 137 feet wide, and 40 feet high, large enough to accommodate a "complete two story building" and its expansive gardens. The interior landscape boasts "forty varieties of flowers and seven kinds of hedge plants, and the entire set is surrounded by a hedge twenty feet high, topped by towering pine trees."[24] By the 1930s it seemed that there were no places or even weather events that could not be simulated within the confines of the studio under the complete control of the director and production designer. The very title of Hedda Hopper's 1937 article "Hollywood Sets Would Fool Mother Nature: Scenic Experts Make Land, Sea and Sky Look More Realistic than Reality" sums up the unbounded ambitions of production design. While the studios had vast tree nurseries and enormous outdoor lots, designers favored artificial trees anchored in cement. And while grass could grow on the soundstage, designers opted for artificial grass "which could be sprayed with a brighter green hue for brighter results in Technicolor." Indoor lakes were dyed to look more like water when filmed. Rain and floods remained on the soundstage "because technicians find they can control floods much better indoors than out." This is artificiality "done for the sake of realism."[25] Keaton's environmental design is best appreciated against these emergent norms of studio production, on one hand, and the disappearing arts of on-location shooting, on the other, both of which aspired to climatic and dramatic verisimilitude.

Keaton's contemporary D. W. Griffith was perhaps the most strident proponent of scenic realism, an exception to Hollywood's simulationist ethos that proved the efficiency of its rule. *Way Down East* (1920), Griffith's adaptation of Lotte Blair Parker's successful 1897 stage play, is a case in point. This familiar tale of a waifish, working-class, virginal maiden (Lillian Gish) betrayed by an urban aristocratic cad and then rehabilitated by a worthy, upper-class lover was already out of fashion when Griffith embarked on the project. His attraction to the story, however, had less to do with the defense of Victorian virtue than with the demonstration of cinema's superiority over the Victorian stage and even over earlier, studio-bound, special effects.[26] The film climaxes when Gish's character is cast out of the house and into the night blizzard, a storm to which the play symbolically gestures and can only statically stage. In the film adaptation, the violence of the eviction and the girl's emotional turmoil are matched by an actual storm that Griffith shot on location. Gish's Anna Moore, wearing only a thin dress and a shawl, drifts through a blizzard, is blinded by the snow, and is repeatedly blown over by the brutal winds. Griffith expands the parameters of the play's cataclysmic weather when Anna wanders onto a frozen river where she falls unconscious, her hand and hair dangling in the water while her body rests on the ice. At dawn the ice breaks and Anna is prone on a swiftly moving ice floe until her lover, David Bartless (Richard Barthelmess), leaping from one unstable floe to another, rescues her seconds before they would both be engulfed by a massive and precipitous waterfall (Figure 1.4). Filming in Mamaroneck, New York, and White River Junction, Vermont, Gish and Barthelmess performed their own stunts, suffering frostbite and exhaustion as a result and jeopardizing themselves for the sake of Griffith's realism. The *New York Times* reported at the film's premiere that enraptured audiences

> realized finally why it was that D. W. Griffith had selected [this play] for a picture. It was not for its fame. Nor for its heroine. Nor for the wrong done her. It was for the snowstorm. And not just the snowstorm alone, but for the peril-fraught river with its rush of swirling ice cakes.[27]

It is one thing for filmmakers to use the natural world as an occasional backdrop, as was already the norm in Hollywood. Griffith, however, structured his production around New England's seasons, waiting for each in its proper time to film harvests, sled rides, barn dances, and summer fields. The biggest and perhaps most costly drag on production was Griffith's

Figure 1.4 Anna (Gish) awaits her rescue on an actual ice floe. *Way Down East* (1920).

insistence that the final sequences be shot in an actual winter storm. In her memoir, Lillian Gish explains the imperative: "This film needed a real blizzard, not any snowstorm. We had to be able to act in a real blizzard, not subtitled with a sentence description. If this film was going to work, the audiences wanted to see the real thing. Otherwise, whatever we did would be laughable."[28] Theatrical effects, too well known and worn for film audiences, were out of the question, but cameraman Billy Bitzer feared that even a real storm would not be photographable or, worse, might not look authentic on black-and-white film.[29] On March 6, 1920, the skies over Orienta Point in Mamaroneck, New York, where Griffith had built his film studio on a twenty-four-acre estate, finally delivered the much-awaited blizzard with gale-force winds raging across the Long Island Sound. Gish with her costar took to the wintry woods, filming round the clock while the storm persisted. The river sequence was staged weeks later in Vermont, where the crew had to dislodge physically the ice on which Gish floated. Impressive shots of deep-winter Niagara Falls were interspersed as a bit of creative geography to convey the stakes of the last-minute rescue, despite that the actors were really endangered on Vermont ice.[30] In addition to the long shots that find Gish a collapsed figure on swiftly moving drift ice and spectacular panoramas of the ice field and snowstorm, Griffith framed

Figure 1.5 Anna (Gish) is buffeted by the Mamaroneck blizzard. *Way Down East* (1920).

close-ups of Gish in the blizzard, her sweet face made raw by the whipping winds and frozen by the real snow and ice that clung to her lashes (Figure 1.5). American literary critic Edward Wagenknecht, who appreciated the deft cinematography and editing of these thrilling last scenes, nonetheless castigated Griffith. "No director has the right to ask ... what Griffith asked, and no film can be worth such risk and suffering."[31]

The production budget for *Way Down East* totaled $800,000, Griffith's most expensive film to date and among the most expensive films in history up to that time. He financed it at great risk to his own personal income and property, and against the film's international distribution rights. He thus felt compelled to justify the expenditures before the film's release. In an unpublished open letter to his fans, Griffith posed the question of how a film depending only on "tears, comedy and human interest" and shot in relatively modest sets could cost so much. The answer simply was that the crew first had to wait for each season "to secure the proper atmosphere," and then devote months of time to the final blizzard sequence:

> We have attempted nothing that seemed so impossible as the photographing of the elemental resistless force. ... The plain truth, that despite its simple setting,

[32]   *On Location . . .*

it is the most expensive entertainment that has ever been given since Caesar plated the arena with silver for the citizens of ancient Rome.[32]

Though the film was as successful as it was hazardous (according to *Variety*, it earned $5 million at the box office and was the fourth-highest-grossing silent film in US history), Griffith struggled to keep his production company in the black.[33]

For his next monumental feature, *Orphans of the Storm* (1921), Griffith built elaborate and historically accurate sets over fourteen acres of his Mamaroneck estate to reproduce France on the eve of revolution. While he could build replicas of Notre Dame, Versailles, and the Bastille, the snow required for the winter scenes had to be real. Chastened by the wait for *Way Down East*'s perfect storm, Griffith took out what was a curious first in the annals of American actuarial science. He insured his production against losses up to $25,000 not in the event of a storm, but rather in the nonevent of snow *not* falling between October and November 20, 1921, in Mamaroneck when production was scheduled to end. As the *New York Times* reported, "A real storm is needed, for only on the stage can the two orphans be lost in a fall of paper snow." The weather risk was distributed among eighteen companies. The *Times* continues: "This is the first time a policy has been written in America for a snow storm. Many have been written against a storm."[34] When November 20 came and went without flurries, Griffith apparently submitted his claim.[35] As a first, this film insurance may also have been the last.

As a set designer, Griffith was a fastidious recreationist, dedicated to constructing buildings and interior rooms on location with maddening exactitude for historical detail. But when it came to filming actual weather, Griffith was a naturalist, and the weather, it seems, eluded exact prediction. Eighteen companies could not foresee the pattern of snowfall and wintry precipitation in New York between October and November, and Griffith, collecting on his policy, had to extend his shooting schedule. Yet in Griffith's sentimental dramaturgy weather is never random, however indifferent it may be to his filmmaking purposes. In both *Way Down East* and *Orphans of the Storm*, rain, snow, and even sunshine are attuned to human emotions and they amplify (though are rarely the root cause of) characters' suffering and joy. It is not snow but the class inequality and the anarchic storm of the French Revolution that besets the poor girls in *Orphans*, and their fragile social state is played against snowy scenes twice in the film. First is when the two infants are laid at the "foundling steps of Notre Dame." Louise is abandoned because her mother, a countess, has married a commoner. To protect his family's reputation, the countess's father orders her husband slayed and leaves the baby (his own granddaughter) on the snow-swept steps. Henrietta, the other orphan, is born to impoverished parents who, unable to feed her, plan to leave her at the cathedral. Yet when Henrietta's father sees this other infant freezing in the snow, he decides against deserting his own daughter in the elements and commits to raising baby Louise as his own. His ruse of leaving an infant in snow to attract the pity of passersby works too well. "So Life's journey begins." In the second snow scene Louise (Dorothy Gish), now grown, is blind and forced by a dastardly family who has abducted her to beg outside of Notre Dame. The snow falls, Louise trembles with cold, and citizens leaving church give her alms, including the countess and the good doctor who will eventually restore her vision. These two snow scenes are not just important to convey the precariousness of these girls to the audience; Griffith's weather sentiment is explicitly part of the characters' plotting. Leaving babies in the snow, forcing a blind girl to beg—the *characters* in this film orchestrate the sympathy of others by exploiting the pathos of these natural conditions. "You'll shiver better without a shawl," says the mustachioed hag to Louise. Stripping her of her last protection against the elements and thus making her plight as an impoverished blind girl even more obscene, the old beggar pushes her back onto Notre Dame's steps. These characters know that weather carries a pathetic charge.

At the end of the film, the revolution gives way to "a REAL DEMOCRACY," as an intertitle emphatically informs us. "Then are the rights restored and do gardens bloom again." Naturalizing this state of political affairs, Griffith stages the sisters' long-awaited reunion and Louise's restored vision in a blooming garden. The radiant sun is a sign and supplement to the sisters' abundant joy. But just off-screen, we must surmise that Griffith was still waiting to film the snow. In *Orphans of the Storm* Griffith plays pathetic fallacy in the film against the unpredictable patterns of pro-filmic weather that erupts utterly independent of any human feeling, no doubt aggravating Griffith and his insurers. It is little wonder that West Coast set designers would take to the great indoors, creating storms, sun, and snow on demand and as required by the script, reserving what Mark Shiel calls "unmediated, chance-based images"— shots of actual storms, clouds, and rain—for those rare occasions when script, production schedule, and California weather aligned.[36]

KEATON'S ENVIRONMENTAL DESIGN

Keaton's environmental design is of an entirely different order. Taking a page from Lillian Gish's memoir, he understands that artificial weather has an inherently comic touch and *Steamboat Bill, Jr.* rather uniquely thematizes weather *simulation* (as opposed to its pathetic registers) within the diegesis itself. One of the many winks to the audience, on this score, comes with the first of two weather reports. Following a shot of Will in sunny skies, an insert of the local newspaper gently warns: "Weather Conditions: Unsettled—wet and cloudy." We then cut back to Will slogging through strong winds and a unrelenting downpour. Moments later we have an update from the same printed source: "Storm clouds in the offing." In the shot that follows we find the town dealing with a full-fledged cyclone. Using comic understatement, the sequence highlights the familiar disparity between the techniques of presumably high-tech weather prediction and local experience, while the film also mocks the inadequacy of modern technology, sciences, and infrastructures—for example, River Junction's bank, new hotel, modern rival steamboat, and twentieth-century meteorology—all of which collapse in the face of a good old-fashioned storm. Or, perhaps it is more accurate to observe that Keaton uses modern technology to produce local weather experience that is designed to insult advanced prediction and assault modern institutions.

Keaton's weather reflexivity continues when Will scrambles into the community theater seeking shelter. A medium shot shows us the stage door. When Will arrives, Keaton cuts to a long shot and we discover that this door frame is freestanding because the rest of the wall to which it was once attached has been blown away. Soon, in slapstick fashion, this door too collapses over Will as he passes through the threshold—a small-scale version of the house-falling gag discussed earlier. Behind him we see piles of debris: bed frames, decimated furniture, bits of roof and scaffolding, and broken trunks full of clothes (or are they costumes?). Tearing down the first and the fourth wall, the storm promiscuously mingles art and life, whereby theater props are indistinguishable from the scattering of River Junction's "real life" furnishings such props presumably replicate (Figure 1.6).[37] But the scene continues to confound artifice and on-location realism: the next camera position juxtaposes storm rubble in the foreground against a bucolic river landscape that mirrors the film's opening image of the tranquil shoreline of River Junction (Figures 1.7 and 1.8). At first glance the shot seems a continuity error or a violation of temporal sequencing, until we realize that this idyll is a painted backdrop hung from the theater's one remaining wall, and thus an unwitting memento of an unruined town. The momentary disruption of the illusion of the total storm is a matter of perceptual organization, one that coyly cites cinema's theatrical inheritance while also sensitizing the viewer to the suspensions of disbelief required to achieve weather semblance. Keaton then literalizes this altered consciousness (and momentary suspension) when he cuts to reveal the theater's fly loft and

Figure 1.6 Will (Keaton) enters the local theater where real and diegetic props mingle. *Steamboat Bill, Jr.* (1928).

Figure 1.7 Will (Keaton) is dumbfounded by the theater's painted backdrop of calm weather. *Steamboat Bill, Jr.* (1928).

Figure 1.8 A view of the town's tranquil riverbank before the storm resembles the theater's painted backdrop. *Steamboat Bill, Jr.* (1928).

the obligatory sandbag that will fall on Will's already bruised head: disoriented from yet another blow, Will attempts to leap to safety in the still waters of theater's painted still life, only to crash to Earth. When the theater's last wall gives way, Will is once again exposed to the cinematic world and Keaton's storm surge. This series of gags performs the obsolescence of theater's two-dimensional effects and early cinema's studio-bound production in the face of cinema's on-location realism. Though nineteenth- and early twentieth-century sensational melodrama created within the theater's space spectacular effects such as conflagrations, floods, avalanches, and tornadoes, Keaton enacts here the transition from the shallow space of theater and painted backdrops to the unbounded dimensions and world-making capacity of the immersive cinematic environment, whose "naturalism" is always in doubt.[38]

The slapstick misrecognition on the community stage does more than literally and figuratively turn theater and artifice inside out; it functions as a mise-en-abyme that captures the technical achievement of manufactured weather on location. Gags such as the falling house require near-perfect environmental control, or as Keaton explains:

> We had to make sure that we were getting our foreground and background wind effect, but that no current ever hit the front of that building when it started to

fall, because if the wind warps her she's not going to fall where we want her, and I'm standing right out in front. . . . [I]t's a one-take scene. . . . [Y]ou don't do those things twice.³⁹

With only a two-inch margin for error on all sides, the real weather conditions on the Sacramento River must be perfectly stable if Keaton is to survive this stunt. In fact, in many of the shots in which rain and wind pummel people and things, we see sharp shadows cast on the ground, suggesting that *Steamboat* was shot almost entirely under sunny skies, a mismatch anathema to Griffith's melodrama (e.g., see the shadows cast by the sun in Figure 1.3). We may surmise, then, that the painted backdrop in *Steamboat*'s theater sequence mimics the actual weather conditions—clear and calm—on the day that Keaton obliterated River Junction. In other words, Keaton's perfect storm does not originate in the clouds, but in the near-perfectly predictable and friendly environment at California's capital, just as Keaton's doomed river town must be built according to the most precise specifications so as to fall apart safely. His disaster architecture is likewise designed to *succumb* to the elements rather than endure their force. That Keaton reflexively reveals and riffs on the distinction between real and artificial weather means that any weather "pattern" is itself discontinuous, fragmentary, and, at times for these reasons, rather funny. One striking feature of Keaton's work is the constant shuttling between, and thus drawing attention to, these spontaneous incongruities of climatic simulation. After Miriam Hansen's famous formulation, we might call Keaton's weather a "reflexive modernist ecology" that foregrounds artificiality and the techniques of environmental design.⁴⁰

The reflexivity of Keaton's gag structure, moreover, puts engineering on display such that we apprehend a distinction between the character's predicament and the metteur-en-scène's arrangement of and intervention into the diegetic world.⁴¹ Will, for example, survives the house-falling sequence only because Keaton carefully placed his character in the exact position of the open window and then cut power to the wind machines. Within the film, Will's survival is merely dumb luck. We are thus ever mindful when watching a Keaton film of the director's intelligent design and technological savvy that pushes the character's adaptability to new limits, a point to which I'll return later in the chapter.

The effect of Keaton's engineering is somewhat distinct from the techniques of the self-reflexive musical, slapstick's generic close cousin. Jane Feuer explains that the heroes of musicals are marked as such by their spontaneous reappropriation of found objects and environments for use in their unrehearsed performances. This bricolage produces the effect of inventive spontaneity by concealing engineering or "technological know-how" of successful numbers.[42] Let us consider what Feuer calls the "nature of this illusion" as exemplified in the well-known title number of *Singin' in the Rain* (1952), conveniently a number about the weather in a story that selectively reveals the techniques of Hollywood's behind-the-scenes artifice in the vast indoor studios. When Don Lockwood (Gene Kelly) erupts into song and dance while walking home in a serendipitous downpour, the apparent simplicity of the mise-en-scène and choreography conceal the number's high-tech production and Kelly's virtuosic technique. This concealment also relegates to the background the manufactured environment, despite that earlier numbers show Don manipulating fans, filtered lights, and fog machines to transform a dark soundstage into an idealized romantic setting. So that audiences would perceive Kelly's carefully rehearsed tapping as Don's mere spontaneous splashing, M-G-M had to pipe in "rain," calibrate water pressure and pattern, and hollow out precise spaces for puddles to form.[43] Within the diegesis, however, it is Don Lockwood who transforms a given space into a place of performance through his romantic burst of energy. To rephrase Feuer, this feat of engineering pivots on a vision of "nature" as convincing illusion against which the performance itself is naturalized. It is virtuous characters and not an off-screen director who order the world by imaginatively manipulating its elements.

Feuer also tells us that the production of this uncharacteristic rainstorm in *Singin' in the Rain*'s fictional Hollywood was threatened by an actual (and far more characteristic) Los Angeles drought. M-G-M competed for water and water pressure with the residents of Culver City who were sprinkling their parched lawns after work. With these extra-cinematic environmental conditions in mind, we may read the following exchange between Don and his girlfriend Cathy (Debbie Reynolds) before the title number as more than just romantic banter. At night, they stand at the entrance to her apartment building kissing goodbye under an umbrella as the rain pours down.

> CATHY: Take care of that throat. You're a big singing star now. Remember? This California dew is just a little bit heavier than usual tonight.
> DON: Really? From where I'm standing the sun is shining all over the place.

Love mentally transforms rain at night into sunny skies, to be sure. In the case of this scene, shot over two sunny days in the midst of a drought, a steady downpour in Hollywood was wishful thinking: the sun really was shining all over the place.

More to the point, however, Keaton's films stand out because the director's will overshadows the characters' abilities. Writing of the extended cannonball-train gag in *The General*, Lisa Trahair claims that what we see is not the character's successful manipulation of the materials at hand, but the work of the director who stages and times the "perfect contingency" on which the sequence rests. The "instrumental malfunctioning of the Keaton character gives way to the ordering forth of the director who orchestrates the mise-en-scène to rescue [his character] from the consequences of his ineptitude."[44] Because we know that Keaton's character is subject to the director's manipulation, we apprehend as an illusion the idea that man is master of his world. It was this feature of slapstick's agnostic fortuitousness that fascinated Siegfried Kracauer. He remarks that the character's triumph is a result of chance. "Accidents superseded destiny; unpredictable circumstances now foreshadowed doom, now jelled into propitious constellations for no visible reason." A character is beholden to "a random combination of external and completely incoherent events which, without being intended to come to his help, dovetailed so perfectly" that he has no choice but to survive deathly falls.[45] Whereas Don Lockwood is in control of his environment, Will (along with Keaton's other characters) is beholden to a nondiegetic force to which he can only react. "Keaton's meditation," concludes Trahair, "is a lucid articulation of what becomes of subjectivity in a world where film doubles reality (and vise-versa)."[46] The modern subject finds himself in ever-diminished control over his simulated world and, at the same time, discovers new features of his ecological dependency—a form of knowledge that, for Sloterdijk, is the signature of twentieth-century modernist aesthetics.

MANUFACTURED CLIMATES AND THE ECOLOGIES OF WAR

The chlorine gas cloud over Ypres in 1915, argues Sloterdijk, is a climatological fabrication that "sheds light on modernity as a process of atmosphere-explication."[47] By gassing the troops and using their respiratory reflexes against them, the Germans explicated features of a habitable environment that were previously taken for granted or were, in the Heideggerian sense, the background givens of our world. Gasping for air, the Canadian soldiers were confronted with their dependency on an oxygenated, nonchlorinated environment. The new reign of terror targets "the enemy's primary, ecologically dependent vital functions: respiration, central nervous regulation, and sustainable temperature and radiation conditions." And thus did World War I give rise to a "discovery of the 'environment.'"[48]

Apropos of Keaton's layered mise-en-scène in which artificial weather foregrounds the fact that there is no "natural" weather in his film, atmospheric explication is both a revealing and simultaneous concealing of atmospheric conditions. Chlorine gas discloses the nonacidity of what had passed for normal nonchlorinated air. In concealing with chlorine the properties of Ypres's typical air, the German military explicated its now-compromised quality. Under such circumstances, "the living organism's immersion in a breathable milieu arrives at the level of formal representation bringing the climatic and atmospheric conditions pertaining to human life to a new level of explication."[49] In this respect, explication corresponds to Martin Heidegger's notion of unconcealment whereby poison gas (in this case) makes available conceptual and then practical knowledge of atmospheric givens. Unconcealment names the event in which things that have always been present become known because they are now deemed useful or meaningful to our lives according to our orientation in the world.[50] The perversity of Sloterdijk's formulation is that whereas unconcealment leads to a new orientation and understanding of things as they are, explication produces an epistemology that is also a terrifying human ontology. That is, to know atmospheric explication is indivisible from being vulnerable to its lethal purpose. The "formal representation" of the atmosphere intimates how the designs for war and designs for art comingle in our perception of the modern world, such that we understand that air, climate, and atmosphere are manipulable "media of existence" whose now-explicated life-sustaining properties are no longer assured.[51]

The correspondence between climatic weaponry and artistry (or the "art of terrorist warfare") is essential to Sloterdijk's historical argument. Poison gas "had all the features of an act of design, one according to which 'within the rules of art' human beings produce and design more or less precisely delimitable microclimata of death for other human beings."[52] Likewise, modernist aesthetics make explicit previously latent processes and backgrounds of artistic creation. Sloterdijk finds parallels between atmospheric war and the combative practices of both Kazimir Malevich's suprematist compositions and Salvador Dali's paranoid criticism. In *Black Square* (1913), for example, Malevich foregrounds and takes as his subject what was previously the background of the painting: "The background as such is meticulously painted and thus turned into the explicit figure of figure-bearing."[53]

Dali makes explicit the unconscious processes—the dreamwork, the automatic writing, the sublimated desires and willed madness—that modern artists channel. Admittedly, these aesthetic reprioritizations are a far cry from poison gas. But they share with this war the principle of objectifying what were once the unperceivable facets of artistic expression and thus are of a piece with modernity's explicating regime. While no one is physically harmed by viewing *Black Square*, the artwork itself is a form of aesthetic hostage taking. The suprematist ambition provokes "the terror of purification," where the negative composition "demands the unconditional surrender of viewer perception to its real presence."[54]

If the gassing of troops at Ypres is the founding event of atmoterrorism, Dali's presentation at the 1936 *International Surrealist Exhibition* intimates its slapstick counterpart. Sloterdijk recounts how Dali addressed the London crowd in a scuba suit to announce his radical otherworldliness and his submergence in a kind of liquid unconscious. His speech was cut short, however, because he failed to provide himself with an oxygen source. "But," writes Dali of this unscripted horror, "my facial expressions fascinated the audience. Soon they saw me open-mouthed, apoplectic, then turning blue, my eyes revulsed."[55] The crowd applauded enthusiastically, unable to differentiate Dali's performance of the unconscious from its near actualization. For Sloterdijk, this anecdote speaks to the amateurism of surrealism, whose proponents misuse and confuse the objects of science for art, while showcasing Dali's participation in atmospheric design attained, in this instance, through unbidden anoxia. The hostile environment is also the bedrock of Keaton's comedy, of which the surrealists were ardent fans. A similar stunt closes *The Navigator* (1924). Rollo Treadway (Keaton) is dallying on the sea floor in a scuba suit trying to repair the eponymous ocean liner when cannibals cut his air supply. Treadway begins comically to asphyxiate and, like Dali after him, struggles in vain to release himself from the suit or detach his helmet. Thanks to Keaton's real-world competency, however, Treadway manages to complete a spectacular underwater sequence, wherein he battles an octopus and then walks to shore, where he frightens the cannibals with his aquatic attire. In the film's final moments, Treadway and his girlfriend flee the scene of near anthropophagy when a submarine unexpectedly emerges from the ocean depths and whisks them to safety.

Sloterdijk explains that the solution to Dali's suffocation is to pry off the helmet and breathe the external air. Today such a response is almost pointless since the majority of us respire in contained and air-conditioned environments more often than not and the air, outside, is hardly uncontaminated. Is it thus fitting that in *The Navigator*, Treadway is rescued from the cannibals when a submarine provides the escape hatch, not out of but into the vessel. Exchanging one underwater breathing system with a larger-scale version, Keaton's dénouement testifies to Sloterdijk's claim that "the process of atmospheric explication bars all return to once taken-for-granted implicit conditions."[56] As modern humans manufacture ever-expanding environments of death, they aggressively create contained conditions for life. Bereft of concealed places to hide, we have rendered ourselves homeless. Rereading Heidegger, Sloterdijk explains homelessness "in the sense of the human being's banishment from its natural air-envelope and re-settlement in climate-controlled spaces; more radically still, the discourse of homelessness can be read as symbolizing the change of epoch implied by the exodus out of all the remaining protective niches and into latency."[57] This "change in epoch" that for Sloterdijk is aesthetic and militaristic modernism may also be read, of course, as the new geological paradigm of the Anthropocene.

Quite apart from climate design, the militarization of the weather has a long history because modern meteorology has always been a martial science. It was in the 1870s that Ulysses S. Grant established the US Weather Bureau housed within the Department of War by which time the language of "storm fronts" and descriptions of lightning's sulfurous odor, akin to the smell of exploded gunpowder, were already firmly entrenched.[58] Mary Favret remarks of the military and Romantic metaphoric: "The vehicle for understanding the weather is war—not vice versa: war is apparently familiar enough to explain the otherwise inexplicable or unknown. Destructive, volatile, and unpredictable in outcome, war and its gunpowder somehow humanizes the weather—or at least keeps it grounded."[59] Indeed, as she argues, the model of a global weather system was, in Britain, the meteorological response to the Napoleonic wars. The changing British skies encrypted news of distant battles, and weather, like war, was understood as part of a threatening global system. Before the late eighteenth century, weather was conceived as a local, edaphic phenomenon that erupted from the earth below and very often defined or naturalized the political spirit of a circumscribed place. D. W. Griffith's sympathetic weather and sunlit democracy in *Orphans of the Storm* come to mind here. Does the sun shine on France's already bright political future after the revolution? Or is the democratic future possible only because the sun shines? This climatological determinism is part of Griffith's pathetic fallacy.

It was during World War I that meteorology became a truly predictive science. Battling on multiple fronts and bombing from above, all participating nations soon came to realize that air currents and rain, cold fronts and storms not only were the remnants of the weather and war that had rained on other people (as was the case during the Napoleonic wars) but also could be read for the conditions of weather and visibility to come. Essential to geo-military strategy, weather prediction, explains Robert Marc Friedman, underwent a "conceptual change" from a "two-dimensional geometrical model . . . based on kinematics of the wind flow" to "three dimensional models of physical weather-carrying systems in the atmosphere" that could account precisely for the movement of storm fronts and air currents for flight and gunnery, as well as small-scale atmospheric patterns closer to the ground for gas attacks.[60] Where other sciences such as chemistry applied directly to munitions, modern meteorology rationalized world war by mapping weather in space and time and, in the process, codifying and regularizing the experience of weather (or the description of that experience) across regional and cultural differences.[61] If Romantic war symptomatizes and humanizes weather, modern weather also systematizes and increasingly depersonalizes global war.

The poison gas attacks exemplify the new meteorological sensibility. The Germans were able to kill and impair the enemy from a safe distance by possessing reliable foreknowledge of the air currents at Ypres. Too much wind would dissipate the fog to ineffectual levels of air saturation. A change in wind direction, and the Germans would be asphyxiating themselves. Atmoterrorism is a highly localized, topographical phenomenon, which is viable as a weapon only when the attacker has mastered the weather system and climatic norms of the battleground. Keaton's climatic antics are similarly local, delimited, but only possible when the forecast for the day's shoot is predictably clear and calm. In fact, because *Steamboat* anchors its stunts in carefully produced wind and rain, "fair weather" becomes, in this film, a meteorological event and not simply a nonremarkable default that the storm interrupts. That is—and this is essential to Keaton's sensibility—there is no "background" or "given" weather in this film, unless it is literally a painted backdrop. All wind and rain, sun and calm need to be read as specifically produced. Modernist weather in the age of its mechanical reproducibility dispenses with norms, or it suggests that fabricated unpredictability is itself "the new normal." In Keaton's weather-minded cinema, there is no climate against which storms and other intemperate variances arise; there is only weather.

It is worth noting that slapstick came into its own around 1915 when it evolved from pie-in-the-face burlesque theater to ever more elaborate large studio stunts and what I will call *plein air comedy* in such films as *Ambrose's Nasty Temper* (1915) and *Fatty and Mabel Adrift* (1916). As Rob King points out, though these early films have nothing narratively to do with war, their stunts were inspired by military technology including airships, scuba technology, and submarines (all of which, we should note, presume forms of air design) and the creation of sets and later locations large and controlled enough to accommodate cinematic world-making and -unmaking. Audiences became as interested in the spectacle of the stunts as they were in the techniques of their productions. Fatty Arbuckle, Keaton's mentor, made his name at Keystone Studios, where slapstick magic was guarded as top-secret information. A 1917 *Photoplay* cartoon represents the studio as a heavily fortified citadel, armed against the spies from lesser film producers: "Keystone's tricks," writes King, "are equivalent to state secrets in a time of war." [62] It is no coincidence that Keaton describes his soldiering in France during World War I as a series of gags and funny mishaps in foul weather that began when he was issued a uniform and shoes several sizes too big: "I was not amused to find slapstick flowing over into my new life in the Army."[63] Fortunately, his misadventures on the vaudeville stage and later on the film set were far more dangerous than war. His only field wounds were temporary hearing loss and a nasty sinus infection contracted while spending night after night on the draughty floors of French mills and stables. For Keaton, World War I had none of the airborne threats of bombs or poison gas. His Great War was the effortful routine of sleeping in barns and slogging through France's sodden countryside in a downpour in clown-size shoes. An almost too poetic touch, his infantry division was nicknamed "The Sunshine Division."[64]

FUNNY WEATHER AND ENVIRONMENTAL COMEDY

Tyrus Miller explains that late modernist laughter exploded from the trenches of World War I as a prophylactic affect that stiffened the subject "against danger, marking that minimal spatial difference between conscious life and the pure extensivity of dead nature: a difference that preserves the subject, however diminished, in situations of adversity."[65] Laughter automatically and defensively (and sometimes against a subject's will) erupts when encountering another body riddled with shrapnel or deformed by poison gas. It also describes a deadening response to the imperiled self. Hardened laughter thus is a form of playing dead to survive. Or as Miller, quoting Adorno and Horkheimer, remarks, "by adaptation to death, life pays the toll of its continued existence."[66] This is not a "sense of humor," as Miller later explains, but an anesthetic response to modern desubjectifization that the Great War presaged. The "dead nature" to which Miller refers is the mute inanimate death world that encases the etiolated, but still vital subject of war. In Keaton's work "dead nature" resonates more as the simulated environment that forms both the background and foreground of his admittedly deadpan and entirely exteriorized performance. But what is so funny about Keaton's weather? What are the features of modernist weather that provoke modernist laughter?

The publicity for *Steamboat Bill, Jr.* pitches the comic and high entertainment value of the storm's destructive force: "Gales of Laughter! What spectacular tornado action—dynamic and awesome one moment, laugh-echoing the next! What a wow!"[67] The alternation between awe and laughter, comedy and horror is more funny than melodramatic because, as one promotional feature explains, the weather bears no cosmological grudge and destroys with no particular purpose beyond amusement. "River Junction perished not because it was wicked, but because the world must be entertained, and in this case the entertainment is a tornado as funny as it is awesome."[68] This causality is in contrast to the conventions of the disaster film, such as John Ford's *The Hurricane* (1937), in which weather becomes a force of divine justice against the hubris of human law and ambition. Set on a fictional Polynesian island under French colonial rule, the film focuses on the tribulations of the native islander Terengi (John Hall), who is unjustly imprisoned in Tunisia and then, after his escape, hunted on his home island by the cold and unwavering French governor. Terangi's certain capture is thwarted by the thrilling hurricane. As the governor stubbornly sets sail in pursuit, the good doctor (Thomas Mitchell) warns him of the storm's *moral* power. "When you feel the might of the sea and the wind maybe you'll discover that there's something greater in this world that the French criminal code! . . . Yeah, Terangi is out there. Go chase him! Then hear God howl and laugh at you." When the hurricane hits with impressive force and decimates the entire island community including most of its inhabitants, we are led to the conclusion that God himself condemns the colonial world order and produces an apocalyptic storm to make this point. But there is something about the storm itself that maintains the narrative's dramatic tenor.

The publicity for *The Hurricane* explains that the storm, attributed to a vengeful God in the film, was in fact the work of men. The fictional island community, including the sizable lagoon, was created on two and half acres of the United Artists back lot, once it became clear that mounting a hurricane on the Samoan island of Tutuila would be too costly and involve a considerable "weather gamble." Water tanks, hydroelectric pumps, carefully engineered spillways, and twelve fans powered by 8-cylinder Liberty airplane motors (each capable of lashing out a 90-mile-an-hour gale) created fifty-foot tidal waves and pelting rain strong enough to demolish the elaborate set and to genuinely batter the actors.[69] Samoan natives, cast as extras to lend the film an authentic touch, testified to the authenticity of this engineered storm—or so the publicity goes. Compared to "their experience with the real thing," this hurricane "was as bad as any that they had seen." According to the press book, they were so convinced by the special effects that their terror in the film was not "acting" but a rational response to the very real deluge of water in the studio under the director's control. Even the primary cast members are no longer in character per se, but trying to hit their marks against the elements. Thus had Goldwyn, Ford, and hurricane designer James Basevi "duplicated nature's furies without exacting nature's toll of life" in the nondiegetic space of the studio.[70] *New York Times* film critic Frank Nugent marveled at the storm's total appeal to the senses. "It is a hurricane to fill your eyes with spindrift, to beat at your ears with its thunder, to clutch at your heart and send your diaphragm vaulting over your floating rib into the region just south of your tonsils."[71] The storm was so convincing and seamlessly presented that those acting in the film (or so we're told), as well as those watching in the theater, were mystified by its mimetic power. "I suppose most of it was done with mirrors," muses Nugent. "Inside stories have whispered of miniatures. . . . If this is make-believe, nature must make the best of it; she has been played to perfection."[72] That the storm is synthetic does not in any way diminish its force. The United Artists press book recommends that producer Samuel Goldwyn be enshrined in Samoa "as the chief of their gallery of local gods, with the appropriate name, He-Who-Makes-Hurricanes-Better-Than-the-Gods."[73] In contrast to both *The Hurricane* and Griffith's storms, Keaton's tornado is funny because it is random and unexpected, spectacular but survivable. In fact, Keaton inverts the weather realism of the dominant paradigm. His storm is obviously anthropogenic, but it is not necessarily, or is only incidentally, anthropocentric. This is this basis of his environmental comedy and what makes him such a fascinating director of the Anthropocene.

Keaton originally wrote *Steamboat* as a flood comedy to debut only months after the waters of the Great Mississippi Flood had finally receded. The publicity department at Joseph Schenck's studio claimed that the floods were too frequent and deadly for laughs and thus an inappropriate subject for Keaton's next film. "That's funny," said Keaton, "since it seems to me that Chaplin during World War I made a picture called *Shoulder Arms*, which was the biggest money-maker he'd made at that time. You can't get a bigger disaster than that, and yet he made his biggest laughing picture out of it."[74] Following from Keaton's analogy, the comedy of war is a precedent for the catastrophe of weather even as weather's destruction is made intelligible by comparison to war. And, of course, *Shoulder Arms* features a grimly funny flood scene in the trenches. Unable to persuade the studio and its sense of actuarial entertainments, Keaton decided to simulate a cyclone. The studio agreed to the revised calamity despite that cyclones and hurricanes killed four times more people in the United States than floods, as Keaton later pointed out. In 1926, two years before *Steamboat*'s release, Southern California was hit by a megastorm that, over the course of two days, generated five hugely destructive tornadoes, several mini cyclones, and deadly lightning strikes. Tornadoes demolished communities up and down the coast, while winds and unruly water currents sent fishing barges violently onto shore. Lightning struck the Union Oil tank farm in San Luis Obispo, igniting the largest and hottest oil fire in US history up to that time.[75] Mike Davis explains in his book on Los Angeles disasters (in a chapter appropriately titled "Our Secret Kansas") that Californians are more bemused than frightened by tornadoes, celebrating them "as not only the most violent but also the quirkiest windstorms in nature. Their capricious behavior—taking the cradle but leaving the baby safe—constitutes an entire genre of American folklore."[76] Perhaps for this reason, California's tornado epidemic (Los Angeles is hit by tornadoes twice as often as Oklahoma City) remains "culturally invisible," or latent and concealed.[77] Sounding this cultural disposition, the studio press book for Ford's *The Hurricane* declares that the tropical hurricane, utterly lacking in humor, is "a complete villain" due to its relentless and lethal power. "There is no compromise, no preparation or prevention for the hurricane. Earthquakes, floods and fires may be beaten, or even stopped, but the hurricane refuses to accept man as the lord of creation." A cyclone—described in this same feature article as the hurricane's "inland cousin"—is "a comedian, more noted for its freakish pranks than for the amount of damage which it inflicts."[78]

Humorless weather, like world war, is totalizing and complete, both in its destruction and, in film, as apprehended through special effects. Funny weather—mischievous and unpredictable—is also partial, its illusion incomplete. In its cinematic simulation, it reveals the gaps between pro-filmic and fictional conditions and thus has something in common with comic acting. James Naremore writes that the comic actor "disrupts coherence at every level of the performance, deriving laughter not only from the foolish inconsistency of the characters but from a split between actor and role."[79] When executing gags, Keaton is simultaneously the character he plays and the deadpan comedian stunt man, and often, the director of the fictional action. What Naremore refers to as an "alienated style" of comic performance pushes slapstick to the brink of "radical deconstruction."

> By its very nature, comedy undermines our involvement with the characters, barely maintaining a dramatic illusion. It might depict violent or deadly action, but it does so in a way that invites us to observe plot machinery *as* machinery. Every comic actor is therefore something of a deconstructionist, calling attention to the way we manufacture our socialized selves.[80]

Similarly, comic weather barely maintains its impression. This is detotalizing artificiality in the service of undermining the givenness of the environment. The effect is comic and climatic alienation.

This formulation begins to explain our response to other forms of simulation. Alfred Hitchcock's *Spellbound* (1945), for example, loses its suspenseful momentum when Gregory Peck and Ingrid Bergman ski down a mountain slope that is obviously rear-projected. Long shots of stunt doubles flying down a snowy run are intercut with medium shots of our actors who calmly knee bend in front of a wind machine while the background flies by. We note the incongruity of depth cues in these closer views and the disparity between background speed and foregrounded bodily stasis. Bergman's horror at the deathly precipice at the end of the run is incommensurate with her obvious safety in a rear-projected world. This is an example of climatic camp, a moment of "failed seriousness" as Susan Sontag would call it, which occurs when the artifice of melodramatic weather breaks.[81] Bergman is fearful of a nonpresent danger because she inhabits the "glaring implausibility" of what Laura Mulvey identifies as rear projection's "clumsy sublime." This composite aesthetic, in which foregrounds are spatially and temporally at odds with their backgrounds, tends to "immobilize" the actor "paradoxically at the very moment in the film when there is a fictional high point of speed, mobility, or dramatic incident," a caesura that exposes the effects of celluloid manipulation and turns acting into a "self-conscious, vulnerable, and transparent" performance.[82] Keaton's character, by contrast, is imperiled when he is forced to respond to phenomenally real, physically proximate danger from which he, by slapstick convention, will safely emerge. Keaton achieves comedy and not camp because, in placing himself within a dangerous microenvironment and framed by authenticating long shots, he demonstrates that the effects of the weather are real even if they are simulated at their source and purposefully inconsistent in their manifestations. Indeed, *because* it does not ask us to take the threat or its consequences too seriously in the diegesis—because it does not court failed seriousness—Keaton's film better conveys the real horror of his pro-filmic endangerment in ways that give us some confidence in our own adaptability.[83]

Even for today's audiences, slapstick may thus be the appropriate antidote to environmental sensationalism on which we fixate in inclement moments. Martia Sturken writes that our contemporary storm fetishism and obsession with forecasts explain the success of the Weather Channel: "In the story of the weather and survival of dramatic natural disasters, the viewers of weather media are asked to reassure themselves that they can survive the everyday difficulties of life as they know it," even as they witness the failure of others from the safety of home. With melodramatic absorption, we helplessly watch other people's weather, which arrives so suddenly, forcefully, and lethally that we shudder at the frailty of human life and our powerlessness over violent storms. But there is a difference and differently registered purpose in laughing at survival in what *Steamboat*'s publicity materials earlier called a "synthetic holocaust."[84]

For many critics, Keaton's laughter is of a Bergsonian variety; it is a corrective response to a mechanical encrustation on human life, to the automatism and inelasticity that renders the human artificial and thing-like.[85] The effect, writes Bergson, is that the rigid body appears "immersed and absorbed in the materiality of some mechanical occupation instead of ceaselessly reviewing its vitality by keeping in touch with a living ideal."[86] In a similar formulation, Noël Carroll argues that Keaton's gags are structured by inattention, in which characters are either too preoccupied or narrowly focused to register and appropriately respond to changes in their surroundings.[87] Comedy occurs in the interval between situational change and the character's belated response. As a result of "deferred attention," the character finds himself "out of synchronization with his environment."[88] Carroll is adamant that this asynchrony is not a contest between man and the natural world: "The environment is not chaotic: it is rule-bound and law-like in Keaton. If it were not, his success would be impossible. He can adapt because the environment is ordered. His failure at adaptation results because characters . . . employ defective habits."[89] As we have seen, however, the diegetic environment in many of Keaton's films is the source of chaos. Unordered and unpredictable, natural forces push standard cognitive habits to new and sometimes impossible limits, and the films, in turn, tutor bodies to bend with and respond to the unexpected weather elements.

There are several examples in Keaton's work, but two films are especially apposite. In *Seven Chances* (1925), Keaton's Jimmy Shannon is fleeing a swarm of tenacious brides who chase him beyond the boundaries of town and into a series of decidedly rural dangers. Jimmy manages to throw the brides off his trail when he ascends a spectacular sand dune. The abrupt change comes when Jimmy's acrobatic somersaults down the sand bank trigger a landslide. A trickle of rather benign rocks rapidly gives way to an avalanche of enormous boulders that appear out of nowhere. In extreme long shot, Jimmy races down the steep slope dodging massive careening rocks twice his size (see Figure 1.9). He takes refuge in a tree, only to be knocked down. He then finds shelter behind a boulder lodged in the earth, only for it to give way. Reaching the bottom of the hill, Jimmy's reward for survival is a reunion with the bridal horde that awaits him. Momentarily caught between the rocks and the brides, Jimmy decides to escape back up the hill and face the disaster. Ascending, he now sidesteps rocks that proceed to scatter or, in some cases, squash the brides below—a marvelous feat of geo-choreography. Contra Carroll's reading, Jimmy's quick-witted adaptation in response to environmental pandemonium is rewarded when he is reunited with his true love before his marriage deadline expires.

It so happens that the landslide sequence was not in the original script. Keaton recounts that the first time they shot the scenes at the dunes outside of Los Angeles, his bustle dislodged a few rocks that pursued him down the hill. The audience at the test screening was delighted with what Keaton refers to as a fortuitous "accident," but then sat in frustrated expectation of a more elaborate boulder gag. Turning erosion into environmental comedy,

Figure 1.9 Jimmy (Keaton) triggers a landslide. *Seven Chances* (1925).

Keaton ordered fifteen hundred fabricated rocks, some up to eight feet in diameter, to be delivered to the top of a High Sierra slope for the reshoot.[90] The unpredictability of on-location shooting was thus harnessed, tamed, and artificially amplified to satisfy audience demand. Like his early cinema forebears such as Georges Méliès, who turned accidental stop-motion animation into a platform for cinematic magic, so in Keaton's film, "a chance event is transformed into an innovation, and from there, into a system."[91] The final run begins in the dunes with real rocks and shifts to the mountainous terrain with synthetic boulders. The rolling rocks, Jimmy, and the persistence of gravity provide the continuity from one location to the next.[92]

The system of creative geography and the manufactured environment in this scene from *Seven Chances* are anticipated in the famous montage sequence from *Sherlock Jr.* (1924). The eponymous character is an aspiring detective who works as a film projectionist. After being falsely accused of theft, Sherlock falls asleep at the projector and dreams that he enters the world of the parlor mystery film he is watching. The well-known sequence comes just after Sherlock enters the projected world of the "film within the film." Eight shots of approximately twenty seconds in length place Sherlock, through the shock of montage, in seven distinct and surprising environments. First, he is shown sitting on a garden bench. In the next shot he continues to sit, but the sudden shift to a bustling city street without a corresponding bench means that he falls into oncoming traffic. Scrambling to safety in the city, he is transported by a cut to a craggy mountain precipice from which he nearly tumbles. Having just regained his footing on the rocks, he is vaulted into a jungle between two formidable lions. He tiptoes away from the beasts and into the path of a hurtling train, and then another cut places him on a rock outcropping above a rough sea. When he dives into the water, a match-on-action has him land deep in the snow of the next locale. Leaning against a tree in the wintry wilderness, Sherlock finds himself back in the garden. With no tree to support him, he falls down right where his environmental odyssey began.

For Carroll this sequence critiques, in Bergsonian fashion, maladaptation and automatism, "summarizing as it does, in almost allegorical fashion, Keaton's whole concern with unadaptability."[93] Yet, not only is Sherlock quick to adapt in these short shots, but also the sudden shifts all occur at just the moment he gathers himself and finds security.[94] Because *we* watch the body (which is graphically matched from shot to shot) more closely than the surroundings, even *we* are slow to register the new location and each new set of environmental hazards. Moreover, as others have pointed out, this sequence as a whole has no narrative connection to the rest of the film-within-the-film. Thus, rather than dwelling in narrative, this series of shots produces an aesthetic of suddenness that defies cognitive habit or causal prediction. The gag revolves around cinema's capacity to place the same human in different habitats in chaotic succession, or what we could read as an adventure in phantasmagoric climate change. We laugh not at the character's inability to adjust, but his uncanny capacity to survive in radically different environments. In fact, for Bergson, the artificial world and the "disguise of nature" is itself a source for humor. He notes the hilarity of the idea taken from a passage in Alphonse Daudet's *Tartarin Sur Les Alpes* that Switzerland is actually an elaborate opera set run by stagehands who, working machines below the country's surface, produce "waterfalls, glaciers and artificial crevasses." "In 'a nature that is mechanically tampered with' we possess a thoroughly comic theme."[95]

KEATON'S HOSPITALITY

Survival in inhospitable milieus is at the center of Keaton's masterpiece, *Our Hospitality* (1923), in which artificial weather and "natural" phenomena are not so much reflexively depicted as they are incorporated into this story of guest/host relations and inclement environments. A slapstick send-up of the Hatfield and McCoy feud—one of the longest-standing wars between neighbors in US history—the film centers on Keaton's Willie McCay, who travels from New York back to his inherited homestead in the antebellum South. He becomes embroiled in this atavistic battle when he finds himself a dinner guest of the very family who is obliged to kill him. As the Canfield patriarch explains to his vengeful sons, Southern conviviality dictates that they may not murder a guest in their home, and for this reason hospitality provisionally interrupts war. But this war itself is interrupted by weather. The second half of the film features the Canfield strategies of eviction and Willie's ruses of survival that are resolved only when Willie marries the Canfields' daughter, transforming himself from an unwanted guest into a permanent resident alien at the Canfield estate.

Throughout the film, storms, flooded rivers, and craggy bluffs provide our hero with a cover from the murderous clan, even as these conditions thrust him into their midst. Thanks to a postprandial rainstorm, Willie is able to impose himself on the Canfields, knowing that once he leaves their residence they will surely shoot him. The father remarks of both the storm and his plan for Willie: "It would be the death of anyone to go outside tonight." Thereafter, Willie's refuge in the house is also a form of capture until he flees into a mortally raging river. In this film, the codes of war and the conventions of hospitality are connected to unwelcoming or damaging ecologies, some of which Keaton found on location and others he constructed.

But the film is as much a reflection on the effects of nascent industrialization on the environment as it is about hospitality—for in Keaton's work these themes are loosely but inextricably linked. Thus, a full fifteen minutes of the film is devoted to Willie's surreal journey aboard "The Rocket"—one of the first steam-powered, wood-burning locomotives designed in 1829 that Keaton meticulously reproduced for the film. Sputtering through what one critic describes as an "alien landscape," this fragile, ridiculous train with its popinjay passengers is at odds with the stark environment.[96] At most points the landscape is tree filled but devoid of civilization, minus the puny train tracks; elsewhere it is so ravaged already by agriculture that we see a vast deforested field of dust—a harbinger of the dust bowl catastrophe to come. The train ride is one of many detours before Willie encounters the literal limits of the Canfields' hospitality. Shortly after arriving in town and alerting the rival family to his presence, Willie discovers that his inherited homestead is a dilapidated, uninhabitable shack. Functionally homeless with only a suitcase, an umbrella, and a dinner invitation from the Canfields' daughter for dinner, Willie is at the mercy of the elements. He bides his time fishing by the river at just the moment when locals explode a dam for the sake of irrigation—a lucky break, for the newly formed waterfall covers Willie just as the armed Canfield brothers pass by. Later in the famous chase sequence, Willie free-floats down the rapids that have been replenished from the evening storm. Bobbing and gasping for breath, he finally catches himself atop a plummeting waterfall thanks to a bit of driftwood and a rope he's tied to his waist. Through a quick-witted maneuver, Willie manages to both save himself and rescue his beloved just as she crests the precipice (a nod, perhaps, to Griffith's ice storm, but made possible through fabricated falls). The couple marries before the Canfield patriarch can get Willie in his crosshairs. Finding the lovers embracing in his daughter's bedroom after being blessed by the town pastor, Canfield gives up his arms, admonished by the "Love Thy Neighbor" adage hanging on the wall. Given the environmental comedy, the hospitality in the film not only describes the conventions of civility reluctantly accorded to a guest, neighbor, or son-in-law you'd like to kill (Keaton's unwitting but equally witty response to Kant's perpetual peace) but also characterizes human relations to an indifferent or hostile environment. In contrast to Kant, who describes the earth's minimal hospitality and a nature that is thoughtful and caring of human development,

Keaton's nature—already altered by the industrial revolution—has no design on or for human beings.

Gilberto Perez writes of Keaton's cosmology in *Our Hospitality* that the universe is "neither for him nor against him, but simply and uncompromisingly *there* . . . not set up to accommodate him." His survival comes down to an "exceedingly precarious maneuver" without charismatic intervention. And though Willie travels to the South to lay claim to his birthright, he is a resolute outsider, tasked (as are all of Keaton's characters) with orienting himself in an unfamiliar, surreal, and often antagonistic milieu. "It's as if the visitor dropped to this earth, unsure that our world is real, were trying to convince himself that it is by recording its strange behavior in actual earthly locations."[97] Far from having a proprietary claim on the earth, Keaton is "a visitor, not a native." He never quite reaches the status of guest. Hugh Kenner (whom Perez quotes in his essay) reflected on the occasion of Keaton's death, on the "inviolable nature" in his films, "entire systems shattering round him." Keaton, however, "was never shattered because never quite of [this] world. . . . He coped with this earth's systems as best he could."[98] "While on earth," Perez continues, "he tried his best to do as earthlings do, and thereby made us aware of the peculiar systems by which we rule our lives."[99] Perez is writing here of peculiar social and legal systems in Keaton's narratives. Yet his invocation of earthly estrangement and an inviolable and shattering nature suggests that "systems" are operative at a planetary scale, and that Keaton's survival pivots on the fact that he is not native to Earth. *In* but not *of* the world, an alien but not a guest, propelled from one cataclysm to another, Keaton tests the limits of the earth's hospitality. After the title of Perez's essay, we might call Keaton a "bewildered environmentalist" whose slapstick scenarios rest on a prior alienation from the place we all call home.

The relationship between unfriendly weather and hospitality is most explicit in his 1921 short, *One Week*. A newlywed couple builds a prefabricated house from a kit, but they are tricked into constructing in the incorrect sequence. During their housewarming party when a storm develops, rain and strong winds spin the wobbly house like a lethal merry-go-round, forcefully evicting the hosts and guests into the mud. This is another storm quite obviously of the director's making. Wind machines and fire hoses once again localize the precipitation on an otherwise (and off-screen) sunny day for carefully calculated slapstick effect. In the aftermath, Keaton's character beholds his broken house, and rather than seeing the errors of construction, he presumes a problem with the weather: "I guess it's not used to this climate."

DEADPAN/DEAD CALM

Such eviction narratives and environmental homelessness push the situation of slapstick comedy to the threshold of what Lauren Berlant calls "the situation tragedy":

> In a situation comedy, the subject whose world is not *too* destabilized by a "situation" that arises performs a slapstick maladjustment that turns out absurdly and laughably, without destroying very much. In the situation tragedy, the subject's world is fragile beyond repair, one gesture away from losing all access to sustaining its fantasies: the situation threatens utter, abject unraveling. In the artwork or in response to other scenes, when an apprehending sensorium senses a potentially significant threat to the ordinary's ongoing atmosphere, it sparks the rhythms of situation tragedy, with its menacing new realism.[100]

Characterizing threat as a disturbance in the normal atmosphere, Berlant opposes slapstick resilience to the "precarity" of post-Fordist desperation, a desperation that Berlant figures temporally as "survival time," and significantly as "the time of struggling, drowning, holding onto the ledge, treading water."[101] While Keaton's genre is resolutely slapstick, his world flirts with his character's abject unraveling in the environmental conditions of a world too destabilized. In his films humorous play gives way to risk with all of its "life-denting consequences."[102]

In *The Boat* (1921), for example, Keaton's character constructs a houseboat in the basement of his own abode. To extract the boat, he destroys the house only to find that the vessel, initially, will not float. The film ends when Keaton's small family is stranded in the Pacific during a sudden raging storm. The father's efforts to plug leaks in the hull produce even bigger, unstoppable breaches until the family is forced to take refuge in the lifeboat (a tub salvaged from their home wreck). But even this repurposed bathtub gathers water and sinks. Though this short film is full of maritime gags of inattention (many of which play tricks of weather simulation), the final moments take a different affective tack, interrupting slapstick fantasy with what seems like desperate realism (Figure 1.10). Huddled in a sinking bathtub in the middle of the Pacific in the dead of night, the storm now past, the family members kiss each other goodbye and prepare to drown—until they discover that they are in shallow water. Leaving the tub, they trudge to a nearby, uninhabited strip of land and walk hand in hand into an abyssal darkness. Beginning the film as middle class, the family is now, not even a day later, homeless, destitute, and adrift. Whereas *Steamboat* at least leaves the main characters with an old boat (and a surviving priest to

Figure 1.10 The family prepares to drown in *The Boat* (1921).

marry the young lovers), in this earlier film the storm decimates the only shelter remaining. The "joke," if we may call it that, is that the family does not die by drowning. But we may well ask: how will they live? Keaton's narrative touches on the situation tragedy where the explication of weather's latency threatens total destruction. And still, Keaton invites us to laugh.[103] The image of humans floating while desperately clinging to the poststorm remains of domesticity is all too familiar to spectators of present-day hurricanes, floods, and tsunamis, just as it was in the 1920s to those who lived along the shore of the ever-flooding Mississippi. What is less familiar is the dislocation of people as a result of obviously artificial, or avowedly human-caused, catastrophic weather.

The precariousness intimated in Keaton's comedy is front and center in Steve McQueen's contemporary video installation *Deadpan* (1997), which silently restages the house-falling gag from *Steamboat* with all mortal seriousness and in the dead calm of a windless afternoon. With his back to the farmhouse, McQueen stands facing the camera not in bemused confusion, like Keaton, but rather with an unflinching composure in almost defiant resignation of the pratfall that awaits him. Sure enough, the facade detaches and, pivoting on its base, falls over McQueen, who survives thanks to the well-placed open window. What is fortuitous in the narrative sequencing of *Steamboat* (the storm just happens to damage the house whose falling facade just happens to not kill Will) is arbitrary but inevitable in *Deadpan*. McQueen just stands there waiting for the fall. Using several cameras to capture the singular event, McQueen edits the footage so that we see the stunt several times from different angles over the course of just over four and a half minutes: as an installation, the entire sequence plays on a loop in its exhibition setting. As one critic observes, McQueen remakes Keaton's gag into a "compulsive" and "compelling study of purgatory."[104] One wonders if this willing exposure to "accidental" death—a suicide that is also a survival—distills the risks of living in modernist climates by absenting their sensational features.

Modernist weather in Keaton's films is itself both the sign and symptom of human self-destruction that begins in the trenches at Ypres. Keaton, however, is not hardened by war—his deadpan is not "dead nature," in Miller's sense. He is made supple by war's other name, weather. His body is not a stiff shell, but flexible, lively, and organic matter that bends with the wind, floats in the water, and whirls in the cyclone, always emerging ready for the next act, poised physically and intelligently to respond to the simulated world over and over again. If melodrama is the tearful response to other people's storms, then modernist laughter at slapstick's environmental comedy acknowledges both our vulnerability to and agency over the climates of our own making.

CHAPTER 2

Nuclear Conditioning

Survival City is a town in Nevada's nuclear proving ground that was built to test and thus predict the durability of American living against the force of the twentieth century's most destructive weapon and lethal paradigm of environmental design. This little city set the stage—and was itself a set—for nuclear testing, military training, and, perhaps above all, filming. It is the featured location in the film *Operation Cue* (1955), one of the official movies explaining this extensive atomic exercise. Our narrator, June Collin, is a self-described journalist, housewife, and mother who has traveled to the test site to witness the explosion and report its effects "on the things we use in our everyday lives." She tours the blast basin and inspects for its realism the American diorama that is Survival City. Eight structures representing typical American architectural styles and building materials are arranged on short dirt streets named "Doom Drive" and "Disaster Lane" (Figure 2.1).[1] Having undergone improvement as a result of previous tests, these domiciles of American suburbia will be nuclear bombed once again, "to find their weak points." Domestic interiors, "furnished to the last detail," replicate "the average home." Each house is outfitted with brand new working appliances that are hooked up to electricity and gas. The kitchens are stocked with food and the family car is parked in the driveway. The residents, some seventy fashionably dressed mannequins representing white men, women, and children, are posed around the houses in suspended states of daily life: adults gather in the living room for conversation; a female figure is sleeping in the upstairs bedroom while another figure appears to be tending to her; in another house, a boy stands by the living room window (Figure 2.2). The mannequins are

Figure 2.1 A typical American home erected in the blast basin before the atomic test. *Operation Cue* (1955).

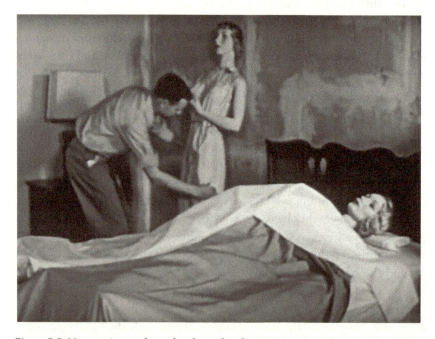

Figure 2.2 Mannequins are dressed and posed in domestic interiors. *Operation Cue* (1955).

not merely put into houses; they are dressed and carefully arranged into narrative situations, as each group would be caught in the fulguration of an enemy nuclear attack. Just outside of this neighborly scene, the food testing program has placed canned goods and fresh meats at various distances to ground zero to learn the effects of radiation on American provisions. The wooden container is labeled "Grandma's Pantry" and contains "a three-day supply of food needs for a family of four," as if Grandma herself had packed a picnic for the nuclear holocaust. A Hollywood film would furnish a script to explain the mannequin gatherings and to have us emotionally invest in their interrupted lives. In this film, the atomic set, along with the bomb that destroys it, *is* the narrative.

The midpoint of the film is the climax that takes us to the predawn desert just moments before the device is about to explode. Narrates Collin: "On the silent desert the test objects waited." The pace of the ten-second countdown is matched by shots of the various waiting "objects": an exterior shot of a two-story wood-frame house, the civil defense volunteers entrenched close to ground zero, and a propane tank. We also linger with a female mannequin framed in profile against the barely visible skyline. She stands out in the open desert dressed for a day at the office. With her brown hair wrapped in a scarf, bangs curled, and lips painted, she looks very much like June Collin—the mannequin surrogate for our surrogate at the test site. It is no small detail that *real* people, those volunteers in the trenches closer to ground zero, are counted among these waiting "objects," and that the objects resemble in detail the real people whose survival and death they are meant to forecast.

At zero point, the atomic flash comes and the impressive mushroom cloud forms. Observers, including we presume Collin, are illuminated by the detonation, and their proximity to the bomb is authenticated in a rather stunning 180-degree pan that begins with a long shot of the group standing at "Media Hill" and ends with the atomic blast a few miles away. What is reserved for remote control cameras is the high-speed cinematography showing us in slow motion, each in its own, individual shot, the houses, electrical substations, radio towers, and propane tanks as the blast wave hits and then, in most cases, decimates these objects, turning familiar American things into divisible, barely perceivable matter. In a living room interior, a mannequin boy stands by a window covered with venetian blinds. When the blast wave comes, the shot cuts to black.

Like the cyclone hitting Buster Keaton's River Junction, the atomic storm reduces Survival City to rubble, as predicted (Figure 2.3). In the post-blast sequence, Collin revisits the materials. We do not see the mannequins blown apart in the remains of their Dooms Day Street living rooms, save a

Figure 2.3 The American home (from Figure 2.1), after the atomic test. *Operation Cue* (1955).

brief glimpse of a fake body that rescue workers excavate from the debris. While the damage is considerable, the test site is festive. Observers line up in the open-air kitchen for roast beef, "done to perfection and roasted in cans that could have been salvaged from demolished buildings." Parts of a town at the farthest point from ground zero can withstand a nuclear bomb, we learn, and the community of survivors will eat grandma's provisions with relish. But the voiceover also explains that the damage is the result of a *small* nuclear explosion, in the kiloton rather than megaton range of a thermonuclear device. Thus, the damage, while real, only approximates in space and by degree the ameliorating capacity of an enemy hydrogen bomb. The one-mile-radius dead zone of this bomb would expand to eight and a half miles, large enough to disappear most American cities and their enfleshed populations.

Peter Bacon Hales writes that as extensive as the damage may appear in the official media of this operation, the results were themselves altered or stage-managed to downplay the devastation of even this smaller bomb to reinforce the Civil Defense's script of nuclear preparedness (the necessity of bomb shelters, good housekeeping, and an alertness to the news) and the fiction of nuclear survival.[2] The film also omits all of the unexpected variables and unforeseen results. The explosion we see is, in fact, of a second bomb that proved to be far more powerful than expected, especially after the first device fizzled and the whole nuclear show had to be postponed.[3] Whereas the microclimates of Keaton's comedy dissipate as quickly as they are manifest on location, the lethal elements of the nuclear device spread far beyond this cinematic laboratory. The bomb's radioactive cloud traveled across Utah, rained over Denver, and then contaminated the Great Plains as it floated down to Texas.[4] The theatricality of the test and the diegetic effect of its supposedly managed environment are part and parcel of the testing regime, and not only for the sake of shaping public opinion and stoking the hope of American endurance. In the regime of nuclear testing and filming, cinema turns the unpredictability and unique destruction of each test into a controlled, contained, and, above all, striking and repeatable image.

This chapter takes place at the Nevada Test Site and considers the cinematic practices that translate nuclear science and its unpredictable anthropogenic environment into an aesthetic—and at times even anesthetic—form. These films may be productively read as "atomic screen tests," films that test the bomb and its targets (including human targets) for their photogenic and photographable properties. Cameras positioned strategically around ground zero generate footage of each object or structure, or of groups of soldiers, volunteers, and civilian onlookers at the instant the bomb explodes, turning film into a probative medium. The data generated may be compared across tests, and the footage may be reassembled for other films. The bomb itself, rarely seen except as a flash followed by the mushroom cloud, colludes with the camera to test the subjects for their endurance as they are simultaneously exposed to nuclear materials and celluloid. Films archive the nuclear condition (the condition of living with the knowledge that weapons of mass destruction exist along with the political will to deploy them) even as they are used for nuclear conditioning. The inseparability of testing, filming, and training, and between the space for experimentation and the unfulfilled promise of a controlled environment, moreover, points to the cultural logic connecting nuclearism to the onset of the Great Acceleration. And it also points to the aesthetic, sensory experience of becoming conditioned on an increasingly unnatural planet. I conclude the chapter noting a curious turn in atomic application toward the "peaceful bomb." Project Plowshare, the last gasp of the Atomic Energy Commission's nuclear program, recommends using weapons of mass destruction as instruments of instantaneous planetary overhaul. Instead of people and their worlds, the Plowshare targets the Earth itself as the obstacle to human flourishing and progress. This phase marks a transition from America's terror-forming atomic culture to the explicitly terra-forming ambitions of the Anthropocene: a humanity at peace with itself and at war with its environment.

According to British geologist Jan Zalasiewicz, nuclear testing introduced to the planet such isotopes as caesium-137, plutonium 239 + 240, and americium 241 that existed naturally nowhere on Earth before the atmospheric testing and everywhere on the planet after it. Nuclear materials, striking for their "globally synchronous" and persistent markers, are clear signals of human-caused planetary change in the geological record. And thus, the first atomic test may serve as a "stratigraphically optimal" starting point of not just the nuclear, but the Anthropocene epoch.[5] Beginning in July 1945, nuclear bombs around the world were detonated "at the average rate of one every 9.6 days until 1988," reaching a peak in the mid-1960s. The trace deposits of synthetic radionuclides rise to the level of significance in terms of scale and "longevity of change (that happens to be currently human-driven) to the Earth system."[6] "Hence," Zalasiewicz writes, "we suggest the Anthropocene . . . to be defined to begin historically at the moment of detonation of the Trinity A bomb at Alamogordo, New Mexico, at 05:29:21 Mountain War Time (+2 s) July 16, 1945."[7] The Anthropocene began not with the bombing of Hiroshima and Nagasaki as the violent feat of war, but in the American desert with a calculated act of experimental science, when scientists (as opposed to a generalized humanity) colluded with the military and intentionally and for the first time tested a weapon that could bring about the destruction of worlds and the annihilation of humanity and most life forms on Earth. Anthropologist Joseph Masco poses the great question of nuclearism in the epoch of the Anthropocene: "How does one define or limit the scope of the nuclear laboratory when its trace elements can be found literally everywhere on the planet?" Conducting ecological and genetic experiments, "turning the earth into a vast laboratory of nuclear effects," the culture of atomic testing enlists all humans as test subjects.[8] The United States was not the only country exploding nuclear bombs and creating atomic test films, but it is the country that inaugurated this regime and its visual culture.

JUST A TEST?

In 1947, the US Air Force created the secret Lookout Mountain Studios in Hollywood, whose sole mission was to develop and test photographic technologies to film atomic explosions and produce the nontheatrical documentaries and newsreels—some 6,500 in total—that have given us the iconic images of nuclearism.[9] The proving ground in Nevada, designated as a nuclear test site in 1950 and host to 928 nuclear tests, became the "most bombed place on earth."[10] With cameras set up to capture every element of these tests, we may presume that this site also became the most filmed place on Earth, resembling a cinematic nuclear back lot as much as an outdoor laboratory. According to the US Department of Energy's official historical account of atmospheric testing, this space was selected because "few areas of the continental United States are more ruggedly severe and as inhospitable to humans." Throughout much of its history, moreover, the site has not been "conducive" to "exploitation."[11] A presumably posthistorical area with only minimal traces of civilization, the "forgotten" site can be fashioned and stage-managed for testing nuclear devices. But the area's apparent emptiness is also a space of appearance. It is here that the contemporary urban world comes into view first as fragments and small samples brought to the site for the sake of their destruction and then in the form of a miniature city worthy of any Hollywood production. With each test, the world appears and is then made to disappear in ever more robust form. Military personnel became the event's "live" audience, its cast of extras, and its test subjects. All of the structures one might find integrated together in the world were isolated in the blast range so that their exposure to both the bomb and the film could be independently assessed and faithfully reproduced in anticipation of future tests and future war.

However much some of these films may have the design of a Hollywood movie, the atomic test film tells the story of how the set is built and how the bomb destroys, with hardly any, let us call it, human interest. The climax (especially of the training films discussed later) is composed of a montage of obliteration minus any narratives of war or scenarios of aggression. Much like Andy Warhol's silk screens and film portraits—made just when nuclear testing was going "underground"—the atomic films are screen tests of repeatability that become individuated ends and aesthetic objects in themselves. This is in contrast to the conventional (Hollywood) screen test in which the actor auditions for a part by speaking lines and following directions while being filmed. The Hollywood test reel, used only for the purposes of casting, gives the director a sense of the actor's photogenic qualities not visible to the naked eye, and it predicts how the actor will appear in the proposed fiction. Warhol's screen tests certainly tested photogenic properties, turning the test into the object exhibited. In them friends and acquaintances, all posed in similar close-ups, endure the camera's interrogation. Whereas Warhol's films play with the power of the medium to expose human frailty and difference, the atomic screen test strives for and largely accomplishes uniformity and repetition of the event and of the image, giving rise to a radical aesthetic emerging from the scientific goal of predictability and repeatability.

Warhol's screen tests and the US government's atomic test thus share an ontological presupposition about the status of the test. These are not exposures in anticipation of the real thing to come; rather, the test makes manifest the real and final thing (the bomb, the exposure, the film). "*Test*," writes Rebecca Solnit, "is something of a misnomer when it comes to nuclear bombs. A test is controlled and contained, a preliminary to the thing itself, and though these nuclear bombs weren't being dropped on cities or strategic centers, they were full-scale explosions in the real world, with all the attendant effects."[12] Among the effects of the test film was to create a regime of survival training that was also meant to test and push the limits of human durability. These films function in the spirit of what Walter Benjamin describes as cinema's polytechnic training. Cinema's "form of shocks . . . established as a formal principle" trains the human sensorium to endure modern industrial practices by subjecting the spectator to industry's unnerving pulses.[13] As he elaborates in the "Work of Art" essay, film establishes an "equilibrium between human beings and the apparatus" that records them. "Film achieves this goal not only in terms of man's presentation of himself to the camera but also in terms of his representation of his environment by means of this apparatus."[14] Cinema shows us the hidden details of everyday objects and their place in a milieu, and it exposes the milieu as such. The atomic test likewise produces a lethal environment that reveals through film the strengths and weaknesses of the human world of which the human is but one among many things that is tested. Thomas Y. Levin speculates that Benjamin's training "could also be said to have an acclimatizing function" akin to the way that video games today prepare young people "for the psycho-sensorial demands of twenty-first century military and industrial conditions."[15] The acclimatizing nature of nuclearism for any human being living in the age of atmospheric testing was, however, more than psycho-sensorial. The conditioning is bone-deep, archived in the dental record, and also indexed in genetic material of anyone living during the era of atmospheric testing.[16] Literally the masses absorb the atomic spectacle into their DNA. Starting with the first nuclear test, the atomic film trains people for this condition and conditions them for this training.

THE ATOMIC EVERYDAY

Most of us are familiar with the Civil Defense films, such as *Duck and Cover* (1952), that tutor our responses to perpetually impending thermonuclear war. Campy were it not so chilling, the documentary explains to schoolchildren that at any moment—during a math class, a bike ride, or a family picnic—a nuclear bomb could detonate and our actions in the interval between white light and the sonic boom mark the difference between life and sudden death. After Hiroshima and as World War II gave way to the geopolitics of mutually assured destruction, anyone in a major city, especially, lived with the knowledge of their vulnerability to nuclear annihilation. Scenarios of future nuclear war and strategies for survival were grounded in the lessons of Hiroshima. John Hersey's 1946 account of six survivors, for example, explains how "each of them counts the many small items of chance or volition—a step taken in time, a decision to go indoors, catching one streetcar instead of the next—that spared him" at "exactly fifteen minutes past eight in the morning, on August 6th, 1945, Japanese time."[17] Providing the minute details of each survivor's location in time and place at the moment the bomb exploded, Hersey confronts us with the terrifying contingencies, some retrospectively interpreted as providential, that allowed some people to live and condemned most others to die.[18] As Cathy Caruth writes, accidental survival is the psychic substrate of traumatic experience because, in its randomness, it "resists simple comprehension." Traumatic experience, in turn, is marked by "the unbearable nature of an event and the story of the unbearable nature of its survival."[19]

The point of the American defense films was to minimize fatalities by turning chance survival into strategic reflex training, and nuclear explosions into legible physical causes and effects. Yet for those living in targeted cities, the rehearsal for survival and the brute everydayness of the looming threat—the waiting and wondering if life will suddenly end in instantaneous carbonization—may have enhanced rather than mitigated nuclear anxiety. Paul K. Saint-Amour diagnoses the pretraumatic stress syndrome specific to the atomic age, a syndrome in which the future, as opposed to the past, lays claims on the psyche and leads to neurosis of a pretraumatic disorder. Preparing for a war that obliterates all civilization and upends the delicate "nuclear balance of terror," we are not likely to survive the apocalypse that proleptically causes the stress. This is the literally "inverted or preposterous phenomenon of traumatic symptoms . . . that exist not in the wake of a past event, but in the shadow of a future one," an event whose destruction will be so total that there will be no "after." Drawing on Jacques Derrida's seminal essay on nuclear criticism, Saint-Amour isolates the uniqueness of the "nuclear condition" that "afflicts humanity with a case of anticipatory mourning, a mourning in advance of loss because the loss to come would nullify the very possibility of the trace."[20]

The presiding scenarios of nuclear criticism toggle between the singular events at Hiroshima and Nagasaki (and their posttraumatic afterlife) and the pretraumatic projections of thermonuclear war.[21] But the regime of atomic tests is of a different order and it summons a different kind of everydayness. These blasts and the films that issue from them feature not the past trauma nor a surprise war to come, but the scheduled and expected, frequent and predictable events that, on one hand, were opportunities to rehearse atomic warfare with live ammunition, but were also, on the other, intended to prove the reliability of the bomb, its targets, and the image. Atomic explosions without thermonuclear war, targeting without malice, repetition for sake of demonstrating repeatability—the atmospheric testing regime of the midcentury may well have traumatized those who looked upon the irradiated desert with a different set of expectations or who were caught unaware. But as scheduled and predictable events, the tests and their films thematized and aestheticized as nontraumatic the repetition of controlled catastrophe. This is how nuclearism overlaps with the Anthropocene every day.

Take, for example, *Military Participation on Tumbler-Snapper* (1952), the cinematic record of the 1952 Tumbler-Snapper test, a series of eight nuclear explosions (four weapons effects tests carried out by the Department of Defense, and four new weapons tests overseen by the Atomic Energy Commission and the Los Alamos Laboratory) carried out in the Nevada Test Site.[22] Because the film's presumed audience is both military planners and troops participating in atomic maneuvers, the account of the test's scientific and military significance doubles as an orientation film. For this reason, it is at pains to normalize the regime of testing in parallel with establishing the norms of the bomb's terrifying destruction. *Tumbler-Snapper* begins with the literal opening of a "Secret Area Document Vault," out of which the official record of Tumbler-Snapper emerges: a thick, nicely illustrated coffee-table book, hand-held for us by an off-screen reader. As the hand opens the cover, a graphic match provides a transition from the printed image on the page to live action. The voiceover welcomes us to the "Boom Town" of Camp Mercy, the military base on the Nevada Test Site twenty miles from ground zero. The name is meant to conjure the sonic shockwave of the bomb and perhaps also to play upon the "hot" real estate of this new atomic neighborhood: "It's a big fraternity, this 'Order of the Mushroom,' and it's growing all the time." Though we are told that there is "no such thing as a normal working day on an atomic test," we glimpse the routine life in the mess hall, the mailroom, and the proving ground as men install various instruments around ground zero. Despite the lack of a *normal* working day, everything else in this film is about establishing norms and reproducing results.

The primary goal of *Tumbler-Snapper* is to find ways of amplifying the bomb's blast curve in response to the diminished damage recorded after previous tests. Over scenes of devastated Hiroshima, our narrator explains that "from a military standpoint, the atomic detonations in Japan seemed to be pretty effective" because the shock wave destroyed or damaged every type of standing structure. "So, Hiroshima and Nagasaki became the norm." The task now was to reproduce predictably both the blast wave and its damage on military and domestic building materials "using every gadget possible," to "find out what really does happen when an atomic bomb kicks out fiercely at the world around it." And so, with Hiroshima as the norm, exploding bombs in the Nevada desert aspired to a new normal. But in the course of this testing and correcting of the blast curve theory, the slow-motion film of the final Tumbler shot reveals another previously undetected phenomenon: a precursor pressure wave that moves out from the zero point in advance of the shock wave. Slow-motion cinematography with the aid of an animated arrow shows us the dust rising above the surface milliseconds before the shock wave will reach the camera. While the detonation provided the needed data to solve the problem of the Hiroshima norm, the film of the test reveals a new phenomenon, the precursor wave, and thus a new pathway for testing. The narrator explains: "We'll have to study, analyze and cross check and then return to our outdoor laboratory again to proof test our findings." The point of weapons effects testing is to continue exploding bombs until there is no new information and no unaccountable variation in the image.

Though we never learn exactly why previous explosions failed to meet expectations, this film describes in almost tedious detail the Tumbler preparations and results. While a number of bombs do explode—some rather spectacularly—in the course of the film, specific detonations become detached from their damaging effects. This is for the sake of both time and organization, as each shot serves a number of different purposes and units. This organization at once assures us that all explosions have a before and recordable after and that new materials will replace the old, despite that we often cannot locate ourselves within these temporalities. For military spectators, the film establishes a relationship between a predictable weapon and a familiar image.

Most visually striking is that early in the film, four atomic detonations are presented on a partitioned screen to summarize efficiently the "Snapper" phase of the test. Moving clockwise, the first bomb appears in its own quarter of the frame, followed seconds later by the next bomb at

Figure 2.4 Partition screen effect. *Military Participation on Operation Tumbler-Snapper* (1953).

the instant of detonation. Eventually all four explosions, each at a different distance from the camera and in different phases of fission, share the quartered screen (Figure 2.4). At end of this thirty-second sequence, the first explosion has faded to black, the second to abstract traces of smoke and fire, while the last is still an infernal column with the signature cloud on top. A kind of animated Warholian silkscreen (produced several years before his work), this short sequence captures the small variations in each bomb's explosion while also demonstrating the repeatability of the image. This sequence of explosions transcribes nuclearism into data sets producing, in the process, an aesthetic of predictable outcomes. The challenge of the atomic scale becomes the promise of a standardized picture.

In the film of the 1953 test series, *Operation Upshot-Knothole* (Atomic Energy Commission, 1953), the scales become even more bizarrely domesticated. Toward the beginning of the film a voiceover explains in rather jocular lingo the laboratory environment of the site: "Many hundreds of tons of materials and months of intense planning by skilled personnel were the ingredients poured into a gigantic test tube of the Nevada proving ground. In spring of 1953 the mixture boiled up in a series of eleven atomic detonations."[23] Rather than watch the blasts individually or see them animated on an apportioned screen, we now scan eleven small color photographs mounted in an album held by the hand of an off-screen reader (Figure 2.5).

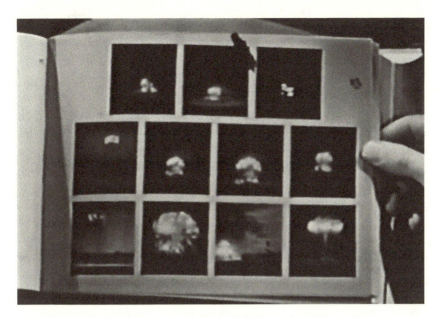

Figure 2.5 An atomic photo album. *Operation Upshot-Knothole* (1953).

The miniaturization of the mushroom cloud is played against the gigantism of the desert test tube that "boiled" them forth. The point of this film is to show not the explosions, hardly necessary because so familiar, but the effects of detonations on military materials, "from a service point of view the main feature of the show." And indeed, subsequent footage of incinerating houses, airplanes, medical encampments, and railcars, all captured with a high-speed camera at 2,400 frames per second, is a stunning demonstration of instantaneous rupture slowed down and abstracted for our delectation. Akira Lippit's characterization of nuclear warfare holds true for the tests. "Atomic bombing produced symbols—as opposed to images—of war which drove the presentation of atomic warfare from fact to figure, towards the threshold of art."[24]

THE ARTS OF TRAINING AND TESTING

By normalizing and conventionalizing the event of detonation, these split-screen effects and abstractions anticipate a pop-art sensibility that transforms the test into an everyday and even banal occurrence. The music that accompanies several of the explosions—a vaguely Wagnerian riff—is repeated from blast to blast in *Military Participation on Tumbler-Snapper* in what becomes a kind of unintentional parody of the sublime, or proof that such seemingly singular experiences and images may be reproduced, repurposed, rescaled, and, on film, reduplicated. The repetition of this image is a feature of mid-twentieth-century photojournalism that Warhol exploits in his early 1960s "Disaster" series: the photo-silkscreen depictions of flamed-out superstars, the electric chair, plane crashes, and the scenes of accidental death and chance survival reprinted on the canvas and abstracted through saturated hues. The critique often leveled against Warhol's headline art is that by reducing such images to a play of surface effects and emptying them of political and historical meaning, Warhol, according to Francesco Bonami, "did not murder painting, but masterminded the killing of content."[25] Yet in the context of late capitalist art markets and modern testing practices, Warhol's repetition compulsion was more than merely glib. His work tested—and testified to—the ordinariness of contemporary catastrophe, as well as the degraded status of art and its human makers.[26] Thierry de Duve argues that Warhol successfully navigated the midcentury art market and spelled out its aesthetic economy by making art *of* commodities. His giant canvasses of Campbell soup cans and Brillo pads "test[ed] the possibility of an art condition."[27] The art object was not its own end so much as a test of its worth.

Rather than fight the symbolic and literal machine of the art market, Warhol famously labored to become a machine even as he exposed its violent effects. He wanted to become a device for both impassive recording (to be, in essence, photosensitized material) and mechanized reduplication—to replace human-made inconsistencies with the machinic glitch. The "pleasure drawn from repetition" symptomatized an impulse Warhol shared with other moderns: namely, "to be the machine and not its slave."[28] As Hal Foster notes, Warhol's oeuvre is a study in the effects of mechanization and automatization on human subjects. The photo-booth portraits and screen tests record human confrontations with technology. The more Warhol's subjects try to pose for the flash photography or remain still for the screen test, the more they become mortified. "Warhol reveals the photo-booth to be a site not only of self-staging but also of subject-testing—in effect, a 'drill.'"[29]

It so happens that Warhol celebrated his seventeenth birthday on August 6, 1945, the day America dropped the "little boy" on Hiroshima. Wayne Kostenbaum speculates that Warhol was sufficiently sensitized to his own life as a catastrophe that his silkscreen *Atomic Bomb* (1965) commemorates both the bomb and Warhol's birth. The black-and-red canvas belongs to the genre of an "explosive self-portrait," "an image of Andy as international trauma."[30] This is a conflation of human and bomb, mushroom cloud as self, self as divisible matter, and "nature" as man-made culture. But the portrait is not of a single mushroom cloud. Rather, the onlooker accounts for the number of repetitions (approximately thirty) and small variations of the same atomic mushroom cloud that drift in place from one reprint to the next. Reading from the top left corner to the bottom right, the canvas begins with the blood-red background dominating the black cloud. The sequence ends with a corner image of near-total black ink. The black cloud eclipses the red background, or maybe the cloud has itself become the background against which another explosion may erupt. It mirrors the form of the atomic screen test and its cinematic movement. This large canvas (104 × 80½ inches) overwhelms less with the *size* of the reproduction than with the *repetition* of reproduction that ends with the end of the image. A commemoration of a birth concludes with the end of signification.

Warhol's machine dream—his image of himself as the bomb—was, writes de Duve, "a desire to be without desire, to be insentient, to be beyond suffering or the fear of death." Warhol's was a desire to escape the pitfalls of the test, the trauma of an aftermath, and "be nothing, nothing of the human, the interior, the profound."[31] Warhol's testing impulse combined with his anesthetic inhumanism and obsession with everyday disaster made him the incarnation of the American dream as the death drive, as de Duve concludes. "One doesn't take on the existence of the perfected machine, one does not turn into a camera or tape recorder, without also taking on the existence of all machines and above all those that kill."[32] As art in the age of large-scale experimentation, Warhol's disaster silkscreens and portraits attest to the inseparability of the death drive and the no less damaging psychology of what Avital Ronnell calls the "test drive," which links testing and torturing to the risks we take in order to make "claims about the world and its contractions."[33]

If Warhol's automatism was intended to in some way shield him from machinic and explosive violence (and project it instead on his test subjects and spectators), the atomic tests were likewise something of a preemptive rite. Anthropologist Hugh Gusterson writes that atomic testing became a scientific ritual aimed not only at eliminating war's surprises by rehearsing detonation but also deterring nuclear war itself by demonstrating the "hyperreliability" of new weapons and nuclear stockpiles.[34] The test deters weapon deployment because the publicized images of the explosions convey to our would-be attackers that our arms are both secure and viable. The test, we may surmise, functions as a threat, or a form of national security performance art. For the scientists, the effect of overwhelmingly successful operations was that nuclear devices, so familiar and predictable, exploded with such frequency—regarded by their makers as being as "benign as vacuum cleaners"—that they were not tools of global annihilation or subject to human error. Instead, they were associated with the "positive experience of reliability," a pleasure, we might say, drawn from repetition and "performed proof of technical predictability." The critique of Warhol's disaster series—that they turn catastrophe into a banal and everyday event—was one of the goals of tests for these scientists. "Where many of us worry that a nuclear explosion will occur at some point in our lives," nuclear scientists, writes Gusterson, "worry that one won't." Yet the tests, argues Gusterson, also had a more magical function as rituals in which deterrence is enacted in the very event of detonation that deterrence is supposed to eliminate. Rather than leading to pre- or posttraumatic stress, the tests relieved scientists' anxieties associated with nuclear annihilation because they provided firsthand knowledge of what these bombs are meant to prevent. In this way, the test helped the scientist to bridge "the gulf between a regime of simulations and the realm of firsthand experience."[35] Predictable and imitable, the test proves a weapon's function. Just as importantly, it also tests and produces the weapon's scientists as such, and, we may add, the entire military apparatus of the nuclear establishment. "Nuclear tests not only test technology, they also test people."[36]

We see the test's performative elements in *Military Participation on Tumbler-Snapper* when American military personnel arrive at the blast range to participate in an atomic exercise. The troops settle into their assigned trenches, share cigarettes, and mentally prepare for the exercise to come: they will watch the atomic explosion from close range and then march to ground zero, as if invading an enemy territory in the wake of a US airstrike. [37] Our narrator explains their collective state of mind as they await the blast:

> Like all too many people both in and out of the military, before these men got their assignment for this operation they had many misconceptions about the bomb and its effects. Some of them thought they would never again be able to have families. Some of them expected to be deaf or blind. Some of them expected to glow for hours after the bomb went off. Like so many people, many of them were afraid. They had never taken the time or invested the effort to learn the facts about what to do in case of atomic warfare. These men have been indoctrinated in what goes on and what to do when the bomb goes off. Any doubts that are left will be eliminated after the full experience of this operation.

These men have already been through extensive mental, ideological, and physical training. After all, this is not a simulated explosion as a preventative measure, but an actual detonation and a real maneuver in a contaminated zone. According to the logic of this film, it is only by surviving an atomic test that one can be fully convinced that survival is possible.

In standard-issue uniforms and protected with only a thin booklet entitled *How to Survive a Nuclear War* tucked into their back pockets, the men bear witness to the test and, in the process, serve as one of its principal objects of study. Just behind the troops are hundreds of "Planning Level Observers from throughout the defense establishment" who study the exercise from close range in this seemingly infinite regress of human testing subjects and predicates. At H minus two minutes, the men hide in their foxholes arranged around the perimeter of the blast basin. Three seconds after detonation they are commanded to stand erect, watch the column of fire ascend, and brace themselves for the shock wave. Boom! Silhouetted against the radiant fireball, the soldiers await the shockwave that ripples across the desert floor in their direction (Figure 2.6). A new camera position shows the men standing in their foxholes when the irradiated desert sand hits them with visible force, and momentarily they are lost in the dust cloud as they use hands to cover their mouths and eyes from the nuclear debris (Figure 2.7). Just as abruptly, the men are now framed in close-up against blue skies. To provide the eye-line matches and demonstrate the soldiers' endurance, the film intermixes footage of the rising mushroom cloud with staged enactments (either re-enactment or pre-enactment, as

Figure 2.6 Soldiers, in the bottom foreground, witness the mushroom cloud formation. *Military Participation on Operation Tumbler-Snapper* (1953).

Figure 2.7 Soldiers are hit with irradiated dust from the atomic blast. *Military Participation on Operation Tumbler-Snapper* (1953).

the case may have been) of the soldiers gazing and approvingly pointing at the fireball with smiles on their faces (Figure 2.8). This series of Kuleshov-effected responses both captures the men's presumed affect and models the appropriate response for future participants—a bit of prospective mimetic theater. After surveying the blast basin and inspecting the test materials, the men march back to the parking area where they smoke cigarettes and reflect on the day. The "biggest value" of this exercise, we are told, was "to prove to ourselves that it can be done," that fear can be replaced with a "confidence that comes only with experience." To verify this emotional state, "psychiatrists are with us to study our reactions before, during, and after the experience." A film about training and testing, *Tumbler-Snapper* is itself a therapeutic or homeopathic exercise that trains the next batch of nuclear soldiers to be atomic spectators, explicitly so. To watch the film of *this* test is to begin to train for the next test.[38] To have endured the test is to be conditioned by human-made nuclear materials.

In fact, the soldiers in Operation Tumbler-Snapper would likely have watched the Atomic Energy Commission's training film *Exercise Desert Rock* (1951) documenting the first atomic tactical maneuvers in Nevada for the Buster-Jangle series.[39] The Desert Rock operation required military personnel to witness the atomic blast from various distances to study the "psychology of panic" from which effective nuclear indoctrination

Figure 2.8 Smiling soldiers watch the mushroom cloud ascend. *Military Participation on Operation Tumbler-Snapper* (1953).

programs could be devised and refined. In 1951, the Defense Department recommended that the military "seek technics for reducing apprehension and for producing psychological resistance to fear and panic, especially in the presence of radiation hazard." Parenthetically, the memo explains that the goal is not to design physical protection but specifically to create an "(emotional 'vaccination')."[40] Faced with real biochemical danger, men inoculated with some kind of an emotional vaccine would be able to carry on their mission in the event of atomic warfare in a highly contaminated area. As if radiation sickness is a form of mental illness, the military seeks to ease fears of radiation first through various forms of cinematic indoctrination and then through exposure to what was considered to be safe levels of radiation.

But there is something even more sinister at work. In the film, soldiers are interviewed before and after the blast and probed for their willingness to *volunteer* to be even closer to the detonation. None are eager, but neither do they declare themselves to be in any physical or emotional risk. By 1953, the US Department of Defense, concerned about the legal ramifications of atomic testing on American soldiers, adopted the Nuremberg Code for medical experimentation on human subjects. The code stipulated that participants in biomedical research would have to be volunteers under conditions of informed consent.[41] Yet, the difference between atomic military training and atomic medical testing was purposefully murky. The Nuremberg guidelines, kept top secret, were not widely distributed to the various government agencies and thus never systemically enforced. Panic tests would eventually require consent. Marching to ground zero after the blast was a matter of indoctrination and training.[42] These films, however, tell us that all exposure to the bomb is finally in the troops' best and even therapeutic interest. For each subsequent test, troops were moved closer to ground zero to determine "the thresholds of intolerability."[43] For Tumbler-Snapper, the next operation, men were stationed seven thousand yards (just under four miles) from ground zero. For the Upshot-Knothole test series of 1953, troops were entrenched just two miles from ground zero, while twelve volunteers were stationed in six-foot trenches two thousand yards (just over a mile) from the blast for shot Annie, a sixteen-kiloton device.[44] And thus soldiers in training watch *Exercise Desert Rock* and learn to move closer and to feel safer in proximity to an atomic explosion because the film itself shows soldiers undergoing exactly such training.

The presumed hyperreliability of the bomb and the repeatability of the image are also presumed to reliably structure the soldiers' affective response to the test. The eye-line matches of the smiling men looking at the mushroom cloud in *Operation Tumbler-Snapper* could thus be inserted into subsequent films. The Federal Administration Civil Defense's appropriately titled *Let's Face It* (1954), which describes to American audiences measures for nuclear preparedness, takes us to a different test but recycles the shots of these happy atomic soldiers in *Tumbler-Snapper* gazing at the mushroom cloud just over their heads.[45] Of course, the tests were filmed to generate footage that could be recombined for different audiences, above all civilians who, themselves, underwent ritualized practice for a nuclear World War III.[46] According to Tracy C. Davis, the whole purpose of civil defense rehearsals—the "duck and cover" drills but also the elaborately staged disaster theater of urban evacuations, mass feedings, and medical triage—was to supplement the persuasive discourse of preparedness with rehearsed action: "Persuasion may have conditioned the public to *believe*, but a rehearsal would enable the public to *behave*, not only in an orderly but in a constructively predictable manner."[47]

Nuclear Anesthetics

These instances of recycled footage and tutored responsiveness suggest that the purpose of the test films is not only to study weapons effects but also to standardize human affects. By bombarding the spectator with repeated images of nuclear explosions and decimated matter, the films translate the terrifying and likely traumatizing experience of atomic detonation into a smile, or expression, that is detached temporally, spatially, and most likely temperamentally from the phenomenon prompting expression. Rather than speak of the aesthetics of the test film or their obviously propagandistic purpose, we may also consider how these films mobilize *anesthetic* techniques as a means of teaching humans to cope with the global terror some humans had created. This is a mode of affective conditioning designed to numb the human sensorium and thereby prevent it from feeling, protesting, or sympathizing too much with the objects under erasure. As Susan Buck-Morss explains, aesthetic experience meets anesthetic operations in Kant's formulation of the sublime. Confronted with such "threatening and menacing nature" as "towering cliffs, a fiery volcano, a raging sea," the ideal beholder does not shrink away from such views in the service of self-preservation. Instead, watching from a "safe distance," the viewer stills his anxiety by regarding himself as an "autogenic," "self-contained" subject, impervious to external phenomena and capable of judging sublime experience "independent of nature." The warrior, trained for battle, is the model for this aesthetic encounter because he remains, as Buck-Morss writes, "impervious to all his sense-giving information of danger." [48] He can behold what is terrifying and hold his ground. When the soldier is also the subject of the film—simultaneously the object of our interest and our surrogate for experience—the phenomenon we witness is a human nature seemingly impervious to damage, or a human nature working against itself. While alert and mobile, the atomic solider in the film is more like an anesthetic object than an aesthetic subject in this regard.

Buck-Morss elaborates that anesthetic techniques first merged with spectatorial practice in such places as the medical operating theater where violence could be done to the body without concern for the pain of the patient who is under general anesthesia and who thus never cries out in distress: "What happened to perception under these circumstances was a tripartite splitting of experience into agency (the operating surgeon), the object as hyle (the docile body of the patient), and the observer (who perceives and acknowledges the accomplished result)." And, she stresses, "these are positional differences, not ontological ones."[49] The human is the persistent figure for and bearer of a gaze that regards the human as mute matter. The effect in the test film is to dissociate cognition from pain by making the alienated human both the object and the subject of the test through an identification of the self with the technology (in this case, the camera) that sees and survives each explosion. For Buck-Morss, technology "extends human power" while "intensifying the vulnerability of what Benjamin called 'the tiny, fragile human body.'" And thus a version of nuclearism's dynamic (building better bombs to destroy more durable worlds) finds its precursor in the nineteenth century: technology produces "a counter-need to use technology as a protective shield against the 'cold order' that it creates."[50] More technology is the problem and solution when war and medical emergencies meet. On the battlefield of the nuclear proving ground, the emergency, we are told, is only a test.

A different kind of film tutorial addresses civilians living close to the test site. The opening sequence of *Atomic Tests in Nevada* (1955) offers this little vignette of St. George, Utah.[51] The voiceover sets the scene: "It's pre-dawn. Five in the morning. Pretty deserted at this hour. Everything is closed down. Everyone's asleep." From images of early-morning Main Street, we cut to three characters—the milkman, the police officer, and the gas station owner. These are "the St. George night-owls," who, as they carry out their daily tasks, are witness to an atomic blast just 140 miles away. The night sky suddenly turns a blinding white. Rather than ducking or taking cover, the men barely take notice and carry on with their morning tasks: delivering milk, checking locked storefront doors, and pumping gas. No dramatic nondiegetic music or postproduction sound of an atomic rumble. The bomb is, we are told, "old stuff in St. George. Routine. They've seen lots of them ever since 1951. Nothing to get excited about anymore." Far from eviscerating the town and searing everyday routine into the specificity of catastrophic time as experienced by the victims of Hiroshima and Nagasaki, the bomb's explosion at precisely 5:00 AM St. George time in any given morning *is* the routine: the explosion, a nuclear nonevent. The test? To remain impassive.

The morning unfolds. The sun rises and children go to school, housewives wash up the breakfast dishes, and shop owners open their stores. Then comes a radio announcement with this warning: "Due to a change in wind direction, the residue from this morning's atomic detonation is drifting in the direction of St. George." Residents are advised to take cover for one hour, but there does not appear to be any particular rush. The announcer stresses: "There is no danger." This, too, is just a routine precaution, "to prevent unnecessary exposure to radiation." Once again, the citizens of St. George are nonreactive and peaceably continue their morning routines—now of peeling potatoes, getting a haircut at the barber shop, feeding the baby a bottle of milk, and working in the shop. What we realize is that this is not a documentary only about preparedness for a future *war*; it is a reenactment of already past contamination from fallout. Reassuring viewers that there are no serious risks, the documentary is a defense of weapon testing in the "backyard workshop" and "outdoor laboratory" of the Nevada Proving Ground. In "the loneliest acres the world has seen," testing will soon resume with even more frequency. Survival City is a pretend town on the test site. St. George, populated with real human beings, would come to be known as "Fallout City."[52]

Yet the danger that threatens St. George, according to this film, is only *a little* unnatural compared to the normal levels of background radiation. Live-action footage gives way to an animated sequence in which the spinning earth appears from a view in space, radiated by interstellar forces. "Since the beginning of time, the earth has been bombarded by radiation from outer space. Cosmic rays and high-energy particles rain down from space on each and every one of us every second of our lives. . . . It is part of nature. We can't control it. Radiation from fallout temporarily adds to this background level." Constantly bombarded by a nature we cannot control, we are already subject to radiation that atomic fallout merely enhances. The nuclear condition *is* a "natural" condition.[53] In the final analysis and over an image that may be a slow-motion capture of an atomic bomb on the horizon or the rising sun, the voiceover assuages any lingering concern: "An atomic bomb is puny compared to the force of nature, and it is completely lost in the vast oceans of the sky." The film's ruses of domestication—at one point the mushroom cloud is compared to "a giant vacuum cleaner"—in the context of domestic small-town life are obviously calculated to convince spectators of how the bomb is already part of St. George's ecology. In any case, "the very nature of testing weapons for national defense requires we accept the possibility of exposure to additional radiation." If the Anthropocene begins on Monday, July 16, with Trinity, then the regime of testing marks another turn in which humans living outside of the blast range become collateral test subjects so that weapons may be proven "frequently, quickly, and more economically" in Nevada. "We have no choice." "Testing must continue." At the end of the film the mushroom cloud takes to the skies floating as "a symbol of strength, of defense, and of security for freedom-loving people everywhere." The price of symbolic freedom is submission to the test.

NUCLEAR UNPREDICTABILITY

Human responses might be easier to standardize than the bombs themselves, whose explosive power and fallout were difficult to predict. Consider the most extensive, elaborate, and controversial atmospheric test series conducted at the Nevada Proving Ground in 1957, Operation Plumbbob. Thirty separate shot tests were designed including twenty-four nuclear detonations and six so-called safety tests, all carried out while the United States was negotiating the first limited test ban treaty, prompted in large measure by the international protests over the effects of nuclear fallout.

The second test, codename Boltzmann, was a tower shot of a 12-kiloton device that exploded as expected, except that an unpredicted change in wind currents separated the cloud into three distinct radioactive units that fanned out west to California and up the coast to Washington state, east toward New York City, via Salt Lake City and Muncie, Indiana, and north into Idaho.[54] Franklin, the next shot, with an expected yield of 2 kilotons, was a "fizzle" of a mere 140 tons. It was not until the Franklin-prime shot, a few days later, that the device yielded an even larger 4.6-kiloton explosion. Wilson, the fourth test in the series, rained radioactive fallout over the Nevada Test Site Control Point, requiring that all personnel be evacuated just as they were supposed to monitor the cloud's activities. And the Diablo shot was a complete dud. The two thousand marines stationed in trenches along with the several hundred invited observers witnessed not a mushroom cloud in the making, but the arduous labor of three "volunteers" who climbed the five-hundred-foot shot tower to disarm the nuclear device by hand. The Smoky shot, of August 31, would only later become famous for the miscalculations of its effects. In the 1980s, the Centers for Disease Control reported that the troops ordered to witness the blast had statistically significantly higher incidences of leukemia, which could be traced back to the test.[55]

In the official film, *Operation Plumbbob: Military Effects Studies* (1957), it is not men but pigs who suffer the consequences of weapon unpredictability. In these difficult-to-watch sequences, pigs, awake and alert, are loaded into aluminum containers close enough to the blast range to be irradiated by the explosion but not killed by the blast pressure. One hundred and thirty-five pigs are individually encased, and without any visual cues of an explosion, a quick cut shows soldiers in hazmat suits unloading the lively pigs. The first Franklin bomb of this series, with its surprisingly low yield, was too ineffectual to produce results and thus the experiment was repeated with the "Wilson" bomb. Wilson's "higher than expected yield" resulted in such elevated levels of radiation that all but two pigs died within the necessary thirty-day observation period. Seven hundred pigs were placed in various situations—trenches, aboveground pens, containers—and also various distances to the massive Priscilla shot of the Plumbbob series, a thirty-seven-kiloton bomb detonated on June 24. Slow-motion footage shows the pigs in one of the pens to which glass panels were affixed. Here the pigs were to "obtain wounds" through exposure to the bomb and flying glass so that doctors could develop techniques for atomic war triage. After the blast, we are told that all pigs in the closest range were killed. While we see pigs in the postblast enclosure scuttling around the men who are charged to retrieve them from this highly contaminated area, we learn that the "massive radiation took its toll" along with "serious thermal burns." "Due to the small number of survivors" with the "desired" injuries, "evaluation of the medical and surgical treatment phase of the experiment did not produce conclusive results." All this death is for naught, because nuclear bombs are not predictable and certainly not as benign as vacuum cleaners. A medium shot of a lone, dying pig whose gut is spilling onto the desert floor is a reminder that the bomb is capable of producing both instant and slow and painful death. A surrogate for hypothetical human victims of a hypothetical war, this pig is also an image of one of the more gruesomely sacrificed test subjects. Unfeeling mannequins have given way to sensate beings whose wounds demonstrate the bomb's lethal power and the futility of postdetonation medical "care."

US Army veteran Joel Healy remembers his experience serving on the Operation Plumbbob series. He was seventeen when he was stationed in the trenches to witness several detonations:

> I thought to myself, if there is a hell on Earth, it's gotta be that. . . . You felt the shock wave of the thing going off and then the heat. And the biggest one that was set off in the desert when I was there was a 74 kiloton—almost twice the size that was used in Hiroshima and Nagasaki.

He describes his terror and sense of betrayal that the US government would knowingly subject its soldiers to lethal tests as a preparation for unsurvivable war. But perhaps the most galling part of the experience was the film crew: "The Army had their own film teams out there to show 'there are our boys whistlin' Dixie' going into a nuclear device."[56]

ATOMIC INHUMANISM

Atomic test films are radical iterations of what Walter Benjamin writing in 1936 understood to be the real significance of the film actor in the age of industrialized labor and the "countless mechanized tests" to which human beings are systematically subjected. He explains that in contrast to the stage actor who performs for a live audience, the film actor performs for technology (the camera, the microphone) before a group of specialists (the director, the cinematographer, the producer) who assess him from the same position as an "examiner in an aptitude test." More like a typist than an athlete, the successful actor must persevere against the technology. And while such tests go on in offices and factories every day (the typing test, the efficiency test), invisible even to those who endure them, film "makes test performances capable of being exhibited, by turning that ability into a test." "To perform in the glare of arc lamps while simultaneously meeting the demand of the microphone is a test performance of the highest order. To accomplish it is to preserve one's humanity in the face of the apparatus."[57] In the capitalist age, one does not *pass* a screen test; one *survives* it. Nothing short of one's humanity is at stake. This victory of man over apparatus, which every fiction film documents, explains the attraction that movies and movie stars have for the majority of city dwellers. Those who "have relinquished their humanity" to the technologies of the workplace during the day go the movies "to witness the film actor taking revenge on their behalf not only by asserting his humanity (or what appears to them as such) against the apparatus, but by placing that apparatus in the service of his triumph."[58] In this, the second version of the artwork essay, Benjamin's audience roots for the screen actor as their victorious surrogate. Miriam Hansen remarks that in the later version of this essay, Benjamin is not as sanguine about the audience's sympathy. In the third version, she writes, "viewers identify with the testing position of the camera itself," assuming the role of both examiner and inhuman apparatus.[59]

The atomic screen test also returns us to the more torturous side of Andy Warhol's screen tests and suggests another connection between the atomic bomb and Warhol's fixation on the repeatability of machinic violence. Inspired by the genre of the mug shot or photo-booth self-portrait, the screen tests were three-minute uncut films in which the subject was well illuminated and framed in medium close-up against a neutral, usually white, background. Commanded to be inexpressive and even unblinking, Warhol's subjects were tested for their ability not to be photogenic so much as inhumanely photographic (a task better suited to Survival City's mannequins). As Callie Angell explains, Warhol "created a set of diabolically challenging performance instructions for his sitters who . . . struggled to hold a pose while their brief moment of exposure was prolonged into a nearly unendurable three minutes." Many nervously twitched. Others, most famously folk singer Ann Buchanan, managed not to blink but were then overcome by involuntary tears as the body fought back (Figure 2.9). The sadistic nature of this filmmaking gradually took over as Warhol intentionally staged the sitting "to make things as difficult as possible for the subjects" and then recorded their discomfort.[60] Whereas Benjamin celebrated the film actor as the survivor of the machine age, Warhol fetishized those moments when the actor's body, as involuntary machine, triumphs over the subject's will.[61] Unto itself, then, each screen test testified to each subject's individual physiology and unique capitulation. We all break down differently—but we all break down, just

Figure 2.9 *Screen Test: Ann Buchanan* (Warhol, 1964).

the same. Collected into a series, as they typically were, the screen tests (like the atomic tests) were experiments in producing likeness across the subjects, capturing the similitudes in Warhol's social collectivities, as Jonathan Flatley writes (Figures 2.10 and 2.11). The screen tests, in their "ability to produce assemblages of likenesses[, do] the work of exteriorizing and presenting the collectivity" of Warhol's factory while at the same time preserving "the singularity and multiplicity" of each person.[62] The "being-in-common" arises out of Warhol's experiment "in which everyone can succeed in failing."[63] The screen tests poignantly archive the vulnerability of the human test subject when likeness is the aesthetic goal. This is the precariousness that the atomic films at once presume for the enemy population and disavow for the American soldiers who are commanded to face the bomb of their country's making and uniformly, repeatedly, and with a smile pass the test.

As a form of endurance cinema in extremis, the atomic screen tests may, like their Warholian counterparts, attract us with their scenarios of putative, even triumphal survival in the face of the bomb's world-shattering destruction, even as they turn humanity into just one of many materials to be tested. But they outright refuse to acknowledge the unlimited reach of radioactive fallout or to consider the slow, invisible violence, to use Rob Nixon's term, of the carcinogenic materials on organic bodies. Indeed, we have to wonder what version of the "human" and what kind of "survival" these tests presuppose. Given that the long-term effects on soldiers, downwinders, animals, plants, and the biosphere have yet to fully

Figure 2.10 *Screen Test: Edie Sedgwick* (Warhol, 1965).

Figure 2.11 *Screen Test: Mary Woronov* (Warhol, 1966).

materialize, the experiment and the test are far from over.[64] For Joseph Masco, the watchword of nuclear nature-cultures and their experimental regimes is *mutation*, which may lead to evolution, injury, or recessive traits whose expression may or may not develop in future generations.[65]

Hollywood may have provided one of the most appropriate scripts concerning postwar human mutation, atomic testing, and nuclearism's domestic uncanny when in 1957, just two months before the Operation Plumbbob nuclear test series began, Universal Studios released *The*

Incredible Shrinking Man. In the final sequence of this science fiction odyssey, our diminutive hero, Scott Cary (Grant Williams), contemplates his microscopic existence in a world that has outsized his irradiated body. He passes through a screened window into blades of grass the size of trees and gazes skyward, abandoning what was once his human house, as well as his earthbound scales of thought. In voiceover, he explains the vicissitudes of a posthuman consciousness achieved through the loss of his corporeal self. Having been exposed to a radioactive cloud just months before, Cary, now himself particulate matter, reflects on the nuclear world from an Archimedean point of view, making sense of his end as the sign of a new beginning:

> What was I? Still a human being? Or was I the man of the future? If there were other bursts of radiation, other clouds drifting across seas and continents, would other beings follow me into this vast new world? So close, the infinitesimal and the infinite. But suddenly I knew they were really the two ends of the same concept. . . . That existence begins and ends is man's conception, not Nature's. And I felt my body dwindling, melting, becoming nothing. My fears melted away and in their place came acceptance. All this vast majesty of creation. It had to mean something and that I meant something too. Yes, smaller than the smallest, I meant something too. To God, there is no zero. I still exist.

In this messianic reverie, Cary's consciousness becomes airborne. The camera cranes up from the garden and the image dissolves into a series of cosmic views: first the stars above Earth, then the Milky Way, and then the celestial bodies and gaseous nebulae beyond (or before) our galaxy—as if in tracking back, the camera is also traveling through time to a vast new world. Sublime experience rescues existentialist doubt and assuages nuclear fears with the promise that the atomic age has generated its Adamic man. Irreducible to zero (in God's eye at least), Cary represents the human limit of infinitesimal calculus in an age in which even the atom is divisible.

What is fascinating about this Cold War tale of inhuman survival is that the peril Cary faces is *not* nuclear warfare. Instead, the film emphasizes the solitary banality of events that lead to his slow, inexorable miniaturization. His "unbelievable story" begins on "a very ordinary summer day." Sunning himself on a boat while on vacation with his wife, Cary is momentarily engulfed by radioactive mist resulting from an atomic explosion we neither see nor hear. A few weeks later, Cary is exposed to garden-variety pesticides that trigger the irreversible molecular mutation.[66] These are events of random airborne exposure, a bad chemical plot standing in for fate. Growing ever smaller "in a world of giants," Cary endures the terrors of domesticity and corporeality in the age of remote nuclear testing.

Cary's shrinking is itself a test, first of his social, interpersonal mettle and then of his survival skills in his typical middle-class home, where the everyday objects—the telephone, chairs, sofas, and family cat—overwhelm our hero in what is first a wrongly proportioned surrounding and then an outright hostile domestic interior. About midway through the film Cary undergoes exponential diminution. From a four-foot man in the previous scene, Cary is now only inches tall. We encounter him, however, in a "right sized" world. He stands at a table in front of the staircase mending his shoes and we momentarily think that he has regained his stature. A wide shot reveals that he has taken residence in a dollhouse that replicates the interior of his home in which it is situated, just at the base of the staircase (Figure 2.12). Whereas in *Operation Cue* mannequins stand in for what the voiceover calls "Mr. and Mrs. America" in the typical family home built in the nuclear proving ground, here Cary, an irradiated human, takes the place of a doll in a no less lethal environment. Just as a version of the world reappears in the nuclear test site, so too does a version of the test site reappear in a Hollywood film, especially its logic of substitution whereby

Figure 2.12 Scott Carry (Grant Williams) talks with his wife (Randy Stuart) on the balcony of his doll house. *The Incredible Shrinking Man* (1957).

dolls stand in for humans, and humans stand as both the objects and the subjects of nuclear testing.

As toxic as the precipitating events of Cary's molecular restructuring is the series of intensive medical exams intended to grant his body a new visibility and transparency. These include x-rays, fluoroscopy, paper chromatography, a thyroid test involving radioactive iodine and a Geiger counter, and then "x-rays and more x-rays." In a series of nuclear tautologies, radioactive materials demonstrate the deleterious effects of radiation. Cary gradually transitions from a medical patient to an atomic test subject.

Cary's diminished size also becomes a trial of image technology, as he is placed in the mise-en-scène of growing props, composite shots, and artfully crafted forced perspectives. Once Cary's body fails to measure against the world's visible objects, he is no longer capable of leaving a photochemical trace and becomes instead a disembodied voice, pure spirit. The film tests the limits of Hollywood cinema to render the infinitesimal and infinite dimensions of atomic experience and its newfound scalar pathos. The science fiction of the nuclear test in this film, then, is not Godzilla come to life, but the trial of one man who becomes peacefully resigned to "dwindling, melting, becoming nothing" in a world of free-floating radioactive mist.

"How immensely the world is simplified when tested for its worthiness of destruction," comments Benjamin in his 1931 essay, "The Destructive Character," in which he observes presciently that "the destructive character is reliability itself." He was, of course, not reflecting on the atomic bomb, but he captures something of nuclearism's testing ethos and the presumed worthiness of the world that survives this deadly showdown. What he describes is an annihilating sociability that acts like a force of nature, dispatching of the world without malice (this is a "cheerful" character), only to make space and to clear away the debris of an era. The destroyer welcomes "a complete reduction, indeed, eradication, of his own condition" and he craves the attention of people who become "witnesses to his efficacy."[67] This self-canceling destructive character is an ambivalent figure for Benjamin because, as Irving Wohlfarth explains, it makes way for revolutionary change by sweeping away an ossified order, but may also be a harbinger of fascist annihilation and the futurist celebration of the aesthetics of war. It is, in any case, "predicated on the assumption that there are critical moments when it is only through 'destruction' that 'humanity [. . .] can prove its mettle.'"[68] The risk is that humanity, along with the world that sustains it, will fail.

By midcentury all biological life on the planet had become conditioned by the nuclear experiment: the test as war by other means, a trial without any particular ends, and a training that elementally changes all of humanity and transforms a "natural" planet into controlled laboratory. For Hannah Arendt, this anthropogenic environment is the real meaning of Sputnik and the possibility that humans might one day live in a fabricated environment on a man-made sphere. Sputnik represented a desire for a life lived in the controlled even if catastrophic space of the laboratory, a willingness to become a test subject. Atomic weapons and the devastating atomic tests suggested to Arendt that we had already begun to relinquish our human advantage and meaning in the world:

> We have found a way to act on the earth as though we disposed of terrestrial nature from outside, from the point of Einstein's "observer freely poised in space." If we look down from this point upon what is going on on earth ... and apply the Archimedean point to ourselves, then these activities will indeed appear to ourselves as no more than "overt behavior," which we can study with the same methods we use to study the behavior of rats.[69]

The surprising claim is that inhumanism in the atomic era is not a radical transformation of people into machines, or a posthuman transcendence of biology, or, like Cary, becoming pure spirit. Nor is it merely our capacity for worldwide destruction, or a vision of human life after nuclear war. It is rather that the cult of the atomic experiment itself fixates on processes and means (tests for tests' sake) rather than producing durable worlds and meaningful ends. Without its world, the human is merely another species on Earth, testing itself against threats of its own creation and in the process becoming a force like nature (capable only of overt behavior) that jeopardizes its own existence. Or, if humanity manages one day to live on an entirely anthropogenic planet, humans would put all their effort into their biological survival while forsaking the meaningful action of politics. "Man may be willing, and, indeed, is on the point of developing into that animal species from which, since Darwin, he imagines he has come."[70] That we had created the weapons of our planetary extinction was only the most obvious manifestation of a kind of inaction, or what Claire Colebrook has recently observed, of a "human *impotentiality*, our essential capacity not to actualize that which would distinguish us as human." In the spirit of Arendt's critique, this is an impotentiality that paradoxically emerges out of a scientific desire to become an exceptional species. Colebook's "human inhumanity" pivots on an ocular-centric orientation to the world, which connects our fascination with looking to the experimental regime: "The eye is geared to spectacle as much as speculation, with speculation itself being both productively expansive in its capacity to imagine virtual futures and restrictively deadening in its tendency to forget the very life from which it emerges."⁷¹ It is at the atomic test site where the results of explosions are interesting in and of themselves and where, without question, the reproducibility of the test is predicated on the technological and biological disposability and replaceability of the subject.

NUCLEAR HOSPITALITY ON A "SLIGHTLY FLAWED PLANET"

The end of atmospheric testing gave way to a new and intentional vision of planetary transformation: *Operation Plowshare*. As championed by Edward Teller, the program would use the "peaceful" bomb to make the earth more welcoming to human habitation by blasting it into submission.

The Atomic Energy Commission produced *Operation Plowshare* (circa 1964/65), whose opening montage sequence, worthy of the Soviet avant-garde, advances a capitalist vision of a planet remade by nuclear explosions. A montage of dissonant sound and image unfolds. A landscape of sand dunes followed by a close-up of dehydrated soil is accompanied by the sound of rain and running water. A lone hut in the wilderness is accompanied by the hum of a massive human crowd. We hear sounds of trains and the buzz of urban life while looking at a deserted mountain range. The juxtaposition of sound and image gives rise to a creative geography and uniquely cinematic temporality: we hear the reverberations of a human-populated and cultivated future while seeing landscapes that are stuck in an obdurate present and beholden to a recalcitrant nature. The voiceover explains the transformative goals of this program:

> To bring water and food where there is only parched earth, and people where there is desolation; to bring freedom of movement where there are imposing barriers, and commerce where nature has decreed there will be isolation; to bring forth a wealth of materials where there are vast untapped resources, and a wealth of knowledge where there is uncertainty. To perform a multitude of peaceful tasks for the betterment of mankind, man is exploring a source of enormous potentially useful energy . . . the nuclear explosion.⁷²

From the weapons laboratory and mock battlefront of the Nevada Test Site, where changes to the earth are merely collateral damage, comes a program that targets the earth itself as the obstacle to human progress. In the new age of nuclear science, detonations move earth to create dams, sea-level canals, harbors, and mountain passes. And this is proposed not to advance the Cold War hostilities, but, in the name of nuclear humanism, to help people in all nations maximize "potentially rich inhabitable land." Blasted cavities will also enable corporations to extract natural resources, or to deposit nuclear waste in cavities created by nuclear explosions. The appeal is that projects "never before practical or possible" can be accomplished with unprecedented speed and, proponents argue, at a fraction of the cost of more traditional excavation techniques. To make this point, the film takes us to the 1962 Sedan cratering test at Nevada. A one-hundred-kiloton nuclear explosion detonated a few hundred yards below ground displaces six million cubic yards of earth "in less time than it takes to describe it." Nuclear explosions remake the landscape faster than the speed of speech: a great acceleration in planetary renovation.

Apart from this film, the campaign for Plowshare had begun earlier in the pursuit of the so-called peaceful atom. In 1959, Edward Teller, famous father of the hydrogen bomb, Nobel Prize–winning physicist, Director of the University of California's Livermore Radiation Laboratory, and Plowshare cheerleader, told an audience in Fairbanks, Alaska, where he hoped to nuclear blast a new harbor into being: "If your mountain is not in the right place, just drop us a card."[73] And in an earlier film entitled *Project Gnome* (1961), Teller explains Plowshare's new detonation regime. Speaking in his characteristically gruff affect, he sits behind a desk, a script in hand, and awkwardly, loudly, and with long pauses midsentence makes a case for nuclear "geographical engineering."[74] The camera slowly zooms in as he enumerates some of the applications for this repurposed technology. Emplaced in "the bowels of the earth," nuclear explosions transform "the earth itself into a crucible to make new kinds of chemicals." Turning the planet into a laboratory—the unintended effect of nuclear weapons testing—is the explicit goal of the "peaceful atom." With the Gnome test, he explains: "We built a physics laboratory right there in the salt mine." Nuclear physics now creates its own laboratory space by blasting a cavity in the earth and then harvesting the new isotopes and human-made elements. With this new orientation comes a different visual culture. The mushroom cloud and slow-motion effects of lethal thermal radiation are now supposedly contained underground and the bomb is experienced as a subterranean rumble or a postblast displacement of earth. In the films of the Plowshare era, the bomb may leave hardly any trace, unless, of course, it is called upon to function as nuclear dynamite.

The perversity of this new regime is that this war on the planet is waged to make the planet a more inviting place to live. The Atomic Energy Commission has always described the area of the nuclear test site as desolate, inhospitable, *and thus* disposable even before testing begins. This is what Valerie L. Kuletz aptly describes as a "wasteland discourse" and colonizing strategy of American nuclearism whereby a *"landscape of national sacrifice,* an *expendable landscape"* is "superimposed" over local and especially Native American use and meaning of the very same place.[75] If it wasn't already welcoming, the irradiation of the atomic surround has ensured that the proving ground will be toxic for generations to come. In 1992, when testing was finally banned, the Department of Defense estimated that experiments had deposited more than three hundred million curies of radioactive materials on the site, making the Nevada proving ground one of the most contaminated place in the United States and still today an ongoing source of water contamination.[76] But *Plowshare* reverses the relationship of nuclear explosions to planetary hospitality. The film explains that this program will atomic bomb "unfriendly terrain" to make it useful and welcoming for commercial development and the needs of global commerce in order to help more people be at home on this planet. Nuclear explosions may transform deserts the world over into lush agricultural land through vast irrigation schemes. Mountain ranges may be leveled to make way for trade routes. Wherever the earth does not yield to human prosperity, nuclear explosions will mold nature to human purpose: instantaneous nuclear constructivism. In a 1961 article written for *Popular Mechanics*, Teller speculates that the heat from nuclear detonations could release oil from both Canada's Athabasca Tar Sands and the shale rock of Colorado, Utah, and Wyoming to fuel the growing demands for energy. He prophesies that a clean nuclear bomb could be used "as a trigger that would modify climate or weather" in a not-too-distant future.[77]

The film *Plowshare* focuses on two specific cartographic challenges under consideration. The first is a two-mile roadway cut through California's Bristol Mountains for the "most direct path" to the coastline. Rows of nuclear explosions could quickly displace sixty-eight million cubic yards of earth and rock. In this sequence it is not sound and image that are juxtaposed, but a superimposition of multilane automobile traffic, trains, and then trucks over an aerial view of the mountain range (Figure 2.13). The superimposition may itself be both the power dynamic and film aesthetic practice of the Anthropocene as such films map navigable pathways onto the natural barriers to commerce, an imagistic overlay of human mobility onto a resistant topography that recalls Kuletz's own analysis of the Trinity test site earlier. The second project is to create a sea-level canal to supplant the Panama Canal, which was under negotiation to be returned eventually to Panamanian control after riots erupted in 1959 amid protests of the terms of the canal's continued operation.[78] An animated sequence leads us through the process whereby "a nuclear blasted route across Central America could provide a channel one thousand feet wide and up to two hundred feet deep offering a virtually unlimited capacity." We then see aerial

Figure 2.13 An interstate highway is superimposed over an aerial shot of a mountain rage. *Plowshare* (circa 1964/65å).

views of Panama's rain forest presented not as a fragile eco-system already endangered by the previous canal, but as an unutilized swath of land ripe for atomic blasting "and one of the greatest civil engineering feats of all time." *Plowshare* expresses a cosmic belief that human potential is equal to its capacity for geo-engineering when the voiceover declares: "Expanding economic and social needs of an ever-expanding population can be met only by moving huge quantities of earth efficiently and economically." The repetition of "expanding" in this sentence, as an adjective characterizing both the rising *needs* of individuals and the rising *number* of individuals, intimates the exponential dynamics of the Anthropocene and its deep connection to the nuclear epoch.

Only as a self-consciously terra-forming species channeling the forces from space may Homo sapiens thrive on an inconvenient—or what Teller called "a slightly flawed"—planet.[79] Yet they do so as part of the very carcinogenic nature-culture they've produced. In *Plowshare*'s final images, the Sedan detonation erupts from the earth in slow motion. Molten materials and the hot glow of atomic thermal energy pierce a rising bubble of sand and dirt while harps and trumpets on the soundtrack resonate triumphant. "This is the peaceful potential of nuclear explosions." Now in a bit of creative causality, the film dissolves from the Nevada Test Site to a series of

[94]   *On Location...*

"peaceful" images: not destroyed suburban houses or charred mannequins in Survival City, but cars driving leisurely through a mountain pass, followed by an image of an active grain elevator, followed by a shot of a cargo ship in a harbor, and followed finally by a shot of a verdant irrigated field of crops. The nuclear explosion does not destroy worlds. It synchronizes sound and image, and it resolves the superimposition of industry *onto* nature as an image of industry *as* nature. An "equipment-free aspect of reality" is what people "demand from a work of art," remarks Benjamin. In cinematic art, as in the landscapes of the Anthropocene, what appears as nature results from "the most intensive interpenetration of reality with equipment."[80] *Plowshare*, in this final sequence, manifests the transformation of mountain ranges into drivable mountain passes but essentially eliminates the nuclear detonation *on location* as the mechanism of deep rock penetration. If cinema gives us the images of reality absent the camera (thanks to editing), this atomic film concludes with a dialectical image of an altered nature absent, or simply after, the nuclear bomb. Or better yet, it is a nature after, which is to say "in the name of," nuclearism. Project Plowshare never came to fruition as planned and was officially defunded in 1975. As a vision or artwork, it was fully realized only on film.

The twenty-seven test explosions conducted for the project in the intervening decades, however, certainly left their traces on the planet. Take just two examples. The salt mine experiment Gnome released an unexpected radioactive cloud that drifted over the Texas panhandle before reaching Omaha, Nebraska's, city limits. Two years later a congressional hearing revealed that children close to the test site had been exposed to dangerous levels of radiation in their thyroids.[81] The experiment was supposed to prove that underground explosions could be conducted fallout free and that the energy generated by the blast could be harvested. The "surprise" leakage of water vapor, as Teller calls it in the film's epilogue, was not a failure of scientific prediction; it offered new opportunities to create new synthetic isotopes and radioactive elements. And with each test, Teller remarks with serious conviction, "we are perfecting our tools, we are ridding our tools of association with radioactive danger." The Sedan crater experiment at the Nevada Test Site—the largest detonation on US soil up to that point, spewed five times more radioactive dust than expected, carrying the cloud eastward as far as the Dakotas. The crater's rim is radioactive to this day.[82] The Atomic Energy Commission flew and then buried several tons of Sedan's highly contaminated soil in Alaska's Ogotoruk Creek to test the effectiveness of water flow to dissolve radionuclides, contaminating the drinking water of the indigenous communities downstream who have since suffered high rates of cancer. It was remediated only in 1993 after classified documents were made public. There was no film about this particular experiment, no spectacle of detonation, no reassuring graph of projected results. But the atomic tests in Alaska did give rise to more than radioactive levels. Indigenous peoples, local scientists, and a newly formed group of activists, called Greenpeace, saw to it that Plowshare would not become a reality.[83] Yet the logic of this geographical engineering program that contaminated the "slightly flawed planet" it sought to correct was in lockstep with the very Anthropocene age that it helped to accelerate.

CHAPTER 3

The Ecologies of Film Noir

Iraq veteran and environmental theorist Roy Scranton offers compelling instruction in the face of world-ending climate change. As he observes, the reservoir of methane about to be released into Earth's atmosphere as a result of global warming will have the effect on the planet of a nuclear winter. The atomic war we thought we avoided is arriving through other means. "We're fucked," he declares in terms befitting a hard-boiled protagonist. "The only questions are how soon and how badly."[1] To prepare for this imminent end, Scranton turns to his own soldierly strategies of coping with war's violence and the threat of death that greeted him daily in Iraq:

> Every morning, after doing maintenance on my Humvee, I would imagine getting blown up, shot, lit on fire, run over by a tank, torn apart by dogs, captured and beheaded. Then, before we rolled out through the wire, I'd tell myself that I didn't need to worry anymore because I was already dead.[2]

Training for death, he argues, is now the task of humanity as a whole in the face not of war but of climate change that is fuelled by our capitalist, carbon-based consumerism, a culture that is both "astoundingly virulent but also toxic, cannibalistic and self-destructive."[3] Instead of embracing discourses of sustainability and military security, we should come to an "understanding that this civilization is already dead. The sooner we confront our situation and realize that there is nothing we can do to save ourselves, the sooner we can get down to the difficult task of adapting, with mortal humility, to our new reality."[4] Learning first how to die, humanity may then, in some other future, perhaps, be refashioned. Whether this future life form will still be humanity is an open question. What role might cinema play in this pedagogy for the Anthropocene? How might cinema teach us how to die?

Disaster and so-called climate science fiction films rehearse the end of the world with apocalyptic narratives of end times and thus may be good candidates for Scranton's project. Yet rather than teaching how to let go, such films typically produce a panicked recommitment to our world as it is (or, diegetically, was) and they do so, usually, in the name of tomorrow's children around whom there is a spark of hope that our current way of life or something very much like it will persist or regenerate.[5] Disaster films represent catastrophe as a sudden end and they depict scenes of mass fatality. But they also give us exceptional characters who manage to survive and they present every sentimental reason to sustain our way life as it is.

Film noir is the genre most devoted to the pedagogy of death and it is an elegy, of sorts, to a deadly and damaging civilization to which characters and viewers are nevertheless drawn. Noir does not terrify audiences with an abrupt and total collapse of civilization, nor does it present us with dystopian futures to come. Instead, these midcentury narratives confront us with the depressing possibility that a corrupting order of things and a dissolute human nature will persist, as they are, forever. These stories do not teach viewers how to survive in this world; they lay bare the attachments to it that kill. Hard-boiled detectives investigate an ecology of misery and crime in a world that is artificial and in some sense already past.

Anthropocene historians J. R. McNeill and Peter Engelke conclude that human-caused climate change reached an unprecedented intensity starting in the 1950s "only by accident, as an unforeseen and unintended by-product of actions undertaken for routine quests for wealth, power, and contentment."[6] Noir is the genre most devoted to the arts of bad living and it turns routine quests into thrilling, doomed narratives in which the everyday grab for power, wealth, and contentment is turned against itself and returns to itself in the form of a violent end. Situated in the postwar American city, noir demonstrates what Dana Polan calls a "negative existentialism." "Environments," he writes, "don't reflect back to a character his/her personality or values—that is, his/her freedom to shape externality according to individual desire—but, . . . rather demonstrate the radical externality and even resistance of environment to the imprinting of a self upon environment."[7] The oxymoron of noir's human-built environment, like the Anthropocene as I read it, is that it is experienced as radically antihumanist, a world that negates rather than yields to the individual human imprint.

In contrast to Hollywood's goal-oriented, active protagonists and compared to the very real industrious, reproductive, first-world populations radically reshaping the planet at midcentury, the noir hero is inactive, unself-actualizing, and morally degraded. Vivian Sobchack notes that noir is a world "of little labor."[8] These are people who wait instead of work, who have foes instead of families, and who kill time and other people. The characters in this genre contribute nothing to the economy, leave behind no legacies, and they often desire, above all, to disappear without a trace—preferably to Mexico with someone else's money. They neither produce nor reproduce the conditions of their existence; this is, she observes, a "degenerate" genre. Banishing weddings and children from its narrative, moreover, noir eschews what Lee Edelman calls "reproductive futurism," embracing instead a queer negativity and a pessimistic ecology without familial hope. Rather than strive to mold a future, to right all wrongs, to create or procreate, the noir hero typically gives up. Film noir thus offers us a vision of not so much a *fallen* but a *fallow* humanity. Specifically, it features the white, middle class, American men and women (characters demographically slated for survival and also most responsible for the activities related to climate change) in stories of their untimely demise in habitats soon to disappear.

Indeed, noir's characters are Hollywood's most ecological figures not despite but because they inhabit and are conditioned by the most unnatural of human-made worlds. They subsist in explicitly artificial environments that imprint them negatively on all ecological levels. I organize this chapter around the three ecologies of film noir, categories that I appropriate with a twist from Félix Guattari's "ecosophy," which is composed of environments, social formations, and subjectivities. For Guattari, these are three ecological registers or levels that may be enlisted for "a new line of human praxis" or a new "modality of group-being" that would bring about a true anticapitalist revolution in response to global environmental ruination. Guattari advocates for a "gradual reforging and renewal of humanity's confidence in itself" that would "counter the pervasive atmosphere of dullness and passivity" through a commitment to "continuous resingularization."[9] I repurpose Guattari's categories, not to counter but to pursue noir's passivity and pessimism to their dead ends. Noir's three ecologies break down as follows. Life in the city, living in shabby rental property, and often on borrowed time, means that the "environmental ecology" of noir is *tenancy*. The city and neighborhood are on the brink of erasure and the hero is always subject to immediate eviction. Locating itself in disappearing urban centers, noir characterizes as both endangered and endangering the habitat of America's built urban environment. The second, "social ecology," keeps our characters in the present moment without pasts they may return to and certainly without a future. Eschewing reproduction and its problematic futurism, moreover, the characters figure out how to relate to each and to the world always living (and dying) in the moment. Thus, *present-tenseness* is the second, social ecology that refuses to think to humanity into a future. And as characters come to understand their serialized nonuniqueness, they come to grips with their *actuarial subjectivity*, the final ecology in which psychology parts ways with intentional action. In their efforts to be singular, noir heroes behave more like members of a death-bound species. Drawing on noir genre criticism and theories of the environment that emerge out of the films themselves, I argue that these anti-humanist ecologies orient us to the ends of a consuming capitalist culture without the promise of renewal, redemption, or hope for regeneration. These tough guys and disheveled dames play out extinction narratives in the genre's bleak landscapes. Giving up, they teach viewers how to die in the Anthropocene.

NOIR'S ENVIRONMENTAL ECOLOGY: TENANCY

As Edward Dimendberg has written, film noir is attracted to the threatened neighborhoods and crumbling infrastructure of American postwar cities. A genre of urban crime, noir is also an archive of the pre–World War II American city, a "memory bank" of "disappearing urban forms," and melancholic meditations on "endangered metropolitan topoi" that will soon disappear.[10] The city is both a site of human misery, where civic neglect becomes manifest in the ghettos and forgotten neighborhoods that foster delinquency, and a unique habitat that vanishes when its residents are evicted to make way for standardized housing, urban renewal, and suburbanization. For Dimendberg, the genre dramatizes the "psychic hazards of dwelling in an urban space whose historical mutation yields real spatial gaps and temporal voids between the modern as 'yet-to-come' and the urban past as 'yet-to-be-destroyed.'"[11] Characters find that they cannot keep up with the pace of change and that their social if not highly individual memory erodes along with access to experience. Film noir's aesthetic world turns urban history into the narratives and affects of a reduced human habitat, where the new and presumably more durable residential arrangements, whether in the form of suburban sprawl, nuclearism's survival architecture, or urban public housing, lead to an even more diminished, psychically negating, but also criminally intriguing form of living.

Kiss Me Deadly (1955), Robert Aldrich's ironic adaptation of Mickey Spillane's vigilante Cold War thriller, is a case study in the erasure of urban history and a history of urban erasure. Private detective Mike Hammer (Ralph Meeker) searches for clues of a murdered women in Los Angeles's Bunker Hill neighborhood. Seemingly navigable only on foot, this compactly built but eerily empty area of boarding houses is perched atop a network of steep concrete stairs, instead of sidewalks. More like the fantastic Casbah in *Pepe le Moko* (1937) than the gridded city of modern Los Angeles, Bunker Hill, in this film, is a dark claustrophobic maze.

Cinematographer Ernest Laszlo's compositions privilege disorientation. Canted angles defy gravity, and the film's fictional residents, often obscured by the cluttered décor of their one-room walk-ups, are hardly calling the shots. In his documentary essay film *Los Angeles Plays Itself*, Thom Anderson comments on Aldrich's use of actual locations. It is, says Anderson, "a literalist film." As Mike tools around the city, "what we see is what was really there"—a city divided by rich and poor neighborhoods, and old and new architecture. "What was new then" in the film "is still with us," and "what is old" has been erased altogether.

At the center of the drama is the Bunker Hill neighborhood, the most photographed area in Los Angeles, says Anderson, and thus a neighborhood whose erasure has been unwittingly documented in fictional films using it as a location. First developed in the 1880s as the address for Los Angeles's elite, Bunker Hill was, by the 1950s, described by urban planners as a high-crime area of substandard wood-frame Victorian mansions that had been partitioned into cheap boarding houses. Within a decade, Bunker Hill transformed from Los Angeles's most coveted real estate to a neglected and densely populated firetrap in the middle of the city. Thus, the Los Angeles Community Redevelopment Agency (CRA) (established in 1948 and empowered to bulldoze the area by the 1954 Housing Act) eventually prevailed in its campaign to acquire most of the land, demolish the old houses, and make way for a private sector building and the "corporate modernism" associated now with this area.[12] Bunker Hill's historic residents, mostly elderly pensioners and Native Americans, were forcibly relocated to mostly substandard apartments and public housing projects. This removal came shortly after Native Americans had arrived in the city through the 1952 Federal Bureau of Indian Affairs, Urban Indian Relocation Program, which oversaw voluntary migration to American cities from the Southwest reservations, many of which were contaminated by nuclear testing and weapons manufacturing plants.[13] Los Angeles was one of seven recommended destinations and boasted the largest urban Native American population in the United States, with Bunker Hill as the community hub.[14] Rather than bring outmoded buildings up to code for better living, the CRA wanted to capitalize on this real estate and maximize it revenue-generating potential, especially when public housing struck right-wing Cold Warriors as a communist plot to manage the city. The CRA prioritized "urban renewal" and slum clearance over programs to create viable public housing. This is what historian Don Parson calls the "slash-and-burn" ethos of neoliberal city development.[15] By the 1980s, Bunker Hill would be home to the LA Museum of Modern Art, the Walt Disney concert hall, and numerous high-rise corporate hotels and office buildings. As Parson writes of Bunker Hill's dispossessed residents, these victims of corporate plotting and urban planning were "caught between the adequacy of their current housing and its annihilation by the CRA."[16]

Slum clearance was also a defensive measure in the nuclear age because, as one CRA proponent argued, Hiroshima and Nagasaki had suffered preponderant damage due to the substandard residential construction. To allow urban blight to persist would be tantamount to "municipal suicide."[17] In 1951, President Harry S. Truman announced the Industrial Dispersion Policy from which followed a host of urban plans to de-nucleate the American city, sacrificing the center so that it would not be a target in nuclear war. To reduce population density and to disburse the armaments centers, the federal and state governments prepared to clear the urban slums, build satellite towns, and create new highway networks and commuter cultures. And thus nuclear war would be deterred for the lack of easy targets. The ideal city would resemble a donut: an empty center ringed with residential and industrial areas, separated by green spaces, linked through highways and light rail.[18] The concentrated old cities, resistant to such improvements, were "the vulnerable heart of America" likely to be lost in the flash of nuclear war according to Ralph Lapp, the acting head of the Nuclear Physics Branch of the Navy and scientific advisor to the US War Department.[19]

Kiss Me Deadly takes viewers to Bunker Hill on the eve of its erasure and at the height of its perceived endangerment to the rest of the city. The film finds there not a hotbed of urban crime, however much the crumbling structures and claustrophobic apartments are evocative of noir dread. Nor does the film feature the elderly or Native American residents of the actual neighborhood. This urban history functionally erased, the film transforms Bunker Hill into a crime scene of a different order. It shelters the victims of an underground nuclear plot who are living in the seedy debris of modernity. Hammer walks the dark streets and steep stairs of Bunker Hill visiting several residences: the nicely appointed, book-lined apartment of the dead woman, and the rundown flophouse in which another woman posing as her former roommate pretends to take refuge. He interrogates a beaten-up journalist living in a dimly lit, cluttered shamble of an apartment, as well

Figure 3.1 Untidy living in *Kiss Me Deadly* (1955).

an unemployed Italian opera singer whose voice fills his decrepit boarding house. Enraptured with his music, he sings while pasta boils on a hotplate in a room crisscrossed with hanging laundry (Figure 3.1). The criminals, on the other hand, live in the posh suburbs. They are upper-class gangsters, doctors, and modern art collectors who frequent not the dive bars in the inner city, but the Hollywood Athletic Club and poolside gardens in Hollywood Hills.

Not only was the tenement—the ur-form of poor ecology—in danger of being nuclear targeted, but also its very untidiness posed a danger to the nation. This is the message in the Civil Defense film *House in the Middle* (1954), which focuses on America's poor neighborhoods, those unsightly blocks "run down and neglected" that you find in any town, we are told, somewhere between tree-lined suburban streets and the industrial downtown where those residents work.[20] "An eyesore, yes! And, as you'll see, much more. A house that's neglected is a house that may be doomed in the atomic age." Tests on mock American homes "simulate conditions seen in too many alleys and backyards in slum areas." The film transitions from an actual city street to the Nevada proving ground where such a house is reproduced in all its flammable details. The living room is cluttered with newspapers, magazines, and clothing, "all the earmarks of untidy housekeeping" that would make the Italian opera singer feel right at home (Figure 3.2). This simulated slum house sits on the right in a row of three houses. On the left stands one that's neglected but not unkempt, and in the middle, a white painted house, furnished and orderly. The house in the middle is the only structure left

Figure 3.2 Untidiness of the nuclear slum house in *House in the Middle* (1954).

standing after the atomic test bomb explodes (Figure 3.3). Produced by the National Paint, Varnish, and Lacquer Association with the cooperation of the Federal Civil Defense Administration and the "National Clean-up, Paint-up, Fix-up Bureau," *House in the Middle* demonstrates that untidiness and life in the slums is death to the person who can't or won't clean up his act, and it is a hazard to anyone else living in the vicinity. Citizens who hope to survive nuclear war are urged to do home repairs and cultivate gardens, as if roses are a form of nuclear deterrence ("trim your shrubbery and trees, weed, and plant flowers"). "Beauty, cleanliness, health, and safety are the four basic doctrines that protect our homes and our cities. . . . The reward may be survival." The threat to the American town, according to this film, is not global nuclear war, but the slum, the rental property, and the neglected nonneighborhood that barely stands in the middle of every city.

Film noir lives in the slum house on the right and its characters refuse to tidy up, plant flowers, or prepare bomb shelters in preparation for nuclear war. These urbanites seek no escape from the inner city that is targeted for both urban redevelopment and nuclear annihilation, and there are no places for them to go, in any case. Significantly, the nuclear event that ends *Kiss Me Deadly* takes place in a lone beach house far from the city center where Gaby (Gaby Rodgers), the ultimate femme fatale, unleashes "the great whatzit." In the film's final shots, Mike frees himself from Gaby

Figure 3.3 Before-and-after effects of an atomic bomb on an unkempt property. *House in the Middle* (1954).

and stumbles into the ocean with his girl Velda (Maxine Cooper). The beach house is engulfed in an atomic glow and the film ends while Mike and Velda run into the water. *This* white house, in the middle (of nowhere), and not the flammable ghetto, is the origin of atomic obliteration, but the bomb likely claims all of Los Angeles (and, for that matter, maybe even the entire world) in its explosive power (Figure 3.4).

While the noir city is targeted for erasure, the heroes are already accustomed to forms of temporary living. Living in down-and-out flophouses, they don't build homes; they just struggle to make rent. For Vivian Sobchack, the American home is "a structuring absence" in film noir that is reflective of the

Figure 3.4 The atomic house in the middle of nowhere. *Kiss Me Deadly* (1955).

postwar housing shortage and the psychological as well as sociological habits that this period of rootless dwelling summons forth.[21] Noir hyperbolically brackets itself off from the rhythms and comforts of domesticity and premises itself instead in the unhomey spaces of cocktail lounges, wayside motels, and shabby apartments. It acknowledges that the idyllic wartime homefront, if it ever existed, is no longer available (or only ironically so). Thus, noir takes place in these temporary shelters, "spaces of social dislocation, isolation, and existential alienation" where public and private affairs intermix and where chance encounters between strangers have morbid consequences.[22]

Noir's affinity with rental property and cheap temporary housing has its roots in Depression-era hard-boiled fiction and its reckoning with the failures of liberal democracy and the rise of the welfare state. These stories made into films during World War II find their visual style when the gritty "red meat" crime film developed a low-budget strategy to accommodate wartime shortages and exploit a more relaxed censorship regime. Sheri Chinen Biesen writes that set designers and cinematographers used fog, mirrors, low-key lighting, and unconventional framing to obscure cheap and often recycled sets and reused costumes from previous, high-budget films.[23] Film noir was not intentionally "green," of course. As a B-picture staple, its production designers had to learn to make do with the remains of larger-budget sets and reduced access to materials, just as its characters live in what always appears as the detritus of consumer capitalism. All Hollywood production had to contend with the shortages of wartime.[24] Noir turned the symptoms of scarcity into a desired aesthetic that would persist and endure as a homeless ethic and form of critique after war.

For Sobchack, the chronotope "lounge time" crystalizes the new spatio-temporal experience of postwar homelessness and transience, and it tends to be read as a threat to the very domesticity it negates. Lounge time "is a perverse and dark response, on the one hand, to the loss of a home and felicitous, carefree, ahistoricity and, on the other, to an inability to imagine being at home in history, in capitalist democracy, *at this time*."[25] This is the period between wartime austerity (when many citizens lived in rundown urban apartments) and the US postwar suburban building boom that from 1945 to 1965 led to the creation of an estimated 35,500,000 new, single-family homes arranged in low-density subdivisions, designed for middle-class affluence and its reproductive happiness.[26] Even when these suburban homes become available, film noir sticks with its urban milieu, preferring the anonymous, cluttered rental spaces to the homogenizing and differently polluting effects of suburban plentitude.

John Huston's *Asphalt Jungle: The City under the City* (1950) is set in a generic midwestern metropolis in which the built world overwhelms and erases all organic life. In the wide establishing views filmed on location in Cincinnati, as well as in the deep exterior spaces shot in the MGM back lot, there is not the slightest sign of "nature," not even weeds or distant trees (Figure 3.5). A police car patrols the vast empty streets and we are introduced to Dix (Sterling Hayden), on the run from his last stick-up, a lone figure weaving his way through the desolate back allies to a dingy diner whose owner, Gus, will provide cover. The "jungle" is a tangle of electric wiring, tenement buildings, and rundown storefronts. Designed for urban life, this city is the death to anyone who calls it home, and not just due to rampant crime. Ciavelli (Anthony Caruso), the ace picklock living in a tiny one room walk-up with his aggrieved wife and a sick baby, explains the source of the infant's cough: "She takes him out first thing in the morning. It's cold then! She says the baby's gotta taste fresh air. I'm always telling her, if you want fresh air, don't look for it in this town." Whether the baby survives into toddlerhood is left open, but his father dies from a stray bullet during a robbery.

Above all, the city offers no permanent residence. Doll (Jean Hagen) has been locked out of her boarding house because the police shut down on payday the nightclub where she works. Teary, she remarks, "I've never had a proper home." She's now bunking with Dix in his ramshackle digs. "Gee this place is a mess." She says. "How can you stand to live like this?" But for Dix, who has lived in this city for several years, this is merely a short-term arrangement. He plans to raise funds by stealing or gambling

Figure 3.5 No signs of nature in *Asphalt Jungle* (1950).

to reclaim Hickory Wood, his family's lost Kentucky horse farm and, as it turns out, the setting for the final scene. With his pockets empty of money and his body drained of blood from a heist gone bad, Dix expires in the grass surrounded by thoroughbreds. When we finally glimpse something that looks like nature or a homestead in this film, it serves as a backdrop to unnatural death.

In his 1945 meditation "Refuge for the Homeless," Theodor Adorno declared: "the house is past."[27] The bombardment of European and Japanese cities during World War II, attacks on civilians, the destruction of homes, and the creation of infernal camps all lead Adorno to the conclusion that "it is part of morality not to be at home in one's home." It is better to live in a hotel or an apartment than to benefit from the presumed stability of bourgeois habitations, which are, in any case, a thing of the past. "Dwelling, in the proper sense, is now impossible. . . . The traditional residences we grew up in have grown intolerable: each trait of comfort in them is paid for with a betrayal of knowledge, each vestige of shelter with the musty pact of family interests."[28] Adorno muses on the insufferable patrimony of the single-family house, the attachment to private property it mandates, and the home's complicity—in the name of "family interests"—with global war and mass dispossession. We could all move into hotels and "attempt to evade responsibly" for our privileged possessions. What we would find in the modern hotel, however, is a "chilly hospitality" in which relations have been reified through economic exchange: from hosts and guests to customers and employees.[29] The less fortunate cannot afford corporate accommodations and thus find themselves in slums or, worse, in the open air. Shelterlessness is the new global condition either intellectually, as in the experience of exile, or materially, as in the fate of most of the world's impoverished citizens. If Adorno preaches the moral discomforts of residential living, film noir invites us to various modes of dwelling in the *improper* sense.

From the mouth of a fictional German exile comes a different sentiment: "Home is where the money is." Recent ex-convict Riedenschneider (Sam Jaffe) in *Asphalt Jungle* exchanges pleasantries in German with a cabbie about the family they've left behind in Europe. A depraved expression of the exile's adaptability, Riedenschneider is a peripatetic bank robber, who spends most of his time in (and trying to break out of) jail. Planting no roots, he lives from one heist to the next. As an itinerant criminal, however, he stands in contrast to the film's other characters who are stuck in the city. Formed by its arrangement but mostly excluded from its wealth, these characters have not an economic but an ecologic relationship to their habitat by reason of their tenancy. "That is the difference between economy and ecology," writes Thomas Docherty. "[The ruling class] may own it in law but not in reason, in *nomos* but not in *logos*." Renters know intimately the property's features; they "inhabit the land ecologically (or by reason) but do not inhabit it economically (or legally)."[30] In the world of film noir these terms become rather twisted and intermingled. Noir heroes exemplify ecological living in ways that enable them to break the law (*nomos*). But, as renters, as people who nimbly navigate the urban world (so often they walk or run through streets and dark allies) and suffer its bad air and corrupt environment, they have a decidedly ecological relationship to the city. They dwell in the city's logic and understand its infrastructure, living and dying intimately connected to the quirky space.

The noir renter is a perverse agent of what Michel Serres calls a *cosmocracy*. A radical rewriting of Kant's cosmopolitanism, Serres's cosmocracy posits a future, borderless planet on which "the disappearance of spatial limits announces the end of legal limits."[31] Serres explains that "pollution-property" in the context of global warming has been the basis of a capitalist drive toward enclosures and "the aggressive and leonine act of appropriation." It started small with the property line marked in ways that sully the land. It became global as countries claimed more territory in the name of imperialist accumulation. Rather than own property and claim human possession of the earth, Serres proposes a new natural contract as a "rental agreement." "The world, which was properly a home, becomes global rental, the *Hotel for Humanity*. We no longer own it; we only live here as tenants."[32] Property ownership gives way to rental agreements; *homo economicus* gives way to *homo ecologicus*. Film noir's characters are dark ecologists who lead the way. They do not claim ownership of their homes, however much they may aspire to it. They don't get rich as landlords, though they often collect rent. And however much they struggle to keep their places tidy, they are not responsible for urban blight and neglect of their neighborhoods and crime scenes. The environmental ecology of film noir is homelessness; in it, malfeasance is habitat erasure. The genre knows yet it hardly mourns the passing of an obsolete humanity whose built environments and patterns of urban development foment different forms of bad living.

PRESENT-TENSENESS: NOIR'S SOCIAL ECOLOGY

Damaged and endangering, the world in film noir nonetheless persists. In the end of most films, a crime (usually a murder) has been solved, an investigation comes to a close, and a femme fatale's scheme is revealed. Yet rather than a triumph of justice or a restoration of order, or the rise of a new state of affairs, noir leaves us with a sense of being stuck in the immoral present. "Film noir is a film of death, in all senses of the word," write Raymond Borde and Etienne Chaumeton in their first attempts to define the genre. Noir's "vocation . . . has been to create *a specific sense of malaise*."[33] A privative and typically nonlocalizable malady ("the absence of a feeling of well-being," according to the *Oxford English Dictionary*), the malaise of noir is in response, Borde and Chaumeton argue, to specifically American forms of postwar living, reflecting "the anguish of a society that no longer knows where it's headed."[34] A genre about death, dead ends, noir emerges out of a culture that can't (or refuses) to think its way into the future. Or as I will reformulate their observation later, it is a genre that critiques the very discourses of optimistic futurity that uphold the culture associated with the Great Acceleration. For Borde and Chaumeton, the anguish is a problem for noir's politics. I argue that the genre's refusal to think forward is one of the most politically progressive features of its social ecology.

Roman Polanski's *Chinatown* (1974) is a second-generation noir that knows its generic history. It is a work of fiction that is also an act of film criticism, a meditation on noir's dead endings and environmental attunements. Most of us are familiar with this plot that takes place in 1939 Los Angeles. Private detective Jake Gittis (Jack Nicholson) stumbles across crimes at both the most intimate and geo-physical levels. At the largest scale, water baron Noah Cross presides over a mass deception. To convince

Los Angelinos to publically fund a new reservoir, Cross has fabricated the conditions of a draught by secretly dumping fresh water into the ocean at night. Having failed to own Los Angeles's water outright, he schemes to buy on the cheap parched land that his proposed reservoir will hydrate into prime real estate. And thus, as he explains, he plans to not simply bring water to the city with the new reservoir, but to bring the city to the water by incorporating the new land into the greater LA County and developing it at a huge profit. He risks repeating the deathly measure of the previous, unstable dam that killed hundreds when it unexpectedly breached, but the rewards would make him the most powerful man in an expanded and fertile metropolis. At the end of the film, the new unstable dam is already under contract.

Closer to home, Noah's empire is built on the violence of incest. Years ago he raped his daughter Evelyn (Faye Dunaway), and this violation of paternal trust produced a child, now a young woman, Catherine. Evelyn's sister and daughter, Cross's daughter and granddaughter, Catherine, at the beginning of the film is mistaken for her mother's romantic rival. She occupies an impossible generational position that causes the family tree to fold in on itself. At the film's devastating end, Evelyn is shot dead and Catherine, now without a mother or a sibling, is in the custody of her father/grandfather, Noah Cross, his sole heir and very likely his next victim. The relationship between geo-engineering and incest, explains screenwriter Robert Towne, is the film's "underbelly." "The two were intimately connected literally and metaphorically: raping the future and raping the land . . . a really strong connection."[35] It is significant that Towne states that Cross rapes not *his daughter* and the land, but *the future* and the land. The film presents us with an unsettling paradox. Noah Cross develops the land and rapes his own daughter in the name of what he calls "the future, Mr. Gitts! The future!" Yet the degeneracy of his family line and the likelihood of another dam's failing tell us that Noah's future is not a movement forward so much as an amplified repetition of the past, more of the violent same.

Film noir is an emphatic—at times satirical—rejection of what Lee Edelman calls "reproductive futurism."[36] This is the political and cultural discourse centered on the cult of the child as the symbol of and motivation for a heteronormative reproduction that mobilizes, perhaps even sacrifices, the immediate present in the name of future generations and our children's children. The American political Left and Right, Edelman argues, invokes the child as the "prop of secular theology on which our social reality rests."[37] The child functions as an anchor for petitions that are all but impossible to reject—who can say no to the child? And yet, the hetero-norm of the child is a future in the form of reproduction and repetition. For all its talk of the child to come, this far-reaching presumption merely "reproduces the past, through displacement, in the form of the future."[38] In film noir, the present is always some version of the past repeating itself and without any false promise that things will improve the next time around. In *Out of the Past*, Jeff is pulled back into his relationship with Kathie and Witt, dragged back to the violent death he thought he had escaped. And in *Chinatown* (literally back in that ethnic neighborhood), Jake once again finds that all of his efforts to protect a woman he loves ensures, once again, that she is brutally killed. With the benefit of hindsight, the noir hero knows that things were bound to go wrong. The past has been written. But one cannot predict the future in these films beyond the certainty of individual death and the constancy of degradation. In place of natality, we get fatality: the repetition of the past without a *particular* future.

Noir cuts against the reproductive impulse at the height of the baby boom and the beginning of an unprecedented and unsustainable human population bomb.[39] When we encounter actual little children and scenes of maternity in film noir, it is in the form of parody. In *Gun Crazy* the sharp-shooting outlaw couple Laurie (Peggy Cummins) and Bart (John Dall) are on the run. Out of money and options, they decide to force their way into the home of Bart's sister, Ruby, just as she's making dinner for her three children. The cramped kitchen in the house, just yards from the railroad track in this small and seemingly depressed California town, named Cashville, is cluttered with baby bottles and big boiling pots, illuminated by bare light bulbs. Ruby is haggard from years of housework and childrearing (Figure 3.6). Hardly the scene of cozy domesticity, this is exactly the impoverished future Laurie wants to avoid, turning instead to a short life of exhilarating, violent crime. In a previous scene, Bart floats the idea that they run off to Mexico, buy a little ranch, settle down, and "maybe even raise those kids we talked about once." But rather than settle, Bart and Laurie first run off to an amusement park where they behave *like* children and then take flight in "Madera National Park" in California's San Lorenzo Mountains, where they are hunted to death after a night of very primitive camping. At one point, Laurie even proposes taking Ruby's baby as a hostage when they make their final getaway. "Nobody would dare shoot if we took the baby with us." Picked up as a shield rather than as an object of maternal affection, the child is thankfully left behind. "No matter what happens," says Bart to Laurie in their final embrace before being shot, "I wouldn't have it any other way." Better to die young in a foggy bog than reproduce a morally upstanding family life.

Noir helps us to reject the National Wildlife Federation's mission statement, "Inspiring Americans to Protect Wildlife for Our Children's Future,"

Figure 3.6 The outlaws intrude on this cluttered domestic scene. *Gun Crazy* (1949).

to conserve natural places "for future generations."[40] In 1907, the child as the beneficiary of environmental efforts became official policy with Theodore Roosevelt's seventh annual address to congress: "To waste, to destroy our natural resources, to skin and exhaust the land instead of using it so as to increase its usefulness, will result in undermining in the days of our children the very prosperity which we ought by right to hand down to them amplified and developed." In this speech preaching sustainability, Roosevelt proposes to transform the nation's rivers into "water highways" and to create a nationwide system of dams to generate electricity, deepen the bed of shallow rivers, and provide irrigation to the "Western half of the country." He calls for the "reclamation" of swampland and marches:

> The constant purpose of the government in connection with the Reclamation Service has been to use the water resources of the public lands for the ultimate greatest good of the greatest number; in other words, to put upon the land permanent home-makers, to use and develop it for themselves and for their children and children's children.[41]

Here we have all of the markers of the Great Acceleration made into policy in the name of the children who will build permanent homes and accrue to themselves the assets of this once public land. By contrast, film noir recognizes that nature conserved in the name of the child becomes a resource for amplified capitalization, usefulness, and an even more robust plunder.

Noir's rejection of reproductive futurism and child-bearing women commits it to a nonprogressive, one might say outright pessimistic, temporality of the present. Sobchack writes of noir's sense of the future in decidedly pessimistic terms: "There are no stages of growth . . . not only because there are no children in its spaces, but also because behavior is compulsive and repetitive and thus becomes cyclical even as it seems initiated by chance and in impulse."[42] In *Brute Force*, for example, the plot to break out of prison is merely part of the cyclical nature of crime and desperation that landed these inmates in prison and then lures them into a mortally futile attempt at escape. The apparent novelty of their plan, hatched by Collins (Burt Lancaster), is a result of group problem solving and cryptic clues being surreptitiously transmitted. Yet, repeatedly, we are privy to perpetual planning and deferrals. Crenshaw, a rather batty prisoner serving a life sentence, is ready to make a break for it. He says to Gallagher (Charles Bickford): "If there's no hitch, we go Tuesday. . . . It's all set *this* time." Walking away, Gallagher, trying to convince Collins that only crazy people try to flee, observes: "It's been 'all set' every Tuesday for twelve years. And twelve years from now, it'll *still* be next Tuesday." Collins, however, stands firm on other precedents: "It can be done. It's been done before and it'll be again." But Gallagher, sure that he's coming up for parole, refuses to participate. "Very soon now, I'll be walking out of here." Collins, calling out Gallagher's own perpetual false hope, replies: "Next Tuesday?"

Collins and Gallagher represent the film's two dominant groups: men deluded by the hope of parole who are prepared to die waiting for release and men intoxicated by the myth of escape, willing to risk death to break out. Both groups consider themselves the exception to history and, in so feeling, fulfill their tragic stereotypes. When his parole hearing is canceled indefinitely, Gallagher joins Collins. In the climax of the film, Collins's crew, working from the outside, are all fatally shot, but Collins summons the strength to mount the guard tower, pull the lever to open the prison gate below, and, as his final act, toss the evil warden to his death. Gallagher, working with his men on the inside of the prison wall, creates the distraction that enables Collins to open the gate, but then, also lethally shot, accidentally rams a truck into the gate, ensuring it stays closed. Dead bodies everywhere, the guards soon quell the riot and force the surviving inmates back to their cells. The film concludes with a goodly doctor stitching up another convict and musing on the senselessness of escape: "Why do they do it? They never get away with it. Alcatraz. Atlanta. Leavenworth. It's been tried a hundred ways from as many places. Always failed. But they keep trying. . . . Nobody escapes. Nobody ever really escapes. Why do they do it?" Repeating the rhetorical question, the doctor's account of history—told through the shorthand of prison names—provides neither edification nor comfort. Die if you stay. Die if you leave. Suffer differently if you avoid prison altogether. The political point of the story may be for prison reform, the rights of America's proletariats, and the need for revolution, but the overt lesson of the film is futility of action to change the present or improve the future.

Noir then places its characters in what Joshua Foa Dienstag refers to as pessimism's "bare condition of temporality," a "linear extension without pattern (progress), goal (telos), or end (eschaton)."[43] Noir is sometimes traumatic in the sense that characters are doomed to reprise the violence that afflicts them. But the dread in the genre is more than individual psychology in that it posits a future in which the world, already productive of human unhappiness, is likely to get worse, but not *radically* so. With each film, we experience a sense of decline or discover characters stuck in a purgatory of the present. This is why films about prison life, in which characters must endure time's duration, mingle easily with the conventions of noir. Noirs can be remade, the same detective may be resurrected, but the best one can hope for in a noir is not a continuation, but an end. Noir repeats itself but struggles to produce convincing sequels.[44]

Living in the present, noir characters wait for their pasts to catch up to them. This is not a feeling *for* history so much as the disjointed sense of asynchrony. The opening scene of Siodmak's *The Killers* (1946) is emblematic in this regard. Two thugs appear in a nearly empty town diner. They rough up the waiter, the cook, and another customer named Nick Adams (Phil Brown) and announce their plans to kill the Swede (Burt Lancaster) when he arrives for his evening meal, which is typically before six. The gangsters twice order from the dinner menu but are told that the food will not be ready until exactly six. The clock opposite the counter is running ten minutes fast, explains the waiter. When it becomes clear that the targeted man is staying home, the thugs take off, and Nick runs to the boarding house to warn the Swede of the imminent danger. The curious detail of the diner's clock running fast combined with the Swede's habit of arriving early and the mandate that the thugs wait for the dinner hour seems like absurd plotting. Then we realize that these characters are generally out of sync with their world. An investigator interviews a delirious crook on his deathbed. "How long has he got?" The detective replies: "He's already behind schedule." Another character who has spent most of his life pacing in a jail cell is questioned about events from the past. He explains: "I can tell you *what* was the last time, but not where or when." Noir's spatial dislocation leads to temporal confusion such that characters are oddly in the moment; they are in "the what" without a particular "when."

The genre's obsession with currency (with cold hard cash) coyly symbolizes its present-tenseness. Cash, the ultimate reified object of the economy and the medium of current transaction, is itself the object of desire and one of the genre's staple spectacles. Even jewels in *Asphalt Jungle* are admired for their potential worth. Without content and rarely exchanged for material goods, money, in film noir, is the empty symbol of a present. Or it is the accumulation of spending potential as an end in and of itself. And this is the perverse if not also radical adjustment noir offers to the temporality of capitalism as characterized by Cornelius Castoriadis:

> And, as an imaginary time or a time of signification, typical capitalist time is an "infinite" time represented as a time of indefinite progress, unlimited growth, accumulation, rationalization, time of the conquest of nature, of the always closer approximation of a total, exact knowledge, of the realization of the phantasy of omnipotence. The present state of the planet attests to the fact that these are not just empty words, that these imaginary significations are more "real" than any reality.[45]

Money keeps noir characters in a state of limbo with limited knowledge but acutely aware of their finite time. They cannot access the unlimited growth or the conquest of nature that capitalist time signifies (in *Gun Crazy* our protagonists are reduced to primitive camping at the mercy of the elements). The cash we see in noir—its literal version of the money shot—is cash out of circulation, money out of time. It's too hot to spend and consumption is too conspicuous to get away with. Moreover, characters infrequently bother to articulate what they want the money for, as if any explanation of future use is necessary. A wistful moment in an otherwise suspenseful scene in Jacques Tourneur's *Nightfall* (1956) has John (Brian Keith), a rifle-toting thug, standing outside a hut in rural Wyoming. He and his dim-witted but sadistic partner, Red (Rudy Bond), have returned to the crime scene to recover the cash they stole in a bank robbery the year before. Or, more accurately, they have returned to recover the bag they accidentally left behind, confusing it for another identical bag full of medical supplies, a failed exercise in exchange value. While Red ties up the good guys who have also come to retrieve the cash, John holds a rifle on them and imagines how he'll spend his half of the $350,000 loot. He explains that with his newly acquired forty-foot yacht he'll scout out and then buy a small Pacific island—that is, until he starts thinking about another bank and another

$350,000, as one of the captives (an insurance investigator) remarks of John's compulsive thieving. When asked about plans for his share, Red's answer is as absurd to us as the question is to him: "I'm gonna set up a scholarship at Harvard." Soon both ruffians will be dead and the cash will be returned to the bank in the form of savings. Noir characters, writes Sobchack, are "fixed in a transitional moment."[46] In the case of *Nightfall*, these thugs are also fixed in transactional potential, perpetually ensnared in futile scenarios and unrealizable economic futures. Hording cash during the boom time of American postwar prosperity, noir characters are bad consumers. They rarely participate in the economy, preferring instead to horde the medium of convertibility.

ACTUARIAL SUBJECTIVITY: NOIR'S MENTAL ECOLOGY

Without a future, film noir also finds little of the past that is worthy of redemption or that may rise to the level of fulfilling meaning. While characters try to take comfort by elevating coincidence to destiny ("That's life. Whichever way you turn, fate sticks out a foot to trip you," says Al in *Detour*), the plots have us see bad luck and poor timing set against actuarial tables that reduce individual experience to statistical likelihood and that predict the future according to risk assessment. Insurance men are as much a staple of this genre as the gangster and the femme fatale—the former there to investigate and explain the compulsive habits of the latter to keep the insurance company in the black. But more than this, insurance puts into relief the degree to which characters in noir are not products of a unique, self-aware psychology or swept up in a divine plan. This depiction of statistical probability lends noir to narratives in which humans act unknowingly (and beyond any particular psychological explanation) at a supra-human, even species level. Behavior overrides intention. Whether he is biologically programmed or simply prone to accidents, the noir hero is not an individual human but an aggregate in the form of an individual.

Michael Szalay observes that hard-boiled insurance narratives such as *Double Indemnity* and *The Postman Always Rings Twice* provide "an 'environmental' account of behavior."[47] Characters are conditioned—socially, economically, temperamentally—by their modern surround, and they cannot comprehend the source of their drives or the consequences of their actions. This is especially the case when they attempt insurance fraud. Staged and real accidents intermix and become indistinguishable even in the perpetrator's own mind. Insurance produces a kind of double consciousness or a double self: one who plots and carries out the "accidents" covered by insurance to collect on the policy, the other who watches, knowing that the scheme is doomed to fail. Szalay remarks that this "bifurcation of identity" is not illuminated so much as produced by insurance.[48] The effect is that characters are unconsciously driven by the terms of their policy or find that the murders they stage to look like accidents return in the form of improbable but actual accidents. In *The Postman Always Rings Twice* (Garnet, 1946), Cora (Lana Turner) and Frank (John Garfield) fall in love and then plan the murder of her husband after watching him narrowly avoid a head-on collision while driving drunk. They first plan to have him fatally fall "accidentally" while getting out of the tub. When a cat crawls into the fuse box and the house goes dark, the husband actually does fall accidentally while getting out of the bath, but not to his death. When they finally do murder him by staging an automotive accident, it is revealed that the husband took out life insurance just before his death. The case goes to court, and the lovers turn on each other and fall prey to pernicious lawyers who compel true and false confessions. At the end, Frank and Cora are driving, finally reconciled to each other and looking forward to a happy future, when they crash and Cora, pregnant with their child, is killed. Frank, found guilty of Cora's murder, is sentenced to the gas chamber for a murder he did not intentionally commit. Or, as he consoles himself, he is sent to his death for Cora's murder as payment for actually killing her first husband. Between the intricacies of the law and the ready motive of insurance, it almost appears as if the husband had been framing the couple all along, unknowingly baiting them to fall in love and plot against him. Insurance throws into radical doubt a character's motives such that even Frank can't be sure why he acts as he does.

Insurance, explains Szalay, sets up a peculiar dynamic whereby companies place their bets on the better of possible worlds—presuming the house will not burn down, or that the various clauses (the double indemnities) in the contract are so unlikely to occur that they are a safe bet to insure. Insurance companies are optimists. The policy holder, by contrast, is sold insurance on the premise that the very worst is likely to happen and, even more, that insurance may prevent the unlikely and catastrophic future it covers. Policy holders are mystified pessimists believing that coverage grants them some agency over contingency. "In point of fact, insurance simply compensates for the individual's complete lack of such control."[49] For the policy to pay off, those accidents need to happen and any insured person risks or bets on having his policy fulfilled. Insurance salesman Walter Huff muses in the novel *Double Indemnity*: "You bet that your house will burn down, and they bet that it won't, that's all. What fools you is that you didn't want your house to burn down when you made the bet, and so you forget it's a bet. That don't fool them."[50] Insurance companies are poised to win because they track behavior and not intention. Insurance policies are based on "statistical patterns as they emerge independently of any organizing will. Large numbers of events follow recognizable patterns in the actuarial table only when they are not intended."[51] Walter Huff (or Walter Neff in the film) becomes the victim of his own plot to help Phyllis kill her husband and then collect on the very accident insurance policy that Walter surreptitiously sells him. When it comes to pass that Walter has been duped by Phyllis, who now plans to kill him and keep the money for herself, this revelation "hardly constitutes a significant moment of epiphany."[52] Phyllis is not in control of her desires and no more able to articulate her goals. Walter's Dictaphone confession, offered up in the form of an office memorandum as he bleeds out in boss's chair, is a story of action without intention. "I killed him. I killed him for money. For a woman. I didn't get the money and I didn't get the woman. Pretty isn't it?" As Szalay remarks, Walter's "downfall is attributable not to the fact that he lacks the means sufficient to execute his will, but rather to the fact that he decides to execute his will at all."[53] Lured by the possibility of a doubled insurance claim, Neff stages an accident that rarely if ever happens, thereby disrupting the statistical pattern and awakening suspicion. Hoping to buck the system, Walter merely confirms its predictive power.

As viewed through insurance plotting, noir theorizes psychology as aggregated patterns repeating themselves. Less fatalistic than probabilistic, film noir's account of history without a future, a chronology without a telos, humanity without agency or intentionality, anticipates what we might call Anthropocene historiography rooted through pessimistic epistemology. It is an Anthropocene historical method because it is the sum of unorganized, unintentional actions accumulated as data over time, without progress or particular human meaning, but utterly of human origin. It is a pessimistic theory of knowledge with a twist. As Dienstag writes, metaphysical pessimism, exemplified by Freud and Schopenhauer, finds the unavoidable root of human unhappiness in man's coming into awareness of his finitude, his "ability to project his imagination into the future," to "the hour of his own death," of which he, in turn, spends a lifetime in dreaded anticipation.[54] It is the knowledge of this future and the capacity to imagine this end that makes human existence a fundamentally if not ontologically unhappy one. "Death," he writes of this tradition of philosophy, "is the ultimate expression of the meaning of our lives, or more precisely, of the absence of meaning of our lives—but even more precisely, of the meaning of our lives consisting in the gradual realization of the absence of such meaning." Pessimism says that "death is thus the logical and desirable culmination of a life that teaches us not to want it."[55] Noir characters arrive into the fiction aware of their mortality and they participate in the disposability of human life and the reification (in the form of insurance collection) of unnatural human death. But the particular epistemological letdown in the genre is the result of characters becoming aware of their own statistical or serial nonuniqueness. Walter is first seduced by what he takes to be his own *exceptional* nature. He later learns, however, that in exercising his will, he is merely fulfilling Phyllis's own secret plot to use Walter to kill her husband and keep the money for herself, a plot that noir rehearses over and over again and that insurance agents know all too well from other cases. The agent of insurance becomes the nonagent of his action. Or, to put it differently, the source of Walter's disenchantment is not, in the pessimistic tradition, knowledge of his own death, but knowledge of his own unexceptional behavior and pathway to death—as just another of Phyllis's dupes, just another data point, just another man who dies young thinking he could game the system. Actuarial film noir is the drama of the individual's inability to counter the supra-human trend of behavior; it is the story of people misconstruing as contingency the absolute predictability of human action at midcentury. Given the centrality of insurance to noir as a whole, the genre may be read as an acknowledgment that each individual act not only confirms but also contributes to the big data set called humanity. This is not a geological history or an explicitly ecological commentary, though it may be a philosophical basis for a more reasoned environmental sensibility. To perceive our individual stories and encounters with particularity at a scale that erases psychology and ambition is to find, in the large, even geological view, accumulated effects beyond human meaning. Noir may be the only Hollywood genre that toggles between the individual subject (conditioned by an unnatural environment) and the meaningless aggregates at these inhuman levels.[56]

WE ARE ALREADY DEAD

Commentating on Hollywood's terror noir, Siegfried Kracauer denounced the sadism and morbidity of these films that offer no solution to the depravity in the world beyond a stultifying passivity. Mental illness is becoming the norm, according to these films according to Kracauer, and it is no wonder that these stories are set in the actual anarchic neighborhoods that feed addictions. "People emotionally out of joint inhabit a realm ruled by bodily sensations and material stimulants, a realm in which dumb objects loom monstrously high and become signal posts or stumbling blocks, enemies or allies. This obtrusiveness of inanimate objects is infallible evidence of an inherent concern with mental disintegration." These films reflect, or worse, produce, a culture swayed by "fascist pseudo-solutions." The hostile animism of noir's environment combined with the characters' "impotence" and failure to "demonstrate any counter-measures that would work to restore mental stability" are signs, in Kracauer's view, that Nazi habits of mind have wormed their way into American culture. "Whether society be a spiritual vacuum or a battlefield of irreconcilable beliefs, it seems no longer to provide a shelter for the individual, or principles that would compel his integrity."[57] In Hollywood's "terror films," as he calls them, society provides no shelter and madness reigns supreme. In the context of postwar politics that pits democratic liberalism against fascism and communism, any sign of passivity is reason for alarm. Viewed in the context of the Anthropocene, however, the lesson of passivity, expiration, and even a bit of incurable madness may actually be politically progressive.

In the opening sequences of *Detour*, Al is sitting in a Nevada roadside diner when a song on the jukebox prompts a flashback to his days in New York where he worked as a pianist with his beautiful singer-girlfriend in a "fleabag" dance hall. "Those were the days," he says wistfully of a setup ripe for a musical comedy. "I was an ordinary healthy guy. She was an ordinary healthy girl. And when you add those two together you get an ordinary healthy romance, which is the old story." They long to make it big, her in Hollywood, him at Carnegie Hall. But when it seems that these goals are at odds with their healthy romance, they agree to part ways. "We've got all the time in the world to settle down," she explains before leaving for the West Coast. After a short stint playing solo, Al decides to hitchhike to Los Angeles to marry the girl and realize the dream, a journey that sets him on the path to the gas chamber when he becomes implicated as a murderer in two accidental fatalities. Like many noir heroes, Al is caught between an unfulfilling life and an early unnatural death, but feels singled out for an especially wretched end. He leaves the diner, after recounting his tale of woe, and the police apprehend him: "I know someday a car will stop to pick me up that I never thumbed. Yes, fate or some mysterious force can put the finger on you or me for no good reason at all." Al rues the day he met Haskell, the first acquaintance who turns into a corpse. But looking back, there is no time or situation of happiness that Al would return to and there is no way for him to simply disappear; there are only more unhappy and deadly ends that might have been avoided had he stayed put. The lesson is to either not want happiness or fulfillment or be content to die trying.

If noir protagonists suffer most when they execute their will, then the genre teaches that it is better to do nothing. Indeed, this is the logical outcome when pessimistic pedagogy combines with the psychology of insurance. Explicating Schopenhauer's response to humanity's death-bound consciousness, Dienstag explains that our task is not to wish for happiness, but to limit our discontentment through an ascetic practice. Withdrawal and resignation are the most appropriate responses to a basic condition: "Our suffering is created by the striving of our will in a universe that can only punish such striving."[58] Without any hope for divine redemption, the pessimist, writes Schopenhauer, should model his behavior on the Christian saint who has learned how to "overcome the world . . . having reached complete self-knowledge, has found itself again in everything, and then freely denied itself, and who then merely waits to see the last trace of the will vanish within the body that is animated by that trace."[59] Noir heroes are certainly not saints, but their learned passivity, resignation, and even, in some instances, world-overcoming ascetic lifestyles are striking characteristics in plots that teach them the hard way what Jake Gittis learns in his Chinatown assignment: "To do as little as possible." These characters learn that no one can disappear without a trace because it is so difficult to extinguish the will that wants to act. Yet it may be that the brush with insurance promotes the critical disposition needed to imagine the self in these terms. Writes Szalay of *Double Indemnity*: "The doubleness in the title signifies the way insurance produces agents who passively observe themselves perform unintended actions."[60]

No other genre features characters so inclined toward passivity, to waiting, and even resigned to their deaths. In *Maltese Falcon*, waiting is the theme of the film's last thirty minutes. Gutman, Wilma, Joel, Sam, and Brigid hole up in Sam's apartment waiting for the sunlight and then for Effie to retrieve the falcon. Then Sam and Brigid wait for the police. Sam even promises to wait twenty years for Brigid to be released from prison on good behavior after he resolves to send her over. Or consider how many scenes in *The Killers* find the Swede in states of repose or awakening from a nap. He spends a goodly portion of his last boxing match down for the count, and he famously remains prone in his bed in the boarding house awaiting his executioners, even after a plaintive warning from his friend. In *Murder, My Sweet*, an eccentric ex-con lures Philip Marlow (Dick Powell) to investigate the whereabouts of his girlfriend. When Marlow becomes embroiled in a much more complicated plot, a wealthy father and husband of this very woman offers to pay Marlow to stop the investigation. "Now this is beginning to make sense in a screwy sort of way," jabs Marlow. "I get dragged in, get money shoved at me. I get pushed out, get money shoved at me. Everybody pushes me in. Everybody pushes me out. Nobody wants me to do anything! . . . OK. Put a check in the mail. I cost a lot not to do anything."

For Elizabeth Cowie, characters in noir "feel compelled by forces and passions beyond their reason to act as they do."[61] And while these protagonists often do not understand themselves or simply react to the forces around them, they seem able enough to articulate a connection between the desire that compels them and the death such desire exacts as the price for enjoyment. "The connection of desire with death is central to film noir, for it is with film noir that American cinema finds for the first time a form in which to represent desire as something that not only renders the desiring subject helpless, but also propels him or her to destruction"[62]. Fritz Lang's *Secret beyond the Door* (1947) exemplifies for Cowie the forbidden allure of the death drive. Premised on pop psychoanalysis and obviously influenced by Hitchcock's *Rebecca* and *Spellbound*, *Secret beyond the Door* finds Celia (Joan Bennet) attracted to Mark (Michael Redgrave) while on a trip to Mexico. Soon Celia abandons her safe, upstanding suitor in New York—a decision marked when she tosses a coin in a Mexican wishing well—and marries Mark, who, in noir's gothic tradition, conflates sexual and homicidal desires due to a traumatic childhood attachment to his mother. Mark's murderous dark side is inseparable from Celia's sexual attraction to him. Toward the end of the film, as he approaches her ominously with the intention of strangulation, she declares: "I knew you wanted to kill me last night, Mark. And I know why you've come back now. Last night I wanted to save myself, but I'd rather be dead than live without you. That would be a slow death for a lifetime." For Mark, Celia is a "cyclone," an "earthquake," a turbulent natural disaster that enthralls him despite a lifetime spent with controlling and catastrophic women. A pastiche of other noirs and gothic melodramas, the film is somewhat unique for its explicit embrace of a death-bound romantic sensibility shared equally between the man and a woman who has no monetary stake in the seduction. Whereas Mark is drawn to murder due to his childhood fixation on his mother (a fixation Celia manages to "cure" when she bids him to remember the cause of his symptoms), Celia's attachments to Mark are less open to ready explanation. Celia is not a victim of trauma or in need of ready cash; she is rather a woman in pursuit of her desire. And we may presume that in curing Mark, Celia extinguishes his allure.

Death is both immanent in noir's world (it suffuses all transactions and relationships, giving them all a sense of terrible urgency) and imminent as characters become resigned to their limits. Many of these heroes, in fact, are already dead. This is the explicit conceit of the voiceover narration in *Sunset Boulevard* in which Joe Gillis (William Holden) introduces himself as the open-eyed corpse floating in Norma Desmond's pool. A screenwriter by trade, Joe is the hero of a film littered with unfinished screenplays and films. The mise-en-scène pits the decadent mansions of old Hollywood, "crumbling apart in slow motion," against the "new" Hollywood's vast artificial back lots, soundstages, and unoriginal ideas. *Sunset* is only the most obvious example of noir's sense of its stories and characters as simultaneously contemporary with their moment of production while also being cliché manifestations of the same old story.

Film noir's lessons in passivity and tenancy negate the very active humanity, specifically these Western or mostly American, mostly white men, at the dawn of their most productive, proliferative, ecologically ruinous age. In teaching us how to die, in tutoring us in the pleasures of death over an abundant and productive life, and in taking stock of the attachments to the unsustainable world we've created, film noir may, despite all of the crime it features, teach us that we do less harm and may even access greater freedom when we give up hope. "Optimism," explains Dienstag in the spirit of Lee Edelman, "subordinates the present to what is to come and thereby devalues it. Pessimism embodies a free relation to the future. In refraining from hope and prediction we make possible a concern that is not self-abasing and self-pitying."[63] Noir characters can certainly be both self-abasing and self-pitying. Yet, as a whole, the genre takes a step back and asks us to identify with these characters who find their hopes crushed, and perhaps also asks us to critique the folly of their desires, which likely match our own. Indeed, because it features crimes, because its characters want but typically cannot have the good life associated with rapacious consumerism and huge, well-appointed homes, noir's hopelessness is pessimistic but not nihilistic. Again, Dienstag explains: "Pessimism expects nothing. But this is not nihilism. Nihilism would be not *wanting* anything. Extreme nihilism? *Wanting nothing.*"[64]

The humanity of noir is asserted by Vince (Vince Edwards), an escaped prisoner in *City of Fear* (Lerner, 1959) (Figure 3.7). He has stolen from the San Quinton medical experiment lab what he thinks is a bounty of heroin that he plans to sell and profit immensely from. He pleads his case and defends his violent prison escape to his girlfriend:

> Do you know the difference between a con and an ex-con? Well, there isn't any. You're just dead meat, dishwashing the rest of your life. . . . We can go places. Live big. . . . Don't you think I know what's good in life and what's bad? I know what's good. . . . I'm not an animal. I'm a person. I want things.

Figure 3.7 Vince (Vince Edwards) asserts his humanity in *City of Fear* (1959).

Figure 3.8 The noir hero as radioactive material. *City of Fear* (1959).

Wanting things and aspiring to live big is noir's version of the human condition at midcentury. But these narratives are less morality tales about such desires than they are about the receding horizon of big-life ambition. As it turns out, Vince has stolen a canister of highly radioactive cobalt 60. Because he literally clings to the substance he thinks will lead him to the good life, he dies of radiation poisoning in the film's final shot. Police cover his body with a trench coat and mark him with a yellow sign warning passersby: "Caution: High Radiation Area." They turn a corpse into hazardous (human-made) material (Figure 3.8). In literalizing as toxic the means of achieving a human life, *City of Fear* is a pessimistic critique of human ambition that never falls into nihilism. The good life, noir tells us over and over again, does not open up a future; it forecloses it. Noir invites us to linger in its present-tenseness with its currency in cold hard cash. Rather than reward those who strive to accumulate more, noir says that we may be better off dead. The finality of death, however, should not be mistaken as the telos of narrative or the progress of history. It is merely the human character catching up to its posthumous world.

PART II
...at the End of the World

CHAPTER 4

Still Life

WELCOME TO THE ANTHROPOCENE!

In 2011, *The Economist* announced that the effects of climate change had arrived. The science is clear, the causes have been proven, and the emergency is underway: in their geologically short time on Earth, humans have become a force of nature, altering the geophysical properties of the planet and accelerating the pace of geological change. The planet is getting warmer, biodiversity is shrinking at an alarming rate, the "wilderness" is an "increasingly irrelevant" concept of pristine land, and the future of all life on Earth as we know it is jeopardized. The Holocene is over. "Welcome to the Anthropocene!"[1] The title of this short but appropriately alarming article strikes a balance between sincere introduction and ironic entrapment. It details succinctly the current environmental state of affairs, at once marveling at human productivity and warning of its potentially disastrous consequences, all under the banner of a kind of sitcom sarcasm. "Welcome to the Anthropocene!" It is as if walking into the author's disarrayed apartment, she turns to us, eyes rolling, and says: "Welcome to *my* world." The world of the Anthropocene is an unwelcoming scene of humankind's making that will likely accelerate human extinction. If there is a joke here, it is certainly on us, but not only on us.

In many respects, however, this title is perhaps the most appropriate form of invitation to think about human agency, climate change, and catastrophe as a matter of and for hospitality. What begins as an invitation from nowhere to dwell on Earth may end in a story of humans overstaying their planetary welcome. *The Economist* brackets such an alarmist scenario by making the case for human solutions to the problem of climate change.

Proposing schemes of geo-engineering and smaller-scale environmental "fiddling," the author reasons that if humans have cast the planet out of the climatological norms, they can also restore it: "Piecemeal actions can quickly add up to planetary change." And thus, even as a force like nature, humanity is still separate from and putatively exercises control over its increasingly designed environment. *The Economist* does not look forward to a new human age, but clings to an Enlightenment faith in human ingenuity. Yet, as the accidental creators of a climate we cannot control—as a species, as unique individuals, as a force of nature—*who* are *we* to welcome anyone or anything to the Anthropocene? Who or what welcomes us?

Encompassing a range of host–guest relations and rituals of welcome and dwelling, hospitality presumes a home as a structure in which people live but also the Earth as the planetary home we all share (or should share) equally. Jacques Derrida explains that there can be no hospitality without a home, and only the sovereign may welcome the guest.[2] The welcome can also be a more insidious claim, or extension of one's power:

> To dare to say welcome is perhaps to insinuate that one is at home here, that one knows what it means to be at home, and that at home one receives, invites, or offers hospitality, thus appropriating for oneself a place to *welcome* [*accueillir*] the other, or worse, *welcoming* the other in order to appropriate for oneself a place and then speak the language of hospitality.[3]

As spatial appropriation, the "welcome" purposefully elides or forgets another's prior residency. There have always been others (other species, epochs, geophysical forces) that have preceded us and perhaps even welcomed us to claim a space on Earth before we could declare possession of the planet. In its more expansive registers, however, hospitality is a welcome that acknowledges both the claims of the dispossessed and the vulnerability and rewards that befall those who open their home or nation to the refugee, to the stranger, to a god, or to a potentially threatening or inclement event. It may even name our receptivity to thought and to a nonforeclosed and unforeseeable future.

Anthropocene hospitality is not only about the ethics and politics of the welcome but also a matter of time, place, and duration. This is to say, it is a matter of aesthetics, specifically the challenge of perceiving, rendering visible, and therefore thinkable, a human dwelling that diminishes or absents the human. I approach the relationship between politics and aesthetics of hospitality in this chapter by focusing on China's Three Gorges megadam and hydroelectric plant, a feat of geo-engineering that is both an event of and monument to the Anthropocene. Jia Zhangke's film

Still Life (2006), Liu Xiaodong's large-format oil paintings, and Yang Yi's digital photography attend to the effects of the dam's human dislocation and environmental ruination, and they pose questions about hospitality and hominess, of dispossessions and resettlements, through the aesthetics of slowness, deep space and deep time, and the place of the human in a posthuman milieu. They tell us that our conventions of looking may not be adequate to perceive the world's human-caused disappearance. Genres of perceptual realism, indexicality, and witnessing—the ethical terms associated with celluloid—must be supplemented (if not supplanted) by painterly and digital manipulation to capture the competing temporalities and disorienting foreground/background relations of our epoch. Or, it is perhaps more appropriate to say that heterogeneous media are necessary precisely because the Anthropocene world is irreducible to a single, comprehensive image or medium. In thematizing hospitality and nostalgia, moreover, and contemplating the place of the human and the withdrawal of the world, these films, digital artworks, and paintings are not able to reverse or improve the conditions of their subjects, nor do they offer up a clear political program. But together they capture and create an archive of the Three Gorge's mystifying ecology and may provide the useful aesthetic registers enabling us to rethink and rescale political commitments in light our environmental situation.

WELCOME TO FENGJIE!

"Welcome, Friends from Fengjie!" Among the first spoken lines in Jia Zhangke's 2006 feature *Still Life* (*Sanxia Haoren*), this welcome is also something of a joke. Our main character, Sanming (Han Sanming), has just disembarked after a five-day journey from the northern province of Shanxi. No sooner is he off the boat than he is subjected to a number of tourist swindles. First, he is forced into a warehouse to see a befuddling one-trick "magic" show. The illusionist sets up the stunt. "It takes US dollars to travel by water. Watch closely and learn." In place of dollars, he transforms a fistful of paper first into euros and then into renminbi with just a wave of his hand. Audience members are forced to cough up "tuition fees" for this lesson in international exchange and nautical mobility. Moments later, with the address of his long-estranged wife in hand, Sanming is lured onto the back of motorcycle taxi. Rather than taking him to a home, however, the driver stops along the riverbank and directs his gaze to a barely visible patch of treetop foliage surrounded by the rising waters of the Yangtze (Figure 4.1). "That little island out there, that was your street," the driver

Figure 4.1 All that remains of the submerged old city are these leafy islands in the middle of the floodplain. *Still Life* (2006).

explains: "The old Fengjie was flooded a while back. Never heard on TV about the Three Gorges Dam?" Looking out over the floodplain, our driver points to hardly visible remains of a submerged ancient city (where the driver himself once lived) whose ruins now form the basin of one of the world's largest reservoirs. This is old news to everyone in this area, but Sanming is quietly stunned and feels like he's been stung. "You knew! You tricked me!" The savvy driver then charges him another three yuan for a ride to the relocation office and, from there, to a flophouse. Here Sanming will bide his time mingling with and then working alongside Fengjie's migrant workers (who are tasked with dismantling the cities and towns in the Three Gorges Dam floodplain) and forced migrants (commanded to leave their soon-to-be flooded homes). At one point, and fulfilling the antinomies of hospitality, he, the guest, is tasked with demolishing his own temporary residence when the flophouse is slated for demolition. These opening and ongoing ruses of magic and misdirection are part of a crueler and more pervasive ecology of China's rapid modernization schemes and engagement with the global economy. But these two short scenes also prepare us for a vanishing act of epic, geological proportion as the dam basin fills to capacity, submerging entire cities, histories, and species. In this way, Sanming's introduction to the costs of the Three Gorges Dam is also his welcome to the Anthropocene.

Most of us by now have heard of the Three Gorges Dam, China's feat of design and mobilization that set at least ten world records. It is the largest dam and power plant, with the most voluminous flood discharge capacity; it required more concrete, earth, steel, and stone in its creation than any other man-made structure on Earth, rivaling even the Great Wall of China. Number ten on the list of world records: 1.3 million people were forcibly relocated from the floodplain's ancient settlements to the distant suburbs of Shanghai and Chongqing, or to upslope land above the new water level that has already proven vulnerable to landslides and mud-rock flows.[4] The Three Gorges Dam website boasts: "This is the largest number of people ever moved in the history of the world for hydroelectric complex construction."[5] But for every world record, an act of un-worlding follows in its wake. Complementary to the dam's construction was the whirlwind deconstruction of the surrounding life world. Migrant workers were brought to the region to dismantle in the time frame of just two years the 13 cities, 1,600 factories, 700 schools, 140 towns, and 1,352 villages built over the course of two millennia.[6] It is thus no surprise that the official visual culture of the official Three Gorges Dam website emphasizes the big picture. Aerial and distant views captured with a wide-angle lens strain to convey the scale of the dam in relation to the mostly invisible humans that bring it into being.[7]

Rob Nixon argues that the global phenomenon of megadam fetishism has become a kind of "national performance art." Independent of its utility, the megadam instantiates the "monumentality of national modernity" and a country's power to alter the world and move its people.[8] Fully operational in 2012, the dam marks China's ascendency into hydroelectric energy just five years after surpassing the United States as the world's largest emitter of greenhouse gases. It now surpasses the Unites States by a factor of two (another world record). Washington's recent withdrawal from the Paris climate accord has left a world leadership gap that China is poised to fill as both the world's leading producer of greenhouse gases and the nation dedicating the most resources to alternative energy projects throughout the world, what the *New York Times* compares to a Marshall Plan–scale funding of massive infrastructure projects.[9] In the context of the Great Acceleration, the megadam, while cutting dependency on coal, is the most visible example of a water management trend, which, in the last sixty years, has averaged one dam built somewhere in the world every day. Such projects have changed the water flow and patterns of silt accumulation. Providing short-term solutions to flooding, irrigation, and the need for clean energy, dam construction is also shrinking the earth's major deltas and coastal areas.[10]

Thus, to call these "world" records is a rather modest boast, even for the People's Republic of China. The dam is nothing short of a geological event. NASA scientists note that the ten-trillion-gallon reservoir shifted ever so slightly the Earth's rotation and the axial coordinates of the North and South Poles.¹¹ As an environmentalist measure, the dam was designed to extend the capacities of Chinese green energy and cut carbon emissions into the future, while also protecting Chinese citizens from the Yangtze's devastating floods. Yet the dam has subsequently brought about landslides, earthquakes, silt accumulation, and the rapid extinction of freshwater species because of blocked migratory routes and preponderant water pollution.¹² The regionally unique Yangtze River dolphin (also known as Baiji), once worshipped as a river deity, was declared extinct in 2007. *The Guardian* reported that this was the first large vertebrate forced into extinction in fifty years, "and only the fourth time an entire evolutionary line of mammals has vanished from the face of the earth since the year 1500."¹³ Next in line is the Chinese sturgeon, a crustacean-era fish that had thrived unchanged for 140 million years until it stopped reproducing naturally in 2014.¹⁴ The extinction of Yangtze's freshwater population (because they cannot migrate) and the forced migration of millions of people (who want to stay put) must be understood not just in the context of an already expansive two-thousand-year Chinese history, but of a larger, more entangled evolution developed over millions of years that rather suddenly ended. This is a quintessential achievement of the Anthropocene age wherein geo-engineering intended to address the crisis of global warming leads, in short order, to other irreversible and unplanned environmental catastrophes on a planetary scale. The Three Gorges Dam, in other words, demonstrates that our efforts to fight the effects of the Anthropocene produce new environmental problems that even bigger future projects will be designed to address. The negative dialectics of the Anthropocene extend Enlightenment reason to its catastrophic ends.

Such projects produce the paradoxical figure of the forced migrants, such as those living around the Three Gorges who have been doubly threatened by the causes and solutions of anthropogenic ecological disasters. The history of the Yangtze's flooding due to deforestation and unsustainable farming reached historic levels in 1998, when it killed thousands and left fourteen million people homeless.¹⁵ The Three Gorges Dam, proposed in part to address such flooding, displaced more than a million citizens, most of whom were forced to the coastal cities, like Shanghai, that are vulnerable to typhoons, floods, and rising sea levels.¹⁶ The dam and its vast relocation project are part of China's ongoing industrialization and resettlement policy that began in 1949 and intensified during Mao Zedong's Great Leap Forward. In 1958, Mao declared a new official policy. "There is a new war: we should open fire on nature."¹⁷ Guided by a utopian monomania to mold the land in accordance with the dictates of Chinese communism, the People's Republic of China has created more than eighty-six thousand dams throughout the country, more than any other nation, accounting for half of the dams built in the world after 1950. The result is more than ten million internally displaced people.[18]

Drawing on the work of anthropologist Thayer Scudder, Nixon explains that the "developmental refugee" is forced to flee not political persecution per se, but development projects, such as the megadam that literally floods out of existence an entire people and culture. Horizontally caught between the "centripetal logic of national development" and the "centrifugal narrative of displacement," the developmental refugee is also chronologically ensnared. As national history accelerates, these people find themselves "stranded not just in place but in time as well." These are "lives of temporal impoverishment."[19] Rather than being carried into the future, the developmental refugee's life is diminished—from the modern cityscape to tents in a floodplain, from communal living to singular dwelling, from a historical world to something approaching, if anything, a nonworld. As John Berger reflects of victims caught in the dam's "submergence zone": "people in such a zone lose all sense of residence. . . . Once that has happened, to restore any sense of domesticity takes generations. Each year of such accumulation prolongs the Nowhere in time and space."[20] Private and customary homeliness is not simply a matter of shelter, but of culture. Berger's convincing but counterintuitive observation is that a person without residence—a person who is physically exposed and culturally bereft—does not live in a heightened sense of place and time, as one might expect, intensely aware of duration and dislocation. Rather, domesticity and the unexceptional rituals of residency are what enable us to experience time and space meaningfully. They form the background against which history unfolds.

It is fitting that rather than making a film about the Three Gorges Dam itself, Jia focuses on the displacement and disorientation it occasions. He follows two characters, Sanming, a coalminer, and Shen Hong (Zhao Tao), a nurse, who come to Fengjie in search of their estranged spouses, each equipped with a piece of obsolete information. Sanming has only a submerged address for his lost wife; Shen Hong has a phone number one digit short of the new numbering system. With only hunches to guide them, Sanming and Shen Hong maneuver around the city, never crossing paths, and their itinerary brings us to the decommissioned factories, evacuated housing, piles of rubble, and new modern bridges and buildings under construction. At the relocation office, where local residents complain bitterly about unpaid compensation and local corruption, Sanming asks after his wife and daughter. All technology and information proves useless, however. The computer (itself a dinosaur) is frozen and the one relative

Sanming manages to locate, his brother-in-law, initially refuses to help. "Don't stir up the past," he warns, stirring a bowl of hot soup aboard his rickety fishing boat that is likely floating above the very past Sanming hopes to recover. Shen Hong visits the now-defunct factory where her husband once worked. Waiting, she too bears witness to a group of angry citizens who have been cheated out of compensation when the factory was sold to a private firm. Repeatedly, we linger with the laborers who manually dismantle the city while sometimes in the background we see signs of new construction above the projected water level. In the background of other shots we see Fengjie's bedraggled refugees waiting for their transport on the same docks that welcome their perverse counterpart, the developmental tourists, the Western and Chinese visitors eager to see the dam, its ruins, and the Three Gorges before the water rises. Between these vignettes, our two characters wait and behold with studied detachment the bizarre scene of nature's and civilization's undoing. Every background, we realize, is in a state of radical flux, and most of the city's population is living on boats, in tents, and in crumbling, half-demolished apartment buildings. The frantic pace of deconstruction and relocation, however, is conveyed to us through a slow style and scenes of waiting. Long takes amplify the tension between the stilled foreground, where our characters wait, and a background where the rest of the world hurries in response to the fast-rising waters. This is not a slow style in time with slow violence (to use Nixon's term). Rather, long takes capture in real time the frenzy of adjustment. As if to sum up the quiet turmoil, Jia writes in his production notes: "Teams of workers running back and forth in front of the camera. I'm in awe of the stillness of their silent expressions."[21]

The Three Gorges Dam is both central to this drama and what motivates everything around our characters, and yet it is merely inconvenient to our protagonists' quests. In fact, we only glimpse the dam itself once toward the end of the film when it serves as an incidental backdrop to Shen Hong's final, undramatic meeting with her husband, Guo Bin (Li Zhubing). With just a few words, they agree to divorce. Jia tracks down the embankment, panning right to frame the couple with the dam and its barely audible water discharge in the background (Figure 4.2). We never see the dam in its totality, and thus the film resists the ready sublimity of this historical experience and the possibility of felt transcendence. Instead, we get only the smaller-scale fragmentation of space, lives, and even time.

Jia's Zhangke's oeuvre, from *Platform* (2000), *The World* (2004), and *24 City* (2008) to *Still Life* and his more recent feature *Touch of Sin* (2013), testifies to the belated but swift pace of China's postsocialist market economy against both the anachronism of Mao's still-sputtering

Figure 4.2 The most we ever see of the Three Gorges Dam itself in *Still Life* (2006).

cultural revolution and the deep time of China's ancient history. His films take us not to the country's centers of growth with the movers of the new economy, but to the peripheries where citizens are shaken, unsettled, and often forcibly dispossessed to make way for the future, only to find themselves scuttled in place. As Zhang Zhen explains, Jia stands apart from the other Sixth Generation filmmakers not just because his formative years were those of the transitional period, or the reform era after Mao's death. He is, himself, from the periphery. Born and raised in a lower middle-class family in Shanxi, one of the most impoverished regions in China, Jia worked as an itinerant artist before leaving the provinces for the postmodern metropolis. A pivotal figure, Jia has worked outside of the state-sponsored film industry (and this is one reason for his appeal to Western elite audiences), but he has also risen to the status of an anointed insider who earned his degree at China's premiere art school, the Central Academy of Fine Arts in Beijing, and has served as head of the Academy's Intermedia Studies Department.[22] In all capacities a consummate professional, in his autobiographical statements, Jia promotes himself as an "amateur."[23] He favors the consumer-grade technologies, including digital filmmaking, low-budget productions, nonprofessional actors, on-location shooting, and regional dialects. This is what Zhen refers to as Jia's "insistence on spatial indexicality and linguistic particularity" that rejects the polish of studio shooting and the socialist-era mandate of standardized Mandarin.[24] His films, some of which are semiautobiographical, follow characters—migrant workers, migrant artists, displaced people, or people left behind—who are both chronologically and spatially at odds with the times. Zhen writes, "As a result Jia has been called, admiringly, the 'migrant-worker director.'"[25] For Jia's characters, modernization, globalization, and capitalization are not much-awaited improvements one enjoys, but uneven processes one survives.

Jia remarks that when he first arrived at Fengjie, it was hard to imagine that the vast scenes of demolition were purposefully created in the name of progress or that they were even human caused. "It's more like after a nuclear war or an alien attack. Upon the remnants, in the background of the fast-vanishing city that holds historical memories, I felt an urge to make a film."[26] Far from a "natural disaster," the demolition of Fengjie and the other neighboring cities is the belated realization of a development project first conceived in 1919 by Sun Yat-Sen, revisited by Chiang Kai-shek, and approved with tremendous enthusiasm by Mao, with the groundbreaking ceremony taking place only in 1994.[27] For all of this history, however, the deconstruction site seems to arrive from an alien and wholly apocalyptic future. Jia literalizes something of this temporality with an odd extraterrestrial interlude that gestures obliquely to another range of host–guest relations. Twice in the film we witness UFOs flying over the rubble, including a scene where a mysterious ruin proves to be a spaceship when it abruptly takes flight. Shen Hong is staying with her husband's friend whose apartment overlooks the Three Gorges and is itself overlooked by this odd structure on which children are playing earlier in the day. At night, Shen Hong hangs a shirt to dry on the line of the balcony. Just as she leaves the shot, the tank top hangs poignantly in the left foreground while in the right-hand background the structure rumbles and then takes flight (Figure 4.3). What appears at first to be a historical remainder is in fact a medium from another time and world altogether. Jia explains that the concrete edifice is, in fact, an unfinished memorial to migrants that he discovered on location, specifically a monument to relocation fashioned in the shape of the Chinese character *hua*, a reference to the Chinese people.[28] The structure is thus thrice repurposed, its status as a real-life "unaccomplished" monument to Fengjie's displaced population converted into a symbol of historical loss and alien renewal, a metamorphosis that radically expands the ambit of planetary dislocation. The image of flight at once gathers together and distills a range of temporal dislocations, but sets them in juxtaposition to the all-too-worldly experience of historical erasure. This is just one facet of a "surrealist atmosphere," which, Jia explains, "is part of China's reality, such as the speedy changes. It's beyond human logic."[29] The arrival of aliens is only the most obvious way in which Jia disrupts the conventions and visual style of realism and, for that matter,

Figure 4.3 The incomplete monument to displaced citizens becomes an alien ship. *Still Life* (2006).

humanism. The film's surrealist impulse reveals less a human unconscious than what Pheng Cheah describes as the "disjunctive synthesis between the temporality of postmodern technological culture and that of the everyday experience of the provincial masses."[30] Through these cross-hatched temporalities, Cheah argues, we find fresh combinations and a new everydayness in this globalized, soon-to-be-disappeared world. And in the context of the earth's rising tides, there can be no doubt that the image of Fengjie's submergence is also a vision of the planet's watery future.

STILL FOREGROUNDS, WRITHING BACKGROUNDS

Jia was initially drawn to the scene of the Three Gorges Dam following the trail of the neorealist artist Liu Xiaodong, the subject of Jia's documentary entitled simply *Dong* (2008), which Jia shot simultaneously with *Still Life*. The first half of *Dong* takes place in Fengjie as Liu creates one of his life-size, multipaneled *en plein air* oil paintings *Hotbed* (2005) featuring the local demolition crew. On a rooftop overlooking the Three Gorges, the workers are posed in a game of cards while on break from their taxing work. In the film, Liu gives them precise instructions on their posture and the direction of their gaze. Among them, but crouching off to the side, is Sanming, a character in this film and in Liu's painting, both of which mix found environments with staged actuality. Indeed, *Dong* shares with *Still Life* several shots in common (mostly of Sanming), suggestive of the way that Jia's fiction and documentary filmmaking differ only in degrees.³¹ I turn to Liu's work here to consider how his painting not only brought Jia to the scene of the dam but also inspired his narrative and compositional style.

As evident in his other painting (not depicted in *Dong*), Liu answered the dam's inhuman monumentality and the official images of its construction by foregrounding the region's dispossessed residents and workers in colossal group portraits. *Three Gorges Displaced Population* (2003), for example, finds six men arrayed across a six-foot-wide, multipanel canvas. Each figure is attired differently to suggest an individuated cross-section of the dispossessed, despite that all are helping to carry what appears to be one very long iron rod (either helping to build the dam or salvage some of the wreckage). Behind and below them in the distance we see the dam's construction site, and on the left is the rubble of the already-demolished city and what looks to be temporary tent housing. The lines across the panels are slightly mismatched, as if the whole were a series of large-form photographs pasted together to replicate a panoramic painting. The iron rod is disjointed, as is one of the human figures caught between two panels, two temporalities, and two spaces. Thus, each section seems to exist in a slightly different time, giving rise to a fragmented space. Such disjuncture undercuts the nationalist epic of the Three Gorges Dam on the official website, and the foregrounded human figures challenge the dam's inhuman scale. Art historian Eugene Wang writes that the painting is jarring also for its revision of Chinese socialist realism, which, under Mao, featured peasants and workers, and of course Mao himself, in the most valiant terms. Here and in the card-playing painting referenced earlier, though they are foregrounded, the men have an "unheroic" and "humble" bearing. "The gigantic bid for systematic control (and hence the mandates of official narrative) is brought into sharp juxtaposition with the specific contingencies of the individual workers."³²

But it may be that Liu's more recent paintings clue us in to the particular aesthetic registers of the Anthropocene and Jia's own compositional strategies. Liu has honed his singular genre of painting in response to a series of visually stunning environmental catastrophes. First is the 2007 cyanobacterial infestation of Lake Tai that transformed China's third-largest freshwater body into a massive swamp of toxic, foul-smelling sludge. Second is the 2008 earthquake that devastated the Sichuan province. These are two disasters that scientists link to China's hydroelectric dams on the Yangtze and Min Rivers, respectively.³³ It is thus fitting that Liu would be drawn to these locations after Fengjie. In 2010, he traveled to Beichuan, the hardest-hit area of Sichuan, two years after the 7.9 magnitude earthquake killed at least seventy thousand people and left eighteen thousand more missing.[34] So totalizing was the damage that the survivors were relocated to new accommodations in presumably more stable territory and Beichuan's ruins have been preserved, as such, as a memorial to this disappeared town and its thousands of mostly school-aged victims.[35] As Wang explains, Liu set the stage for his painting, *Out of Beichuan* (2010), by hiring young aspiring female models from Chongqing to pose on a cargo tricycle in front of the town's berubbled remains (Figure 4.4).[36] Posing as themselves, as opposed to pretending to be Beichuan's stricken victims, the young women appear apathetic and "untheatrical": visitors to the site of catastrophe, teenagers unmoved by even an earthquake.[37] Just as striking is the Beichuan landscape itself. It seems as if rock and debris are still tumbling down the deep slope to the city's destroyed center. In contrast to the multipanel compositions of Fengjie that fragment the space of a panorama, *Out of Beichuan* is a gigantic *single* canvas, approximately nine feet high by thirteen feet across. Created on location, the painting, Wang explains, does not cleave to the conventions of pleinairism or documentary realism, as indeed is the case with all of Liu's *en plein air* work; nor does this scale match the intimacy of human portraiture. Yet it draws all of these genres into a peculiar new

Figure 4.4 Liu Xiaodong, *Out of Beichuan* (2010). Oil on canvas, 9' 10 1/8" × 13' 11/2" © Liu Xiaodong; Courtesy Lisson Gallery.

dynamic. Wang writes: "The painter [Liu] has stated that he wanted to treat the landscape as portraiture in a state of 'writhing,' while the group portrait was to be rendered with all of the dispassion of a still life."[38] This combination of genres inverts the expected spatial-temporal field. Rather than placing humans against a transhistorical landscape, it is the people in the foreground who have become timeless (as in a still life) while the portrait of the frenetic landscape claims a historical and thus time-stamped singularity. Liu stills human affect—reifying it through the genre of a still life—while an unnatural history agitates and writhes in the background.

It is also no coincidence that the English-language title of Jia's film is *Still Life*, even though it was shot in the region that inspired classical Chinese landscape painting and, as other critics have noted, Jia uses long-take tracking shots to simulate Chinese scroll painting.[39] What do we make of this generic designation, still life, for a digital film and moving picture? What, if anything, does this quaint and outmoded pictorial regime have to do with the hospitality of the Anthropocene?

Norman Bryson explores the tension in the still life that both invites and banishes the human from its world. On one hand, the genre is almost as old as humanity itself. The earliest examples date from preantiquity, and its objects—bowls, glasses, fruits, fowl—are as recognizable to us today as they were to spectators thousands of years ago. Set in the domestic space, the still life summons the rituals of daily consumption and reminds us of our biological being. On the other hand, the still life refuses to figure the human itself or to prioritize human actions that separate us from our mere metabolic existence. The genre "expels the values human presence imposes on the world," values associated with history, narrative, and the "scale of human importance."[40] Whereas historical paintings depict the events of human enterprise (wars, revolutions, and exceptional or heroic acts), the still life captures the "culture of the table," the everyday scene of eating, absent the person who consumes. This is the quotidian, virtually timeless ritual that, he argues, forms history's "permanent and inevitable background." At the end of the day (or perhaps at the beginning), we eat at a table and carry out the "small scale, trivial, forgettable acts of bodily survival and self-maintenance."[41] And thus the still life is the genre of domestic things so enduring that these forms (plates, glasses, jugs) "point backwards to a long evolution of culture that designed them."[42] These are not, however, scenes of conviviality or celebration, but compositions of scattered objects. "Still life is unimpressed by the categories of soul, consciousness, achievement, grandeur or the unique. The human subject that it proposes and assumes is a . . . material entity on a par with anything else in the material field." The flat ontology of the still life is one of many "insults to the humanist subject."[43] If history is what makes human life meaningful, the still life frames precisely what is "ignored or overlooked by the human impulse to create greatness."[44] Yet as John Berger commented, without these rituals, historical experience is impossible.

Typically an arrangement of customary objects, the still life radically defamiliarizes our relationship to the world in ways betokening the paradoxes of the Anthropocene. Bracketing history and the human form, the still life often achieves its realism in its random assemblages: the debris, waste, and scraps are thrown together with food and leftovers, including the insects on overripe fruit. "It is as though we were shown the appearance the world might have without a subject to perceive it; the world minus human consciousness, the look of the world before our emergence into it, or after our death."[45] This description may remind us of Alan Weisman's ecological thought experiment, *The World without Us*, which provides a history of the future in which humans have suddenly vanished from the planet.[46] But whereas Weisman takes us five hundred years into the future, the still life lingers in the more immediate aftermath. The perishables on the table are still recognizable as such, and nature has not yet reclaimed the abandoned house. Indeed, the still life presumes a living, anthropological onlooker who is tethered to a culture field and who *could* be at home in the world of things. The paradox or "painful dualism" of the still life is that it presents a "dramatic objecthood" "inimical to human presence," which, at the same time, "works to return that cold outer world to human warmth." It does so by addressing the viewer "through the most unmistakable and universal ritual of hospitality, as a guest at the table"—or at a table the previous guest has already abandoned.[47] The Greek term for still life, Bryson reminds us, is *xenia*, which refers to ancient customs of hospitality. The antique still life thus depicts the raw foodstuff left so that guests may prepare their own solitary meal according to their custom (the guest as foreigner), an offering made with the idea that the guest may also one day be host. And thus *xenia*, like *hôte*, refers "equally to host and guest," to the *equality of* host and guest, and it presumes the "spirit of reversible hospitality."[48] Such that the food is raw and presented as a bountiful offering, moreover, the hospitality of *xenia* (or its painted representation) originates with nature's welcome, a "nature that performs all the work of culture."[49] In this way the still life naturalizes human relations "with earth and sea yielding their fruits for all in a moment prior to hierarchy and social division."[50]

As if to signal the key objects of a still life, Jia's film is broken into four segments: cigarettes, liquor, tea, and toffee, two of which are introduced with pointed reference to still life compositions. In the first, for example, the shot begins with a medium close-up framing of Sanming in profile sitting on the rickety bed of the flophouse. To his right is a cluttered table illuminated by the sunlight shining through the room's open door. After he calls his brother on his cellphone, the camera leaves Sanming and tracks in toward the table, framing it against the open door through which a teenage boy emerges. Without a word, the boy grabs a cigarette from the table, puffs on it vigorously, comically, and then leaves as abruptly as he arrived. The shot concludes when the table and its odd assortments command the frame. Eyeglasses, bowls, water glasses, bottles of soy sauce and fish sauce, various containers, plastic bags, chopsticks, cigarettes, and an ashtray are among the objects of this scene (Figure 4.5). And then the title, "Cigarettes," appears. While this will later be a setting for shared meals among the demolition workers, the table is neither set nor exactly deserted (Sanming is sitting just off-screen). But separated from human actors and given the weight of the title, this still life composition highlights the luminosity of random objects and their quietude in a city of frantic dislocation.

The third section of the film, "Tea," is introduced in a similar style but to different effect. Shen Hong is in the defunct factory and manages to unbolt her husband's rusted locker. The camera tracks in to the top shelf on which are positioned a bag of tea, a tarnished box, worn gloves, notebooks, and an assortment of tools (Figure 4.6). The back of the shelf appears to be lined with faded blueprints for a building, likely no longer standing if it was ever built. These are the remnants of Guo Bin's previous life as a factory worker. He's now manager of a demolition company (and unofficial leader of a gang of thugs who force people out of their homes). Shen Hong has had no contact with him for two years, and these abandoned remains are the only clues of her husband's past life, of the husband she once knew. In

Figure 4.5 The still life composition in Sanming's boarding house. *Still Life* (2006).

Figure 4.6 The still life composition in Guo Bin's abandoned locker. *Still Life* (2006).

both shots, the still life signifies a leave taking, a departure, and perhaps also a transformation beyond the frame. And yet, in contrast to painting, all of these objects seem to have a limited shelf life in the face of the rising waters, or they will persist in the silt to come.

While there are other examples of what we would call still life compositions in the film, such depopulated images are rare. Corey Byrnes notes that the things around which each section is putatively organized function not as "immobile still life objects, but as commodities that circulate between individuals, creating links and strengthening the mutual embrace of landscape and figure within cinematic depth."[51] Indeed, Sanming will share cigarettes with the other workers as means of making new friends, and he'll offer his ex-brother-in-law liquor as a gift (which is rejected). Shen Hong will make herself a cup of her husband's tea. Because these objects leave their de-animated compositions, Byrnes and others have dismissed this title as useful for decoding the film's image world.[52] In his production notes on the film, however, Jia writes of still life as not simply a painterly mode or pictorial arrangement, but an elegiac regard for the world and its abandoned objects that inspired the entire film.

> I entered an empty room one day and saw a bunch of dusty objects on the table. I seemed to have uncovered the secret of still objects. Those furnishings that sat in the same places for years, the dusty utensils on the table, the wine bottles on the windowsill, and the decorations hanging on the wall all carried some sort of poetic sadness. Still objects are one part of reality we neglect. Although they endure, they remain silent and hold secrets.[53]

The still life is an archive or archeology of a past existence, or a silent, secret truth of existence—of what is "ignored or overlooked"—and thus the film *Still Life* in its totality may be said to record the processes of a culture's sedimentation whose traces and workings are everywhere.

Jia also conceptualizes the four consumables of the film in a manner consistent with still life's invitation. Cigarettes, liquor, tea, and toffee are not just any commodities, but were designated (and hoarded) as "luxury" items during the planned economy: "Only during special holidays such as the Lunar New Year, could you get these special supplies." He remarks that these objects, like the dam itself, are remnants of Mao's China—they share with the dam a belated relationship to the present. For this reason, they do not merely circulate like any other items for sale, but carry with them a prior significance. "When you visit someone's house, you have to bring some sweets or tea with you as a gift," comments Jia.[54] This is to say that, taken together, the objects of the film are historically connected to a bygone era of the socialist economy and its persistent culture of hospitality. And it matters that the narrative focuses not on Fengjie's residents, but on visitors who pursue clues from a disappeared time in a city that, as Ackbar Abbas writes, "disappears people."[55]

For Abbas, this film bears witness not to a postsocialist China—the state-supported free marketeering and commodity economy introduced in the 1990s—so much as to a culture of *posthumous* socialism, socialism's afterlife in "a present made of up absences." "The no longer there" of communism and the "not yet there" of the "as yet unrealized hope that the 21st century will prove to be the Chinese century."[56] This temporal no man's land is the theme of Jia's film and it is evident also in the architectural forms of contemporary urban China, as Abbas explains. Fengjie is the abandoned city about to be submerged, sacrificed for the "speculative overbuilding" of other metropolises and commercial districts. "Many of the new areas in China's biggest cities look nothing so much as ghost towns that bear an ironic resemblance to Fengjie: not ghost towns where people have left, but ghost towns where people have not yet arrived."[57] The still life, with its vanquishing of the human form, its image of the world before our emergence or after our death, and its movement between luxury and necessity, finds its architectural corollary in the empty buildings (those yet to be destroyed and those yet to be inhabited) of a posthumous socialist China. This is socialism after its death, or a socialism after the human, or, better yet, a socialism that absents the human by submerging human worlds and artifacts, burying them in the *humus* (earth) in the name of both humanism and socialism. The geological overtones, of course, suggest how the political ambition to remake or unmake the world leaves a thin stratigraphic signature. In her search, Shen Hong visits Guo Bin's army buddy Wang Dongming (Wang Hongwei), who is now an archeologist. She finds Dongming frantically unearthing artifacts from the two-thousand-year-old Han dynasty discovered only when the modern city of Fengjie was dismantled. This is the very earth into which modern-day Fengjie will soon settle. Scratch any surface and you are likely to encounter the shallow grave of human residency on Earth.

We may note in passing that the Chinese-language title for Jia's film, *Sanxia haoren,* translated as "The Good People of Three Gorges," is a reference to Bertolt Brecht's 1943 play *Der gute Mench von Sezuan (The Good Person from Sichuan),* written six years before Mao would come to power and while Brecht himself was a German Jewish refugee in Hollywood. Surrounded by the glitterati of the film industry and the intellectual exiles from Germany, Brecht was theorizing epic theater, inspired, in part, by his brief encounters with Peking opera.[58] The title of Jia's film gestures subtly to this trans-Atlantic, trans-Pacific exchange, to two periods of mass dislocation, and to the projections for the possibility of a good life before and after communism. Brecht's play, which takes place in the very region of the Three Gorges, opens much like the film: a scene of swindle followed by a search for accommodation. Three gods have come to the "semi-Westernized" city in search of one good person who will host these deities for the night. A crooked water seller (his cups have a false bottom) offers to help but can find no willing townsperson until finally the prostitute Shen Te reluctantly agrees. As reward for her hospitality, the gods give her money. But goodness proves impossible to sustain in the face of the town's greedy and parasitic residents, who quickly move into Shen Te's tobacco shop. These gods are putting humanity and its world to a test. Reading from a scroll, the Third God declares: "'The world can stay as it is if enough people are found living lives worthy of human beings.' . . . Good people, that is." Whether or not a good person is to be found is the play's unanswered question. Shen Te is only able to protect her newfound life by inventing an alter ego, a cousin who evicts the lecherous group and harshly handles other debtors. Rather than change this corrupt state of affairs, the gods flee back to the heavens and leave us, the audience, with the task of world repair.

Sheldon H. Lu writes that Jia's film, like Brecht's play, argues for a "materialist critique" of the "concrete conditions of life rather than the imposition of unrealistic moral demands on the people."[59] In Jia's film, the area's demolition and the forced scattering of its residents breed corruption at every level of society and social encounter. Even our main characters, Shen Hong and Sanming, are morally opaque to us. Sanming is searching for a wife he purchased from this region sixteen years ago, exploiting Fengjie's surplus of women, as one character puts it. Now his ex-wife, Missy Ma (Ma Lizhen), is forced to work on a barge to repay her brother's debts. Missy Ma is a victim of human trafficking and it shows no sign of ending when Sanming promises to buy her back. Shen Hong seeks out her husband, Guo Bin, who is manager of the demolition company and its brutish young thugs, and he is rumored to be having an affair with a ruthless businesswoman who owns the company.[60] One of the demolition crew, Mark, befriends Sanming. Upon hearing Sanming's ringtone "Bless the Good-Hearted People," a song from the communist era, Mark declares that there are no good people left in Fengjie. And yet, throughout the film we witness numerous acts of kindness and small gestures of welcome, not least between Sanming and Mark. That the test of humanity begins with a test of hospitality suggests that the film's two titles are different ways of articulating the same problem of dwelling in a postsocialist or even simply an environmentally posthumous world and understanding the effects of the Three Gorges Dam as an act of radical erasure. Flooding these ancient cities may well be a way to change or end a world that does not allow people to live lives worthy of human beings; or the flooding may itself be a means of allowing that inhuman world to persist, as such.

"The old country is already submerged in water, and the new site is still under construction. Things to be kept should be picked up, and things to be discarded should be left behind."[61] The final two sentences of Jia's brief synopsis of *Still Life* express the limits of nostalgia (there is much of this history that should be left behind) and the possibility of salvage. Rather than give us the world of things without the human, as is standard in the still life, Jia, by the end of the film, frames an uncertain but open future absent a world and its familiar spatial coordinates. In contrast to Shen Hong, who ends her marriage on the site of the Three Gorges Dam, Sanming and Missy Ma decide to reunite surrounded by Fengjie's wreckage. Though being his wife in a town far from home was a miserable existence sixteen year ago, especially for a woman sold so young into marriage, Missy Ma confesses that her life thereafter has not given her any more joy. Sanming vows to work in the coalmines and raise the thirty thousand yuan needed for her release. Their reunion is sealed through the minimal, or bare, hospitality of a shared piece of White Rabbit toffee, the most ubiquitous of China's cheap candies. But the sequence shot featuring this banal exchange is extraordinary. The couple is positioned in long shot in the right-hand corner of an empty, half-demolished room. Missy Ma stands in profile while Sanming crouches, smoking a cigarette. She hands him a piece of White Rabbit, which he carefully unwraps and bites in half to share (Figure 4.7). She then squats, facing him, and slowly chews the toffee. As this quiet interchange unfolds, we take in the striking composition, which like a *trompe d'oeil* painting stages multiple thresholds that challenge the onlooker to differentiate between flattened surface effects and recessive space. Black mold on the white portion of the wall behind the characters provides an almost decorative background, while the lower third of the wall is painted dark green, the same color as Missy Ma's tunic.

Figure 4.7 Missy Ma (Ma Lizhen) offers Sanming (Han Sanming) toffee. *Still Life* (2006).

Figure 4.8 Missy Ma (Ma Lizhen) and Sanming (Han Sanming) turn to watch a building collapse in the distance. *Still Life* (2006).

To the couple's left, a huge jagged hole in the wall opens onto the rubblescape below, perfectly framing the urban gray ruins beneath the gray sky of the deserted city. This view is so still and monochromatic (I would say melancholic), and the edges framing the city so perfectly serrated, that it looks to be airbrushed onto the wall rather than seen through it. Then, suddenly, almost in Keaton-like slapstick fashion, a distant skyscraper spontaneously collapses.[62] The squatting couple then rises, turns, and totally deadpan watches the ashes ascending from where the faraway building once stood (Figure 4.8). Vertiginous confusion gives way to the reassurance that space still has three dimensions, and yet the falling structure is as bizarre as the alien spaceship. In this way, the vignette of reconciliation shuttles between the concentrated familiarity of foregrounded fiction and the disorienting, even writhing, background of otherworldly ruination. It is the fiction, in other words—the sharing of toffee, the promise of a less coerced marriage—that anchors us in an otherwise inhospitable, trampled world, or a postworld of the Three Gorges future.[63] A tiny bit of luxury offered as a kind of compensation for the lost world and a wasted life, this is a scene of minimalist hospitality—a welcome to a marriage staged in recent ruin above a ghost city.

This minimalism is answered in the next (the film's penultimate) scene of robust conviviality. In the room featuring the earlier "Cigarettes" still life, Sanming now shares cigarettes, his hometown liquor, and a meal with other demolition workers in the soon-to-be-flooded flophouse. In another odd twist, the poor evicted owner is now subsisting in a hovel under a bridge across town, while the guests enjoy this, the hotel's last supper. All of these men, visitors to Fengjie, will disperse the next morning in search of work, and Sanming promises to find his new friends high-paying jobs in Shanxi's dangerous coal mines (the dirty energy industry that too often disappears people and leads to calls for more hydroelectric dams). But the scene itself is about the simple pleasure of these near-naked men sharing a meal. In the face of geo-political transitions and the disastrous geological change of the Anthropocene, still life (the genre and the film) asks us to linger with what is overlooked and to consider the local and immediate possibilities of the world undone but in which the objects of hospitality, the invitation to an unknown future, still function, even when (and perhaps because) the home, the walls, and indeed the world itself is past.

The final moments of the film follow Sanming headed to the boat that brought him to this disappearing city, but something off-screen catches his eye. In the film's last shot, his back is to the camera and over his shoulder we see what captures his attention: an aerialist in silhouette walking a tightrope strung between two abandoned buildings (Figure 4.9). This is no alien spaceship, but the magic of human invention. Though the dam's rising water level is a forgone conclusion, the rubblescape suddenly seems to be full of new, however short-lived, potential. We thus find neither a melancholic nor tragic relationship to the future, but a salutary lesson of transiency that may inform a new domestic order and a small-scale political practice of hospitality on Earth.

Figure 4.9 A funambulist catches Sanming's attention. *Still Life* (2006).

And yet Sanming, Shen Hong, and even Jia Zhangke, for that matter, are not among Fengjie's dispossessed residents. They are *visitors* with homes to which they'll return. The film ends on this note of hospitality followed by leave taking. What of those who stay behind?

DIGITAL NOSTALGIA, OR THE "NO ANALOG WORLD"

"I love my hometown!" declares Yang Yi, a digital artist and a native of Kai Xian, the last of the Chongqing County villages to be flooded by the Three Gorges Dam.[64] His series *Uprooted* (2007–2008) is composed of twenty-four photographic compositions featuring the town's residents—one, two, or six of them at a time—posing in front of deserted ruins and vast, totally devastated rubblescapes. The residents are attired in ordinary clothes, holding everyday objects, and, in a few images, carrying on with quotidian activities such as haircuts, card games, or hopscotch, as if "the ordinary" still makes sense in this ghost town.[65] Contravening the prosaic calm, we find that all of these subjects are wearing goggles, but not in anticipation of the flood to come. Through the sleight of Yang's digital compositing, these people are already underwater, posing for the camera as air bubbles from their snorkels ascend. *They stand*, it is important to emphasize, not swim, and this immobility or grounding cannot be reconciled with their submergence, or even the series's title, *Uprooted*. It is as if they are weighted down—body, clothing, and hair—having exhaled their last breath, or they are simply impervious to their aquatic surround. Above them we find not sky, but sunlight eerily refracted through the water's surface producing a reddish tint and a sense of enclosure. On one hand, these are images of expansive space. *No. 21* (2008), for example, features six snorkel-masked men, standing arm in arm, posing frontal to the camera (Figure 4.10). Behind them are two multistory apartment buildings whose facades are missing, beyond which stand more half-destroyed buildings and glimpses of a hilly terrain. And yet the prismatic lighting distorts the structures, giving rise to a literal fishbowl effect, thereby miniaturizing the scene, as if we could scoop these people up by dipping our hands into the bowl. This is the queasy scale of Yang's digital imaginary. "I instructed the models to wear diving goggles, and shot the scenes in medium format. Then I shot the river water, light and air bubbles in a transparent fish tank with a digital camera. Later I used Photoshop to combine both elements."⁶⁶ The result is a world both underwater, with no signs of marine life, and above water, yet without homes or breathable air. The sepia tone of river water, moreover, is suggestive of the look of old family photos, even as the image itself points to an impossible future. This is preposterous milieu featuring impossible, perhaps even hysterical subjects. These are people who are either left behind or who, like the characters in

Figure 4.10 Yang Yi, *Uprooted 21* (2008). Courtesy of Yang Yi and Galerie Dix9's Hélène Lacharmoise.

J. G. Ballard's prophetic novel, want to stay in this drowned world, or who want the world to stay drowned. Their nostalgia commits them to a posthuman/nonhuman existence in this elsewhere and else-when of China's posthumous modernity.[67]

Who are these impossible subjects, and what is the object of their nostalgia? Against convention, Yang does not frame his subjects standing by their homes (the *nosta* of this ailment), but in the environment of ruination, as if to memorialize not the space of his childhood, but the time of its erasure. As the exhibition program notes, his hometown will have been submerged on July 24, 2009, Yang's thirty-seventh birthday.[68] Whereas nostalgia typically afflicts the exile, the immigrant, or the soldier far from home (the *algia* of nostalgia is the longing to *return*), in Yang's images people stay put while their town and homes disappear or are refashioned in another place to where residents are forcibly relocated. Or, in a more generalizable sense, people remain while their world disappears. Of course, nostalgia is the longing for the impossible return to a home that likely never existed, or to the womb that evicted us at birth (and hence the hysteria, or womb suffering element of the disease). It is no coincidence, then, that Kai Xian's submergence aligns with Yang's celebration of his emergence. Who would have thought that a person could survive his or her hometown?

As Svetlana Boym writes, we should not confuse nostalgia's spatial dislocations for what may really be at the heart of this loss, namely, a longing for another time and slower temporality, perhaps for an era when the pace of demolition matched the pace of construction, or when environments changed at a pace too slow to be perceptible to humans. As the "historical emotion" of modernity's time and space, nostalgia gives rise to its own aesthetic registers.[69] Apropos of Yang's woozy stylistics, Boym writes that the image of nostalgia may be expressed as a "double exposure, or a superimposition of two images—of home and abroad, past and present, dream and everyday life."[70] Indeed, as she explains, the eighteenth-century Swiss physiologist Dr. Albert von Haller diagnosed nostalgia as an error in perception, a desire for the homeland so strong that the afflicted suffered an "erroneous representation" in which real events and people are conflated with the past and ghostly apparitions.[71]

The real and imaginary, the present and the future coexist in Yang's composite images. This form of digital nostalgia marks the inadequacy of celluloid to record the longings of Anthropocene humanity in the time of its disappearing world. To put it differently, this photo series and Jia's film together represent the aesthetics and imaging ethics of our "no analog" world. For earth scientists, recall, the no-analog declaration refers not to the medium of film or limits of analogical transcription, but to the impossibility of using the geological past for the purpose of climatological prediction. Our present environmental crisis is without analogy or resemblance to earlier geological epochs. But I would like to consider why the world of the Anthropocene defies analogical *transcription* and thereby pushes the analogical arts into digital fabulation and prophesy.

For *Still Life*, Jia turned to digital cinematography in place of what he describes as the temporality and "stable tone and texture"—let's call it temperament—of celluloid. High-definition video:

> enabled me to improvise in reaction to the rapid changes taking place in China. If we use the traditional 35mm, which relies a lot on lighting and also requires a high budget and a long period of investment research . . . I think it's impossible that way to capture the vanishing of the Three Gorges and the flow of immigrants. . . . Digital technique really suits the fast-tempo change in China: it enables us to really catch up with the speed.[72]

Celluloid may mummify change, as André Bazin famously declared, but it cannot catch up with the shifting terrain and moving populations in this artificial landscape. The digital image and its ready manipulation allow Jia to capture the immediacy of a disappearing past, to fabricate aliens from the future, and to change the tone of the image to "greenish-blue," a hue, he explains, that pays tribute to the ancient Chinese ink paintings created in the Three Gorges region. In contrast to a presumed rigidity of binary code, the coloration suggests something about the digital as a kind of liquid medium that superimposes the look of ancient watercolor onto an ancient world quickly vanishing under water. In fact, the digital may be the most appropriate code to convey what Jia calls the "surrealist" numerology of Fengjie's rapid dismantling. This is not an arrangement of *ones* and zeros, but *twos* and zeros. "The contrast between the number 2000 and two," he remarks, is "very surrealistic."[73] Fengjie's "gradual, heavy history" built over two millennia is "taken apart in two years." Celluloid cannot keep up with this speed.

Shen Hong is governed by her own eccentric numerology that Jia slyly compares to an antiquated horology, or even a media archeology. She has traveled a great distance in search of Guo Bin, yet has given herself only twenty-four hours to find him in the chaos of this disarrayed city armed with a phone number that is two years old and one digit short. She is now in Dongming's apartment (adjacent to the alien monument overlooking the Three Gorges), and he is cooking them a "Sichuan dinner" after a long and fruitless day of searching. Shen Hong walks slowly away from the kitchen passing Dongming's desk, where the camera tracks and then lingers on yet another melancholic still life. Suspended over various objects—a globe, an empty bottle, some books, a desk lamp, and what appears to be a small stereo—is an array of old, broken analog timepieces (Figure 4.11). The archeologist, we surmise, collects lost time and amasses the missed moments of alternate pasts and futures. Wristwatches strung on a wire over the desk are in the company of antique pocket watches and old alarm clocks, all frozen at the instant when they stopped keeping time with (or watching over) this world. These arrested clocks (I'm inclined to write that they are "alarmed") are now relics of a different temporality. Analogical time, like the celluloid thirty-five-millimeter image, is too slow for the contemporary rate of change, and too continuous for the fragmentary scales and times of Anthropocene history. This particular still life marks the onset of a no-analog world somewhat literally and acutely aware of what the image (and the watch, for that matter) no longer indexes.

Analog media—including celluloid, videotape, and magnetic tape—are what D. N. Rodowick calls "intaglio" arts, or art as "worked matter."[74] In the case of photography, light rays sculpt the chemically treated surface of celluloid, resulting in a mechanically produced image of a reality exterior to the camera. Analogical arts are, he explains, isomorphic and continuous with the phenomena they capture; they are analogs with the things and people whose images are etched on their surface because they share not only a space but also the time of recording with their subjects. *These things or people featured in the image were there at that place, then, with*

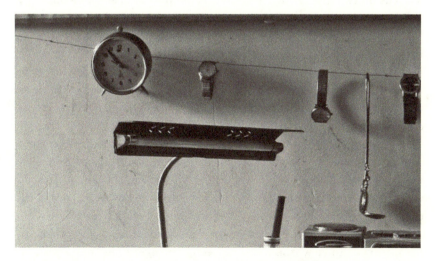

Figure 4.11 Broken clocks suspended in space and time. *Still Life* (2008).

the camera, and the resulting image resembles the scene it captured. The beholder of photographs, writes Roland Barthes, is struck by the poignancy of this "emanation of *past reality*": "The photograph possesses an evidential force, and . . . its testimony bears not on the object but on time."[75] The particular melancholy of photography is that it allows us to view and then to embrace what is past, what is no longer, what is now or will at some point in the future be dead. "Every photograph is this catastrophe."[76] When analog media are too slow, too expensive, and too cumbersome and fixed to capture things as they change, when digital supplants analog, we find ourselves in the realm of digital immediacy, a new testimony of a different temporality. The shift from the image of the world sculpted by light to the world transformed into binary code and transmittable information brings about a new ethics of the medium, which has deep connection to the psychology of the Anthropocene and these fables of the Three Gorges Dam. The transition signifies not simply how we feel about the image and its world, but the degree to which we *act* on the world and mold it in our image.

Stanley Cavell makes a compelling case for a kind of passivity that arises in the presence of the cinematic image whose world, importantly, is past. This pastness is the case both because the recording is prior to and distinct from the scene and time of the projected film and because this is the only way to account for, or define, cinema's reality based as it is in photographic processes. "The reality in a photograph is present to me while I am not present to it: and a world I know, and see, but to which I am nevertheless not present (through no fault of my subjectivity) is a world past."[77] The appeal of the cinematic experience is manifold for Cavell, but I want to focus on two aspects that rest on this temporally disjunctive ontology. The first is that cinema allows us to view a world over which we exert no control. The screen on which images are projected is also, he insists, "a barrier." "It screens me from the world it holds—that is, makes me invisible. And it screens that world from me—that is, screens its existence from me."[78] However invested we may be in the image, the story, and however much we may connect with a character, the world in film is not one we can enter into, not even if we leave the theater and seek out the location of production. The filming has already occurred. For better and worse, a world that is past and from which I am screened is a world I can neither help nor harm. Watching projections of the world on film, allowing us to see a world that cannot return our gaze, we spectators find ourselves not in the classical paradigm of voyeurism whereby we think we control what we see, a perversion of looking predicated on sadistic manipulation. Rather, "by permitting us to view [the world] unseen," cinema fulfills "not a wish for power over creation . . . but a wish not to need power, not have to bear its burdens."[79] Cinema makes us "mechanically absent" from the spectacle on screen such that "my helplessness is mechanically assured: I am present not at something happening, which I must confirm, but at something that has happened, which I absorb (like a memory)."[80] Cinema offers a respite from power and a call to action. In the darkened theater, viewing a world past, we may enjoy our passivity and we experience, as he calls it, a relief from private fantasy.

Writing in 1971, Cavell makes an argument for cinema as technology that permits (perhaps even promotes) invested passivity. The inaction of spectatorship finds a potential parallel in production. Making a film, the cinematographer or director must make selections, choose actors, and write screenplays to create a fictional cosmos. But film does not require such active intervention. "It is equally a possibility of the medium ... to let the world happen, to let its parts draw attention to themselves according to their natural weight."[81] Film satisfies our collective desire for the world to exhibit itself, "to let the world as such appear."[82] That appearance, however, is not reality itself, but a projection of a past reality.

The second part of Cavell's argument I wish to pursue builds on the first. Because the camera mechanically produces an image of the world, because it allows the world's self-exhibition, cinematic images also restore our belief in the world as it was. Or more precisely, film enables us to overcome our subjectivity and reconnect with a world we may share with others. In a characteristically recondite sentence, he declares: "Movies convince us of the world's reality in the only way we have to be convinced, without learning to bring the world closer to the heart's desire (which in practice now means learning to stop altering it illegitimately, against itself): by taking views of it."[83] We overcome our doubts about the world's existence when we see projected images of it—views that mirror our own perceptual operations. Cinema helps us to overcome our doubts about the world we share, but it does so on the condition that the world we see on the screen is past. Parenthetically, Cavell suggests that this mode of spectatorship is an alternative to changing the world, *illegitimately*, according to our wishes, or altering it against itself. Cinema maintains the reality and credibility of the past world, screening it from our modifications. "Film takes our very distance and powerlessness over the world as the condition of the world's natural appearance."[84] With the onset of the no-analog epoch of the Anthropocene, there is no "natural" image—if such an image or a nature ever existed. Sensing that "traditional" cinema is already past and its world is one we postmoderns no longer believe in, Cavell attaches to cinema what Rodowick would later ascribe to digital media. "The future," writes Cavell, "has replaced the past as the object of timely elegy."[85]

If celluloid cinema presents a "natural," past world we can believe in, over which we have no control, Yang creates still images of incredulity where the wish to change the world against itself has been realized. This change refers both to the Chinese government's deconstruction and then flooding of the town before the arrival of any photographic equipment and Yang's technique of digital manipulation. Rodowick writes that, in contrast to celluloid, digitality operates in the mode of "mutation," "interactivity, and practically infinite manipulability."[86] Ever open to new inputs and a dazzling array of effects, after-images, layering, and the discrete rearrangement of ones and zeros, the digital interface does not preserve what it captures. It captures in order to gather, move, share, and reorder data. "The digital will wants to change the world, to make it yield to other forms, or to create different worlds."[87] Digital art is oriented not to the world past, but to an "emerging future," "future events to which we must respond."[88] The utopian promise and perversity of digital desire before and after the camera's appearance on the scene, of course, is that Yang's future world can accommodate neither the life world of human beings nor our genres of perception. The temporality of Yang's digital photography defies experience: there is no viable time or place from which to behold these scenes of a not-yet present, which is now (at the time of this writing) past; there is nothing "natural," and there is no world for us to see or feel. In a similar spirit, Jia's digital cinematography in *Still Life*, with its alien animation and surreal flights of fancy, is "duplicitous." This is not a deception, nor is it in reference to the duo of twos to which Jia refers earlier. As Ackbar Abbas writes, Jia's duplicity is

> rather a provocation to thought, opening up the possibility that the real is not the true, that the visible is not the intelligible, and the intelligible is not the visible. The digital composite images in *Still Life* allow Jia Zhangke's cinema to work in the gap between the visible and the intelligible: as if it were only by means of spectral images and the spectral history of socialism [and, we might add, its ecological costs] could be evoked.[89]

To view the world of the Three Gorges Dam, in other words, requires the supplement of digital duplicity to be believed. Though both of these artworks commemorate an area, an era, perhaps even a geological epoch that is now past, their digital manipulations give rise to an image of an Anthropocene future, insensible because only imaginable.

As a duplicitous digital text, *Uprooted*'s nostalgia looks ahead. This series strays from the "restorative" variety of nostalgia, what Boym defines as a "transhistorical reconstruction of the lost home" that clings to the past as an emblem of "truth and tradition."[90] Homes gone, Yang instead contemplates the nature of "longing itself" indicative of the other tradition, "reflective nostalgia," which Boym finds exemplified in the work of so many East European exiles. Reflective nostalgia is concerned with "the irrevocability of the past and human finitude." "*Re-flection*," she writes, "suggests new flexibility, not the reestablishment of stasis."[91] It is, above all, a lingering in a mode of critical thought that is unsettling. Yang takes flexibility and finitude to an extreme fantasy of human extinction represented as Anthropocene adaptability—digital anagenesis. If these are human subjects, they have already learned to be at home in a submerged world of ruination with no intent on (or capacity for) rebuilding what is gone. In keeping with the critical spirit of reflection, Yang implicitly acknowledges that the home at the heart of homesickness is often what ails us, and that the world built to shelter a modern human (Enlightenment) subject is precisely what makes that world unsustainable.[92] Without a home to return to, Yang invites us to take up residence in the image, to find refuge in the digital ruins.

And yet, digital technology is not only *forward* looking. The broken analog timepieces in *Still Life* are in the company of other outmoded objects, including the broken computer at the relocation office. If the digital image orients us to the future, digital technology is itself resolutely bound for obsolescence and, like the timepieces hanging in the apartment, ripe for new meaning. Jia and Yang are not media purists or strict chronologists, and the Anthropocene, or at least the Three Gorges Dam, inspires them to engage in a kind of media archeology. What Siegfried Zielinski calls a media "anarcheology" is a rejection of teleological history and the presumed uselessness of discarded media. The artists seek out individual variation, alternative possible pasts, and unpredictable futures from the media that were left behind, or thought of but not developed. Above all, the artist values nonstandardized media and the "dynamic moments in the media-archeological record that abound and revel in heterogeneity."[93] Contemplating the abandoned futures and possible media pasts, the anarcheologist, argues Zielinksi, thinks more like a paleontologist, excavating and rejuvenating extinct media from the sedimentation of time and the apparent telos of history.

We find the seeds of such an archeological project in a final image: Yang Yi's *No. 20* (2008) (Figure 4.12). Two men wearing snorkeling masks are in a sepia-toned field of rubble. They are surrounded by the skeletal remains of apartment buildings and are submerged in the Three Gorges reservoir.

Figure 4.12 Yang Yi, *Uprooted 20* (2008). Courtesy of Yang Yi and Galerie Dix9's Hélène Lacharmoise.

Light dances on the water surface above them and the "horizon" dazzles like a Milky Way sky. This too, of course, is a digitized liquid environment. One man stands while the other kneels, his hand resting on what appears to be a sixteen-millimeter film projector. Are these the ruins of the town theater? Is this Kai Xian's last picture show, projected in the town square because the cinema, like everything else, has been rendered homeless? What we see in the middle of Yang's phantasmagoria is a screen projecting not a film, not the world past, but the nonworld of the future envisioned as a play of reflected water and light, empty of things. Perhaps this ending is something of a beginning, or an alternative history of humanity on Earth: the light of a projector before the filmstrip is loaded, the promise of an image to come, or the ambient environment that may one day produce new aquatic life forms. Or maybe we have left the material world altogether and retreated into the fever dreams of a posthumanity, the unconscious of Kai Xian's future underwater residents. In his book subtitled "An Essay on the Imagination of Matter," Gaston Bachelard writes of an unconscious journey figured as the future of humankind in which submergence and disappearance are connected not to death and extinction, but to infinity and thus some form of inhuman persistence. "To disappear into deep water or to disappear towards a far horizon, to become a part of depth or infinity, such is the destiny of man that finds its image in the destiny of water."[94] Is this the infinity of an aquatic human on a submerged planet? Is it possible we will survive ourselves? Welcome to the dreamworld of the Anthropocene.

CHAPTER 5

Antarctica and Siegfried Kracauer's Extraterrestrial Film Theory

Antarctica is the most inhospitable place on Earth, and thus it is a fitting location for this book's final chapter. Read any account of this continent's features and you will find a string of chilling superlatives: it is the coldest, driest, and windiest mass of land and ice on the planet. During its sunless winter, temperatures drop to minus eighty-one degrees Fahrenheit, and even in summer, writes one nature writer, the air "causes instant pain to any exposed skin. It's not even wise to smile—your gums and teeth will ache. Frostbite can set in quickly."[1] A different writer comments on the amenities: "In the interior of the continent there is nothing to make a living from—no food, no shelter, no clothing, no fuel, no liquid water. Nothing but ice."[2] America's National Science Foundation (NSF)-run McMurdo Station, on the southern tip of Ross Island, testifies to the artificiality of human existence in this bitter cold. The largest scientific outpost on the continent, McMurdo was established in 1955 as a fragile "blizzard-prone pastiche of a small American town, complete with a cinema and a chapel."[3] Children are banned along with most creaturely comforts, and today it is a small but "grubby, ugly mess," in an otherwise pristine frozen landscape.[4] Everything needed for survival must be shipped or flown in during the summer months because humans have never lived "naturally" on this continent. Earth's hospitality and human expression reach their limits at the South Pole.

Because of its extreme remoteness, moreover, for millennia it fascinated as a hypothetical continent, presumed to exist as a ballast to the North Pole until the late eighteenth century when Captain James

Cook confirmed both its geographic existence and its uselessness to science and empire. The continent was fully mapped (but still not fully known) only in 1997 when satellite technology could provide detail for what was still considered to be a largely uncharted, *terra incognita* at the bottom of the planet.[5] Always of the earth, it was the last continent to become part of the human world. Antarctica's belatedness thus confronts us with a natural history on the far side of human meaning. For most of human existence, Antarctica has been an image of "the world without us." It is a "frozen part of the Garden of Eden that has been off limits to us," writes geophysicist Henry Pollack in reference to Alan Weisman's speculative science of humanity's sudden disappearance (in which, incidentally, Antarctica does not figure).[6] Unlike Eden, Antarctica is not where human life and its world begin so much as end. The very name, *Antarctica*, designates geography by negation: *opposed* to the North Pole, *opposite* the North Star.

Antarctica is also a challenge to if not negation of cinema—in particular, expressions of cinephilia that constellate around ecophilia. These are two forms of love and attachment that seem to intensify when celluloid and certain ecosystems draw near their moments of disappearance. The latter expresses a love of dwelling in the world, the former a desire to dwell in the image. Or, taken together, they express a singular love of dwelling in the world *through* the image. Antarctica is tough to love, in this regard, because it resists analogical transcription—not because it changes too fast, like the Three Gorges Dam, but because its extreme conditions are too bright, too dark, too cold, or too still and too undifferentiated to register on film. Its relentless sun in summer can lead to snow blindness and overexposure of skin and celluloid alike. Its winter defies vision and cinematic capture. At the time of its earliest "nondiscovery" by Cook, the seventh continent figured cartographically as a negative space, and, in many films and photographs shot during the long winter, the landscape captured with flash photography produced what appears to be a negative image (Figure 5.1).[7] Stephen J. Pyne explains that in the heroic age of exploration of the late nineteenth and early twentieth centuries, the South Pole defied not just narrative, but the "metaphysics (and metahistory) of nature," philosophy, representation, and genres of art:

> The abundance of the observed world was stripped away.... In place of increasing information, there was less. In place of abundant objects, there was only ice; and in place of tangible landmarks, such as mountains or lakes, there were only abstract concepts, such as the poles of rotation, magnetism, or inaccessibility, all invisible to the senses.[8]

Figure 5.1 Frank Hurley's flash photography of *The Endurance* during the Antarctic winter. *South* (1919).

In early exploration films, the journey to the pole eludes the cinematic and even photographic record altogether, and not simply because few of the early filmmakers reached this prized geographic coordinate. Roald Amundsen had to plant a flag in the otherwise empty, indistinct space before he could photograph a location he discovered by virtue of crude meridian calculation. And even after planting the flag and taking the photo, he realized his team had still eight kilometers to travel before reaching the "absolute Pole," the coveted destination that eludes perception.[9] Arriving at the same spot just months after Amundsen, Robert F. Scott, without a trace of sublime reverence, described the pole's "awful monotony" of ice, snow, and inhuman cold.[10] Richard E. Byrd, accompanied by Paramount cameraman Joseph Rucker, was the first to fly over the pole in 1928, as recorded in the documentary *With Byrd at the South Pole: The Story of Little America* (1929/1930). The triumphant moment captured on film, however, is nothing but white spied from the plane's small window; not even a horizon provides a measure of context or grandeur (Figure 5.2). Byrd tosses a US flag out of the window that disappears into the utterly blank white below, reducing this claim of discovery to its most bare symbolic gesture. Upon his return to North America, Byrd recounts to an off-screen crowd of admirers what he and his men missed while on the expedition: "all that you

Figure 5.2 The triumphant shot of the South Pole as seen through the plane's window. *With Byrd at the South Pole* (1930).

have about you here—land, grass, green trees, voices other than our own, the warm rays of the sun, nearly everything that makes life worthwhile." The value of human life finds no confirmation on a continent that is "white, silent and dead." In a different register, geophysicist Bill Green writes of his Antarctic obsession: "It is precisely what is not there, what has never been there, that makes . . . the whole continent . . . so strange and so important."[11] Antarctica, as a place, and the pole, as a coordinate, seem to offer *nothing* to the lovers of cinema or nature. Or maybe it is the void that we love. Channeling the last thoughts of one of Captain Scott's doomed traveling companions, Annie Dillard imagines the dizzying Antarctic freeze as a "lightless edge where the slopes of knowledge dwindle, and love for its own sake, lacking an object, begins."[12]

As a result of this apparently empty, shimmering topography, even modern Antarctica has reflected back more the temperament and culture of the people who have traveled there than it has revealed about itself. Survival in the early days of exploration, as Pyne describes it, "meant surmounting the inactivity and lethargy of the polar night and enduring the introspection and deprivation that were the supreme Antarctic attributes." Paradoxically, he continues, Antarctica did not produce a sensible experience of nature despite its complete isolation from civilization: rather, its numbing whiteness—"utterly without 'human interest'"—made it the most anesthetic continent on Earth, causing visitors to explore their own inner depths.[13] A map of Antarctica tells the story of triumphant claims and crushed human spirits. Entering Hero Bay, you will come upon Desolate Island. On the continent's Akra Peninsula, Exasperation Inlet is just north of Cape Disappointment.[14]

Today, Antarctica's affront to humanity is of a different order. Far from fixed, it is on the verge of collapse. The effect of global warming is that the ice shelves and glaciers will melt, sea levels will rise, and the great coastal cities including New York, Venice, Shanghai, Sydney, and Rotterdam, and several low-lying island nation-states will disappear. The geographical end of the world (the South Pole) is now tethered to the temporal end of many coastal worlds. Despite these imperatives, however, citizens are hard-pressed to invest in the conservation of ice for its own sake, as an object in its own right. Environmental advocates long ago realized that the public could be persuaded to care and donate money for preservation if they were faced with familiar species onto whom they could map intelligence, happiness, suffering, and other signs of human experience, and thus feel toward them something like love.[15] The charismatic animals of the American West inspired the Endangered Species Act. Yet, as legal scholar Bradley Bernau concedes, "the vast majority of endangered species are the small, the microscopic, the unseen, the unnoticed and the unheralded" whose existence matters to the public only insofar as it supports cuter life forms.[16] Loving attachment also underwrites efforts to preserve habitats. The Nature Conservancy pleads to would-be donors to "Protect Nature You Love." Today, as I write, the Conservancy's homepage features the following images: a field of yellow wildflowers at sunset; an aerial view of elephants running through a dusty savanna; an inviting glass of water framed in front of a waterfall; and a child, dressed in a T-shirt, jumping between boulders against a blue sky, his campsite in the background. Just opposite the "Nature You Love" donation button is a photo of a verdant, tree-filled landscape.[17] The humanism presupposed by environmentalism suggests the limits—geographical, emotional, and sensible—of our love for a world that wants us, on and into which we may project ourselves thriving. With public resources for preservation dwindling and human populations expanding, we choose which places and species merit preservation and which may just have to disappear. When we rescue from extinction only the creatures and places we love, what becomes of the unlovely, ugly, invisible, or dangerous animal or seemingly indifferent, remote, and utterly inhospitable land?[18] Against these reigning criteria for preservation, Antarctica is a lost cause. Or it matters to us only insofar as its coastline hosts charismatic penguins, whales, and seals and that its melting, over time, threatens the world's more populous shores.

This once-hypothetical continent, in other words, raises the ethical questions about care and even moral judgment across great distances that Adam Smith first raised with the parable of the "hypothetical Mandarin": if suddenly the empire of China were to be destroyed by an earthquake, how would citizens in Europe respond to an event they did not see or feel? Could they summon sympathy for so many people so far away, or would the earthquake resonate meaningfully only when—sometime later—it affected local commerce? More locally still, would a European willingly sacrifice the lives of thousands of Chinese men he would never encounter to avoid a survivable misfortune to himself? For Eric Hayot, "the hypothetical Mandarin" and the scenarios of mass, but far-off, suffering have tested European sympathy. The Mandarin has become a philosophical figure marking where "moral responsibility ends and indifference begins."[19] Antarctica presents a different, but no less remote, challenge to feeling and sensibility. Why do we care and how do we come to love a place that is such an affront to our senses?

Guided by Antarctica's radical negativity, I am interested in the way that film and film theory may intervene in and temper our emotional and even sentimental relationship to nature, the earth, and even the human world, and help us to form more meaningful ecological attachments outside of conventional feeling, narrative, and genres of representation. In this endeavor, I turn to Siegfried Kracauer, for whom cinema does not preserve a world we love any more than it reflects our subjectivity; rather, it is the medium par excellence that estranges nature and our contemporary moment with the effect of dissolving reified history and the emotional and political investments that sustain it. We may read Kracauer's pre- and post–World War II writings as advancing an alternative and denaturalized natural history of the present. Can such disinterest lead to an ethics of seeing in the service of our mutual survival? Must we vanquish love and human feeling to see our current predicament clearly? Or may Antarctica inspire some kind of nonbinding, detached love beyond what we typically ascribe to human feeling?

Kracauer's explanations of photography and cinema—regarded as essential technologies for decoding urban modernity—illuminate film's role in environmental aesthetics and, in particular, help us to theorize a continent that has never been host to midcentury shopgirls, white-collar workers, or hotel lobbies. I read Kracauer together with early films about Antarctic exploration to think about cinema's relationship to brute and brutal physical reality and, more pointedly, to a vanishing natural history that marks the experience of living in the time and place of catastrophe.

As we anticipate the seemingly inevitable melt of the polar ice caps, Kracauer's writings model an environmental stance akin to that which Gerhard Richter posits, more generally, to the Frankfurt School's relentless but redemptive negativity. In the face of irrevocable loss and of an always already damaged life, "the last and the traumatic void can be made the poetic and philosophic occasions for a vigilant stance that will neither simply revel in resignation nor fully relinquish that madness and enigmatic stimulus of non-deluded hope."[20] In the spirit of this provisional optimism, Kracauer's film theory may be read in the service of ecocentric thought in which human life and humanistic modes of dwelling find themselves in exile if not outright extraterrestrial estrangement. Like damaged life, nature is also already lost to us: it is already past, pastoral, cultivated, mapped, and historicized according to the contours of human meaning. Kracauer urges us to see nonidentical nature and physical reality through the unloving, antihumanist, and perhaps above all postapocalyptic medium of film. We should learn from photography and film to perceive the earth as having multiple pasts and futures—a product not of divine will, political theologies, or inevitable natural development, but one that is fragmented and accidental in design: "nature in the raw, nature as it exists independently of us."[21] And Antarctica, through its very challenge to representation and human history, serves as the most extreme and apposite example of a nature outside of the human world.

While Kracauer's investments in experience make him an odd choice to pair with a continent that has been so insensible to human explorers, his model of filmmaking and spectatorship posit, as Miriam Hansen remarks, a "stoically cool, post-apocalyptic 'subject of survival.'"[22] Drawing on the recent scholarship on Kracauer that challenges his status as a realist or humanist, and guided by his own ecological remarks, this chapter turns to his film and photographic theory to explore a productive model of postcatastrophic self-alienation as the basis for environmental thought. Taken together, Kracauer's theory of photographic vision (which productively alienates the viewer) and Antarctica's negativity (which, as I'll discuss, turns humans into extraterrestrials) lead to a clear-eyed perception of human estrangement on and from Earth. Beyond the exilic sense of nonbelonging, this pairing also liberates us from a naturalized present and foreclosed future.

FILM THEORY AFTER THE APOCALYPSE

In his 1960 *Theory of Film: The Redemption of Physical Reality*, Kracauer ponders cinema's antireferential depiction of nature and the possibility that this unfamiliar view may actually redeem a disenchanted reality after the apocalypse.[23] The apocalypse, however, is not climate change or the Anthropocene planet we currently inhabit and which inspires all manner of traumatic, futuristic disaster cinema. Rather, as Heidi Schlüpmann explains, though there is only oblique reference to Hitler's war and Kracauer's own biography as a German Jewish refugee, Kracauer's book "thematizes film after Auschwitz—in both the subjective and objective sense. This not only entails finding words of description, finding language, but also a prior difficulty, namely that of regarding film in the context of this reality."[24] In the wake of man-made apocalypse, Kracauer proposes humankind's rescue not through revived religiosity (the apocalypse of war did not bring about divine revelation) or scientific truth (which leads only to abstraction). Instead, Kracauer turns to cinema as a technology that will redeem physical reality (as his subtitle announces) and bring us to a planetary consciousness.

> It is my contention that film, our contemporary, has a definite bearing on the era into which it is born; that it meets our inmost needs precisely by exposing—for the first time, as it were—outer reality and thus deepening, in Gabriel Marcel's words, our relation to "this Earth which is our habitat."[25]

Imprinted by the earth's radiance, film answers humanity's urgent need to see and think beyond itself and perceive—perhaps become photosensitized to—our earthly habitat. Out of this process of exposure comes a relation to the world impossible before film and perhaps also before war.

The crisis in perception, as Kracauer understands it, is that the physical environment, cluttered with material and historical debris, has been "persistently veiled by ideologies relating its manifestations to some total aspect of our universe."[26] In his historical sequencing of modernity, religious totalization has been superseded by scientific abstraction. In the former, outer reality reflects metaphysical and "holistic notions as sin, the last judgment, salvation and the like." In the latter, material life is subsumed into immaterial laws and data: "No sooner do we emancipate ourselves from the 'ancient beliefs' than we are led to eliminate the quality of things."[27] Science, like religious art, removes "the world from the field of vision" such that "things continue to recede."[28] Cinema, however, can wrest the natural world from the holisms of both artistic and scientific abstraction:

> Film renders visible what we did not, or perhaps could not, see before its advent. It effectively assists us in discovering the material world with its psychophysical

correspondences. We literally redeem this world from its dormant state, its state of virtual nonexistence, by endeavoring to experience it through the camera. And we are free to experience it because we are fragmentized.[29]

While cinema has existed since the turn of the twentieth century, it is only in this post–World War II era, in the context of *this* fragmented reality, in which all master narratives have been shaken by the war's imponderable violence, that we may, in watching film, encounter the physical world in its incomprehensible singularity. A postapocalyptic subject, in other words, is as fragmented as the world she hopes to experience, and this correspondence between fragmented nature and fragmentized human experience gives rise to this new horizon of perceptibility. From this follows that the material world's "virtual nonexistence" to which Kracauer refers has a double meaning. In one sense, the reality we perceived before the advent of cinema was a virtual projection of ideology. Postwar cinema has the potential to shatter this illusion of coherence, especially if it embraces the affinities of its photographic substrate, namely, if cinema leaves the dark studio and discovers a reality that is unstaged, fortuitous, endless, and indeterminate.[30] In another sense, the external world is itself so fragmented, particular, and dormant that, as a comprehensible whole or meaningful totality, it is practically nonexistent. Writing at the height of the Cold War, Kracauer is not declaring the end of ideology or the triumph of capitalist history.[31] Quite the opposite. Cinema in his account may guide us to nonteleological, highly particularized, and above all estranged modes of perception. This is as close to enlightenment as we are likely to come after the apocalypse.

Kracauer elucidates the ontologically estranging effects of photography through a passage from Marcel Proust's *The Guermantes Way* (1913). The grandson, Marcel, arrives in the living room unannounced and catches sight of his beloved grandmother. For the first time in his life, he beholds her not through his affectionate idealization, but objectively and coldly, like a photographer who has happened by the house. Kracauer quotes this long passage in which Marcel reflects on this horrifying reality and feels himself a passing stranger in the most familiar of places:

> I was in the room, or rather I was not yet in the room since she was not aware of my presence. . . . Of myself . . . there was present only the witness, the observer with a hat and traveling coat, the stranger who does not belong to the house, the photographer who has called to take a photograph of places which one will never see again. The process that mechanically occurred in my eyes when I caught sight of my grandmother was indeed a photograph. We never see the people who are

dear to us save in the animated system, the perpetual motion of our incessant love for them, which before allowing the images that their faces present to reach us catches them in its vortex, flings them back upon the idea that we have always had of them, makes them adhere to it, coincide with it. How, since the forehead, the cheeks of my grandmother I had been accustomed to read all the most delicate, the most permanent qualities of her mind; how, since every casual glance is an act of necromancy, each face that we love a mirror of the past, how could I have failed to overlook what in her had become dulled and changed, seeing that in the most trivial spectacles of our daily life our eye, charged with thought, neglects, as would a classical tragedy, every image that does not assist the action of the play and retains only those that may help to make its purpose intelligible. . . . I, for whom my grandmother was still myself, I who has never seen her save in my own soul, always at the same place in the past, through the transparent sheets of contiguous, overlapping memories, suddenly in our drawing room which formed part of a new world, that of time, saw, sitting on the sofa, beneath the lamp, red-faced, heavy and common, sick, lost in thought, following the lines of a book with eyes that seemed hardly sane, a dejected old woman whom I did not know.[32]

Kracauer writes approvingly: "Photography, as Proust has it, is the product of complete alienation."[33] Its "foremost virtue" is "emotional detachment." The grandson's shock at this revelation demonstrates how "photographs transmit raw material without defining it." The photograph arrests the image in the here and now before its content is flung back into memory and sentimentality, as indeed occurs with Marcel shortly after this defamiliarizing happenstance.[34] Counterintuitively, Marcel's "necromancy" is not a vision of his grandmother in fumbling old age, approaching death; rather, his memories maintain a projection of her in her unchanging youth against the fact of her decline. Thanks to photography, we can begin to see qualities of reality through the suspended gaze of an unloving stranger and what we find may horrify us. In stark contrast to André Bazin, for whom cinema brings "a virginal purity" of reality "to my attention and consequently to my love," for Kracauer, love and memory are implicated in the very meaning-giving totalities that abstract the world from view and that cause us to preserve a mental image against the truth of a person's or thing's materiality.[35] Because "the nature of photography survives in that of film," film also redeems reality from the animated system of love and memory.[36] The effect of *cinema*'s perpetual motion is to "alienate our environment by exposing it."[37] Such exposure is not conducive to tragedy and its always-belated but inescapable revelations, as Marcel remarks in the passage earlier. The fated vision of tragedy attends only to the details that satisfy a contained narrative and, specifically, its foreordination. Because the camera does not know the meaning of the future, it records and exposes every detail, and thus photography signifies its own mechanical indifference to signification. Not even grandmother is safe from its cold gaze.

From the book's first chapter comes a theory of film rooted in a literary account of photography that celebrated as alienated both the subject and beholder of the image. The salutary effect of this technology is that it erodes human subjectivity and the individual's confidence in a world perceived through feeling. Not only does Kracauer's impersonal cinema thus part ways with Bazin's account of loving attention, but also he is working against the grain of what would become dominant psychoanalytic film theory—what would count *as* film theory in the 1970s. From Jean-Louis Baudry's "Apparatus" theory, to Christian Metz's "Imaginary Signifier," and arriving at Laura Mulvey's "Narrative Cinema and Visual Pleasure" blockbuster manifesto, film theory would posit a spectator duped by the technology and seduced by scenarios of narrative cinema into a false sense of mastery and often sadistic control.[38] Cinema would not be an instrument of the subject's undoing. On the contrary, it fashioned a world and experience built to the measure of human, specifically and increasingly *masculine,* desire. Publishing his book more than a decade before this turn to apparatus theory, Kracauer celebrates cinema's capacity to render "life at its least controllable" and to snap us out of our reveries.[39] The point, however, is more than the undoing of the human subject. Kracauer's polemic is for a vision that is receptive to unknown entities and as-yet-undiscovered phenomena that present themselves to a camera that records without thinking. In particular, far from shielding the subject or confirming its attentive inclinations, cinema's "revealing functions" turn on a set of phenomena that the camera alone brings to consciousness. In the third chapter, he enumerates these categories of the cinematic: those that are normally unseen (because too small or too big for human perception), those that are typically overlooked (because too familiar and thus rarely noticed), and those that overwhelm consciousness (because too cruel or too catastrophic to be witnessed without the intervention of extreme emotion). Importantly, cinema has the capacity to maintain the alterity of the unseen world before it is domesticated into narrative.

In describing a theory of redemption through alienation, *Theory of Film* advances a natural history of the photographic present. This is a curious claim to make for a book that, as Miriam Hansen rightly notes, all but represses film history and Kracauer's own intellectual, exilic biography in its exegesis of cinematic properties.[40] Bracketing off master historical narratives, however, is precisely how the book opens itself up to a different postcatastrophic historicism. By drawing on Kracauer's Weimar-era and post–World War II writings, I want to track in his work the nature of natural history and the nature of nature as it culminates in *Theory of Film*. "Nature" in most of Kracauer's work is a load-bearing and ambiguous term. In much of his early, prewar writing, nature designates a mythical appeal to a supposedly immutable status quo, the appearance of the present moment as the telos of the past, or a sense of the natural world as a comprehensible totality. In these uses, nature is akin to ideology, a false doctrine that hides the truth about contingency and alternative possibilities for the past and future. On the other hand, he will appeal to nature as what history does not account for and what challenges ideological claims to coherence or totality. A "natural" image may appear to the onlooker as almost incomprehensible matter. In Kracauer's later writing, especially in *Theory of Film*, this second definition (nature as beyond or outside of history/ideology) becomes most pronounced. Nature is no longer aligned with ideology or master explanatory narratives (a natural image that naturalizes the status quo), but is sub-subsumed into physical reality. In his postwar writing, nature *is* the fragmented truth that ideology prevents us from perceiving. In both the prewar and postwar writing, photography and cinema are deeply connected to the political significance of nature.

NATURE AND NATURAL HISTORY

Writing in reference to Walter Benjamin, Eric L. Santner explains that natural history (*Naturgeschichte*) refers not to a history of nature, "but to the fact that the artifacts of human history tend to acquire an aspect of mute, natural being at the point where they begin to lose their place in a viable form of life."[41] As a result of this process, which affects people and things alike, we experience artifacts detached from history as denaturalized. Or, as Beatrice Hanssen notes, "Natural history entails a falling away from pure 'historical' time in inauthentic 'spatialization' and a temporality of transience" that typifies Benjamin's modernity.[42] Whereas Benjamin turns to the figure of allegory as the representation of "irresistible decay," Kracauer in his Weimar writings finds repositories of a differently inflected version of this natural history in the alienating technologies of photography and film.

We find the origins of this line of thinking in Kracauer's well-known 1927 essay "Photography" published in eight parts in the *Frankfurter Zeitung*. Here he compares two photographs to explain the petrifying effect of technological reproduction. The first is a contemporary image of a film star who is immediately recognizable because everyone has seen "the original on the screen."[43] We automatically accept a contemporary photograph's iconic relationship to its subject because not only the starlet but also her hairstyle and clothing correspond to the historical world as we experience it; indeed, it is all so familiar as to be transparent. The second example, however, challenges photography's iconicity; it is a sixty-year-old photograph of a grandmother taken when she was a young woman. Her grandchildren behold this image and discern no similarity between it and the "long since decayed" original. Failing to recognize their grandmother, the children fixate instead on the "fashionably old-fashioned details" of her clothing that might more appropriately be found in a museum exhibit under the title "Traditional Costumes, 1864."[44] Whereas a contemporary photograph is "translucent," suffused as it is by the historical present, the old photograph renders grandmother into "an archeological mannequin."[45] The children laugh at the outdated fashions and shudder uncomfortably at obsolescence itself. Old photographs "make visible not the knowledge of the original, but the spatial configuration of a moment. What appears in the photograph is not the person but the sum of what can be subtracted from him or her."[46] Because they arbitrarily and mindlessly record a spatialized field, photographs utterly fail as portraits: "When the grandmother stood in front of the lens, she was present for one second in the spatial continuum that presented itself to the lens. But it was that aspect and not the grandmother that was eternalized."[47] Eventually the connection to human history will be lost: the grandmother's costume "will be peculiar, like an ocean-dwelling octopus."[48] In contrast to painted portraits and to history, which rely on selective data and significant memory and even myth, photography preserves a "natural image," defined in this essay as an object perceived mechanically and without cognition, one whose subject might become peculiar, like a strange animal, over time. Even landscapes do not escape this desubstantiating gaze. The hills of the Rhine that look like mountains in etchings are "reduced to tiny slopes" in photographs such that "the grandiosity of those aged views seems a bit ridiculous."[49]

Incapable of conveying the Rhine's symbolic import, the photograph destroys its mythic status. This is photography's political utility: where traditional history requires subjectivity and selective memory to achieve false coherence, photography eradicates all subjective meaning and reflects instead "the residuum that history has discharged."[50] In his introduction to Kracauer's essay, Thomas Y. Levin writes: "Photography stages nature as the negativity of history." Or put differently, photography's natural history denaturalizes historical process, coherence, and inevitability. Levin continues: "Only when the current state of things is revealed as provisional (that is, not nature) can the question of their proper order arise."[51] Here nature as a concept refers both to history's remainder and to the illusion of an immutable, comprehensible truth over and against a provisional reality. In one sense, nature is outside of history; in another, it is that force that naturalizes the present through historical meaning and makes the present transparent, natural, and given. This is what old photographs reveal: they show us our past not as history, memory, or art would have us see it—memorialized, laden with meaning—but instead as spatialized data arbitrarily organized. In the natural history of Kracauer's early work, the person recedes and the photograph "gathers fragments around a nothing."[52] If we could recognize this same negation in contemporary photographs, we could perhaps see even our current state of affairs as the product of a contingent and malleable order. It was Kracauer's hope that photography would bring about a transformation of consciousness that could resist the myths and self-declared inevitability of Nazism by exposing its brute nature. On the other hand, photography is itself a force like nature. Kracauer tropes the historicity of the photograph in ways that harmonize with my interest in the inassimilable Antarctic: photography buries history "as if under a layer of snow."[53] "The blizzard of photographs," he writes of the illustrated newspapers of the day, "betrays an indifference toward what the things mean."[54] Kracauer senses the affinities between photography and ice to obliterate significance.

It is not incidental that Germany witnesses a resurgent fascination with polar exploration in the first decades of the twentieth century based not only on the numerous published accounts of pre–World War I expeditions by Erich von Drygalski but also on the interwar desire to claim parts of the poles for Germany to offset territorial losses dictated by the Treaty of Versailles. The public was able to experience something of the polar world when Antarctic dioramas were installed in the Berlin Institute for Oceanography in 1906 and the Berlin Museum of National History in 1912.[55] Quite apart from the nationalist land grab, David Thomas Murphy writes that stories in German newspapers of the poles' "freakish beauty . . . of [their] auroras, solitude and danger . . . fostered an environmentalist sensibility that went beyond the sentimental naturalism embraced by the romantics."[56] As knowledge of a prehistoric ice became more widely accepted and as fears of another global freeze took hold, the poles came to represent earth's prehuman, natural past and posthuman future. Only a sober turn toward brutalizing nature could shock humanity out of the illusions of its warm but fuzzy sentiments, not just about the natural world, but, as Helmut Lethen explains, the shorter history of capitalist and social alienation, which was often described "as a journey into eternal ice."[57]

Subzero temperatures and temperaments became the master tropes for Weimar's cool objectivity. From the bracing experience of modernization to the chilling confrontation with polar climates, German intellectuals tried to come to terms with and fashion modes of enduring "the cold of modernity."[58] According to the codes of interwar objectivity, Lethen tells us in his reading of Max Weber's 1919 *Art of Worldly Wisdom*, only an "attitude of defiance" could counter the "meaninglessness" of history and the failed processes of evolution. The stalwart figure was the polar explorer. At the poles, meaning was so radically and self-evidently annihilated that men would have to embrace "disillusioned realism" or else become victims of the indifferent world.[59] In his prewar writing, Kracauer figures photography in terms akin to arctic extremes: it both upends romantic, sentimental history and introduces a new and potentially revolutionary nothingness at the heart of mechanical representation—an image depleted of historical and subjective meaning that stands as the ultimate challenge to ideology and progress.

In Kracauer's post–World War II writing, we find a change. Nature qua nature, now subsumed under the umbrella category of physical reality, has a new primacy in his account of what cinema redeems. In his earlier work, photography destroys nature as myth. In *Theory of Film*, photography and cinema enable us to see the physical, fragmented world, including nature, outside of myth, and not only in hindsight. Whereas the single photograph may reveal the physical world through the unloving lens of a camera, cinema not only combines images but also, through its experiments of time and duration, stages the process by which physical reality is dissociated from meaning-giving, externally imposed form. Not all films achieve this potential. Because of their closed narratives and hypercontrolled mise-en-scène, Hollywood movies revert the physical world back into literary convention because they use raw material in the service of establishing what Kracauer calls "a significant whole" (as opposed to the "significant hole" of photography's gathering fragments around a nothing): "The result is film which sustains the prevailing abstractness."[60] Better are those with an episodic structure, as in Italian neorealism, and permeable mise-en-scène in which fragments of material life "inadvertently tell a story of their own, which for a transient moment makes one completely forget the manifest story."[61] In contrast to the always-replaceable subjects and always-repeatable images of the atomic test movies, Kracauer values films that seek out singular and impenetrable details, phenomena, people, and things in "the maze of physical existence." These entities, "snatched from transient life," refuse to yield their secrets. Instead, they summon the viewer "to preserve them as the irreplaceable images they are."[62]

Kracauer's cinephilia, indeed the primal scene for his lifelong critical practice, originates with such a transient image—one from a movie he watched as a boy whose title and plot he cannot recall. The scene itself, he writes, "I remember, as if it were today":

> What thrilled me so deeply was an ordinary suburban street, filled with lights and shadows which transfigured it. Several trees stood about, and there was in the foreground a puddle reflecting invisible house facades and a piece of the sky. Then a breeze moved the shadows, and the facades with the sky below began to waver. The trembling upper world in the dirty puddle—this image has never left me.[63]

This image of a suburban world is twice transfigured. First the scene is transcribed to black-and-white celluloid, which turns the pattern of light and shadow in an otherwise ordinary street into a thrilling vision. Second, and more intriguing, the dirty puddle both reflects the facades of houses and sky that stand beyond the frame and registers the force (in the form of a ripple) of an otherwise invisible phenomenon—a breeze that disturbs the reflection. In the first transfiguration, cinema is an index of a marvelous world *absent* the human figure (not that Kracauer remarks on this feature). In the second sense, with the puddle at its center, the image is an index of the puddle as an index. As Johannes von Moltke observes, this passage condenses Kracauer's theory of film "as a medium of reflection" that "captures an unseen upper world, sets it in motion, transforms it through the 'wavering' surface, and renders it available to experience."[64] But there is something more that disturbs in this image. The puddle, as an analogy for cinema and its animated material, may either reflect back an image of the human world or bare the traces of an invisible elemental nature. The representation of one disturbs and even threatens to negate the other. The suburban world is unpopulated, still, silent, and unmoved, but also invisible except for its reflection in the dirty puddle. Then it appears to undergo a minicatastrophe. "The trembling upper world in the dirty puddle" suggests a fragility of the image and, of course, the "overlooked" vulnerable things it animates. So moved by this rippling still life as a boy, Kracauer ran home and penned the title to a book he planned to write: *Film as the Discoverer of the Marvels of Everyday Life*.[65]

In fact, the filmmaker in *Theory of Film* is nothing short of a discoverer or an endangered explorer who sets out to tell a story but, in shooting it, is so overwhelmed by his innate desire to cover all of physical reality—and also by a feeling that he must cover it in order to tell the story, any story, in cinematic terms—that he ventures ever deeper into the jungle of material phenomena in which he risks becoming irretrievably lost.[66]

We can imagine the filmmaker literally setting off into a jungle in search of a natural world. But what Kracauer figures here is a more profound risk of the subject dissipating and disappearing altogether. Another "hypothetical Mandarin" illustrates the process of self-abandonment. As recounted, a "legendary Chinese painter" so yearned to live in the world he had created with ink and paper that he "moved into it," vanishing into the faraway mountains of his brushed landscape, "never to be seen again."[67] The painter does not absorb the artwork from a position of aesthetic distance, but is absorbed by it, dissolves into it. Likewise, writes Kracauer paraphrasing Valéry, a cinematic film "divert[s] the spectator from the core of his being" when it exposes him to the jungle of material existence.[68] And he too is drawn into the orbit of things and launched by the film "into unending pursuits."[69] Quoting a silent film critic, Kracauer remarks on a kind of cinephilia or idealized fanaticism in which detached absorption in the image both reduces and expands perception to an almost insensible level. It is "passive, personal, as little humanistic or humanitarian as possible," and the diffused subject is "self-unconscious like an amoeba; deprived of an object or rather, attached to all [of them] like fog."[70] This is not a spectator with a sense of herself as distinct from the world, but an individual who willingly absorbs matter into her being, a single-cell organism attuned to a multisensory indistinctness of what Kracauer calls "the murmur of existence."[71] A truly cinematic film will enable the spectator to "apprehend physical reality in all its concreteness," specifically as "a flow of chance events, scattered objects, and nameless shapes."[72] What is "concrete" is not necessarily formed or even hard matter, and we may presume that the human comes to regard herself as a being among these objects, placed in the scene of "a trembling upper world in the dirty puddle."

As von Moltke argues, this model of antihumanist spectatorship should be understood as Kracauer's attempt to redeem experience (as opposed to physical reality) and rescue some form of subjectivity after the disastrous historical events of totalitarianism and authoritarian rule. In Nazi Germany, "the utter dehumanization of the world" correlated with "the loss of experience."[73] Postwar film, writes von Moltke, had the potential to lay bare the material world and recover experience at this minimal, cellular level by "confronting viewers with the estranged fragments of their existence and allowing them to recoup these fragments in the medium of experience."[74] But we can also see the political necessity of describing the world—the real world—as fragmented, scattered, and ruled by chance as a refutation of fascist totalities, of what Hannah Arendt, Kracauer's contemporary, referred to as Hitler's "entirely fictitious world." Kracauer shares Arendt's sense that the power of totalitarian regimes rested on their capacity to construct and maintain (through propaganda, terror, and violent repression) a total fictional world in the form of a fiction that the world is a consistent, graspable totality. Writes Arendt of Hitler and Stalin:

> Their art consists in using, and at the same time transcending, the elements of reality, of verifiable experiences, in the chosen fiction, and in generalizing them into regions which then are definitely removed from all possible control by individual experience. . . . [T]otalitarian propaganda established a world fit to compete with the real one, whose main handicap is that it is not logical, consistent and organized.[75]

In *Theory of Film*, Kracauer is insistent: "There are no wholes in the world: rather, it consists of bits of chance events whose flow substitutes for meaningful continuity."[76] The task of cinema is to explore and affirm this fragmentation, not only to re-establish experience, but also to reject totalitarian totality. Such a modernist cinema, taken to the extreme, would by some accounts become incomprehensible and thus indicative of world refusal.[77] For Kracauer, however, such cinema allows us to slip into "the flow of life" and become enchanted by particularity and open to a world of possibility. The optimism of *Theory of Film* is that after war's catastrophe, we know our fragmentation. That is, we know we are not products of myth, religion, or history, but inheritors of a contingent and fragmented reality that film reflects back to us.

Looking ahead to Kracauer's final, posthumously published work, *History: The Last Things before the Last* (1969), Inka Mülder-Bach notes that, with a historical continuum now reliably foreclosed, "photographic self-alienation is a prerequisite for the cognition of history" itself.[78] In this, his last book, Kracauer returns to Proust, Marcel, and the grandmother to model objective modes of historical inquiry. Back in the living room, Marcel's "inner picture yields to the photograph at the very moment when the loving person he is shrinks into an impersonal stranger." "Self-effaced," Marcel may "perceive anything because nothing he sees is pregnant with memories."[79] Similarly, the historian must purge all preconceived historical laws before he may encounter the remnants of the past and be open to the multiple stories they tell. In this paradoxical scenario of history stripped of memory and law, the ideal historian, like the photographer, exists in the "near-vacuum of extra-territoriality," a stranger to the phenomena he investigates, a "sheer receiving instrument."[80] Whereas Marcel is quickly restored to his loving senses, the ideal historian lingers in—and is radically and forever altered by—his estrangement. Opening himself up to the suggestion of his sources, the historian must surrender his identity to the point of "near extinction" so that he may tap an ecstatic, depersonalized imagination. "Self-effacement begets self-expansion."[81] He is therefore able to "assimilate himself to the very [historical] reality which was concealed from him by his ideas of it."[82] Rather than finding material to fit the narrative, this historian/explorer assimilates himself to this foreign archive. Thus, in both *Theory of Film* and *History*, to be a filmmaker, spectator, or historian is to risk everything in the search for a randomly generated, nonidentical image and alien past. The payoff? "We stand a chance of finding something we did not look for, something tremendously important in its own right—the world that is ours," or "in Gabriel Marcel's words," we may access "our relation to 'this Earth which is our habitat.'"[83]

Kracauer is not proposing a posthuman mode of inquiry based on a fantasy of humans morphing into some other surviving life form. The amoeba is only an analogy. Nor is he giving up the promise of politics; at least this is implicit in his remarks. Instead, he urges a kind of active passivity, selflessness, or self-unconsciousness that can discover a lost past, a new horizon of experience, and unanticipated modes of political thought and action. Alienation or self-alienation—feeling not at home in the world or in one's own habits of mind—leads the explorer to a path of enlightenment (with a lowercase "e"). *This thinking at the edge of extinction* is a kind of ecological attunement that presumes the subject's alien relation to the planet, a place both unfamiliar and strange, but home nonetheless. And in this way, a postapocalyptic theory of film and history confirms that after the "end of time," time persists, and after the end of grand narratives, the "flow of life" and the singularity of particular matter take on a new primacy. This is not divine revelation (those narratives are also foreclosed). On the other side of catastrophe emerges a new and rather alien natural history.

Indeed, echoing his critique of modern abstraction in *Theory of Film*, in *History*, Kracauer again, but more systematically, urges history's detachment from vaguely described philosophical (predominantly Enlightenment) generalizations—be they political-theological, evolutionary, revolutionary, natural, or world historical. Such explanatory models, which may tell us a great deal about human nature, come too easily to be regarded as natural law. As such, they conceal the particular and nonhomogeneous materials of the past. Even worse, when presumably immutable laws shape historical inquiry, they "preclude man's freedom of choice, his ability to create new situations" now and in the future.[84] Even "natural history," reduced to the hard laws of science, transforms the present into the *telos* of the past. Or, as Kracauer states, natural history tells us "why that which has occurred actually must have occurred."[85] Nature also has a history, but we should not presume that it is necessarily natural, much less inevitable. We may now begin to speak of a nature apart from the conceptually loaded term "nature," and also apart from love.

Kracauer of course is not the only person to critique the naturalization of history—but he is among the more prominent postwar intellectuals to promote alienation, dejection, and experiences of desubjectification not as symptoms of late capitalist exploitation but as foundations for critical thought and even future-oriented optimism. Above all, he turns to cinema as a photographic technology that reveals a past and future by redeeming an alien present that would otherwise elude us. Because it "leaves its raw material more or less intact . . . such art as goes into film results from their creators' capacity to read from the book of nature."[86] The environment captured in film is not consumed by its representation. And this notion of alien nature in the raw returns us to the glacial splendor of Antarctica.

ANTARCTICA'S MODERN EXCEPTIONALISM

Mariano Siskind argues that Antarctica stands as an exception to, and thus a critique of, Enlightenment political philosophy, particularly Immanuel Kant's and G. W. F. Hegel's models of world history and the concomitant globalization of reason, commerce, and enduring peace. Against a theory of global modernity that incorporates the entire earth into a narrative of human progress, Antarctica stubbornly refused to yield to this project of planetary enlightenment. In addition to possessing no indigenous people to colonize or bountiful natural resources to mine, Antarctica was, up until the eighteenth century, an exception to modern exploration and projects of empire because it appeared to be impossible to reach.[87] After two unsuccessful attempts, Captain James Cook finally crossed the Antarctic Circle in 1773 and again in 1774. In place of land, he discovered only ice and thus declared Antarctica inaccessible to man and best left to its awful nature. Cook's nondiscovery replaced romantic myths of Antarctic exoticism and fantasies of untapped abundance with a new notion of modern incalculability. Siskind argues that the southern continent's modern specificity is predicated on its resistance to being assimilated into Enlightenment projects that perceived the world "as a modern totality" open to an "ever-expanding colonial network" and what would become the globalization of commerce. The "non-coincidence" of Antarctica with "world history"—or its relegation to a natural history outside of human usefulness (and beyond human knowledge)—makes it "the ultimate exception of the universal premises on the basis of which globalization is imaged, discursively formulated, and carried on." More forcefully still, Antarctica "denounces" as universal these Euro-centric principles of reason and history.[88] In Siskind's reading, Antarctica functions much like photography in Kracauer's writing. Like photography, Antarctica exposes Enlightenment conceptions of nature as culture and requires us to think of history and representation against the norms of German reason.

As Siskind explains, the specificity of Antarctica's modernity is not only its resistance to empire; it also confounds sublime representation, the benchmark aesthetic of extreme natural encounters in the eighteenth century. When Captain Cook first ventured into its icy waters, he beheld "the unexpressable [sic] horrid aspect of the Country, a Country doomed by Nature never once to feel the warmth of the Sun's rays, but to lie for ever buried under every lasting snow and ice." Propelled back to warmer waters, Cook justifies his decision to navigate no farther south. "It would have been rashness in me to have risked all which has been done in the Voyage, in finding out and exploring [sic] a Coast which when done would have answered no end whatever, or been of the least use either to Navigation or Geography or indeed any other Science."[89] Siskind explains that Cook faced a particular horror, of a "nature doomed by nature," for which Edmund Burke's definition of the sublime can only partially account. In the first stage, the encounter with the sublime so overwhelms experience that the distinction between subject and object collapses, and reason abandons the beholder. The second stage re-establishes that distance through the process of representation, narrative, and communication of the sublime impression, and with it, writes Siskind, "the imposition of the codifications of a culture upon nature."[90] He argues that the specificity of the Antarctic sublime produces the overwhelming sensations of the first stage but defies all recourse to reason, or representation and culture. For this reason, Cook was not capable of discovering, naming, or even narrating his Antarctic encounter and so turned away in horror and thus the continent escaped the totalizing logic of reason—this despite the fact that Cook's adventure was a thoroughly modern event.

Siskind's formulation of the Antarctic sublime raises interesting questions in relation to the first cinematic representation of Antarctica. Could it be that cinema, especially as Kracauer theorizes it, is the medium to capture this physical world and bring it into optical consciousness without subsuming it into culture codification, such as narrative? Kracauer argues that there are such horrific phenomena—including war, natural disasters, and sublime nature itself—that may be known only through photographic capture: "These images having nothing in common with the artist's imaginative rendering of an unseen dread but are in the nature of mirror reflections. Now of all the existing media the cinema alone holds up a mirror to nature."[91] In these last two sentences, "nature" describes the quality of cinematic reflections that give us access to a world indirectly, like the dirty puddle in which the world is seen to tremble. "Nature"—what he also calls "crude nature"—is also a catastrophic manifestation in the external world too dreadful to behold.[92] An artist might contain and distort such realities, or invent them whole cloth through the conventions of representation. The camera, however, is more like a mirror reflection, which, like the shield Perseus uses to behead Medusa, "redeem[s] horror from its invisibility behind the veils of panic and imagination." We depend on the camera to reveal scenes that would paralyze us with fear, enabling us to incorporate them into memory. "The film screen is Athena's polished shield," but what is reflected is not something we can act on.[93] If, as Kant argues (after Burke), the sublime is the subjective projection of the perceiving subject and not a property of the object perceived, then might photography and cinema enable us to glimpse Antarctica as raw nature in the caesura between horror and reason?[94] Might we behold the earthly nature of this continent before and apart from the world into which it will eventually become incorporated?

To answer these questions, I turn to two early Antarctica exploration films—or, to be exact, two films about heroically failed expeditions: *South* (1919), an account of Ernest Shackleton's Imperial Trans-Antarctic journey undertaken from 1914 to 1916, and *90° South: With Scott to the Antarctic* (1933), which recounts Robert Falcon Scott's fatal 1912 journey in which he discovered the South Pole a month after Roald Amundsen and then died in the company of two other members of his expedition during the trek back to camp. Though these expeditions were undertaken putatively in the name of science and explicitly for the vainglory of the British Empire, the films were unabashedly commercial ventures. *90° South* cinematographer Herbert G. Ponting, for example, negotiated with Scott for the exclusive right to disseminate images and films from the trip. He was at times regarded as the crew's sole for-profit member.[95] Films were commissioned to offset costs, encourage future expedition investments, and repay debts. While the trade in sealskins and whale oil developed into lucrative ventures on the Antarctic islands (South Georgia, Deception, South Shetland), decimating the seal, whale, and penguin colonies, the Antarctic interior contained no raw materials or riches from which the explorers or Britain would profit and the benefits to science was regarded as negligible.[96] The only guaranteed yield from the adventure was narrative—stories—that explorers would bring back to the home country in the form of lectures, memoirs, and, for the first time with Ponting, a film. As a British publisher assured one polar explorer, his financial future and historical stature would be set provided he returned with a tale "full of human, popular interest."[97] *This* is his demand of a continent "utterly without human interest."[98] The promise of representing and narrativizing Antarctica on film, likewise, would be the trip's primary commodity. Given this mandate, it is curious but not surprising given the conditions of the pole and the state of feature film production that the system of cinematographic representation in both films, fragmentary at the outset, breaks down completely.

The film of Scott's journey, *90° South*, is most interesting with regard to the bifurcation of human history and what appears as a timeless elemental nature. The first cinematographer to accompany an Antarctic expedition, Ponting initially made his film to be serialized, in keeping with the cinema of the early teens. First exhibiting it in installations as a silent travelogue in 1911–1912, Ponting recut the film in 1922 as a silent feature. Then in 1933 he reissued *90° South* with a soundtrack and voiceover narration.[99] The final film retains traces of its exhibitionary history as it labors to both narrate Scott's tragic adventure and represent Antarctica's icy attractions on a continent where, as Ponting himself declares in the film's opening prologue, nature exists "in her most wildest and relentless moods." The film commences with the ship's departure from New Zealand and Ponting treats us to a series of actualities about everyday life on the Terra Nova. A Slavic dance performed by Anton, the Russian "pony man"; a boxing match between two sailors followed by a comic boxing match between two cooks; a shipmate giving another a haircut; the feeding of the dogs—these are scenes that recall the very earliest films by Thomas Edison shot in the Black Maria studio. Upon arrival in icy waters, the film becomes a series of studies in coastal marine life—anthropomorphized accounts of mother and baby seals, penguin parenthood, and the threat killer whales pose to their young. These scenes of "wildlife" compete for photogenic attention with the sled dogs and ponies that stay fit hauling supplies to the various depots that will serve Scott on his southern trek. Ponting's voiceover provides general information about human habits and animal habitats, but it lacks any kind of chronology or sense of narrative purpose. Indeed, Scott and his crew are setting up camp and waiting for the next summer to embark on the journey, and Ponting uses this time to capture images of his polar surround. He then trains his camera on the spectacular "grand desolation" of Antarctica itself: the precipitous Ross Ice Shelf; smoking, looming Mount Erebus; the glacial formations that at times resembles ruins of a strange decayed world; and the deep crevices that threaten ruination to any who traverse them (Figure 5.3). In the momentary stillness of this ancient freeze, cinema becomes indistinguishable from photographs (or, to be more exact, from filmed photographs), except in those instances when sea ice breaks, a penguin appears, or one of Scott's crew members wanders into the frame for the effect of perspective and animation.

The film reveals ice to us as a soulless, inassimilable phenomenon outside of historical significance. This becomes most evident when, fifty minutes into this seventy-minute film, Captain Scott commences his fatal journey to the pole as promised in the title, the most emotional, harrowing, and disappointing slog that would be at the heart of any narrative film about this expedition.[100] Yet this shift to adventure narrative is paradoxically also the shift away from modern cinema, as Ponting's voiceover narrative momentarily gives way to intertitles, and sound cinema momentarily reverts to its silent system of signification. Because the movie camera was too cumbersome for Scott to carry to the pole (and because it was too dangerous for Ponting to accompany him), the cinematic record ends just

Figure 5.3 The Ross ice shelf. *90° South: With Scott to the Antarctic* (1933).

as Scott's journey to the pole begins. In the film, cinema gives way to still photography and then photographs give way to drawings and maps. Once he embarks for the South Pole, never to return to base camp, cinema, in sympathy perhaps, also withdraws.

Ponting justified his exclusion from the expedition by noting that in the landscape beyond the Great Ice Barrier, "there would be nothing to photograph but the level plane of boundless, featureless ice, with the long caravan stringing out towards the horizon." Twenty-five miles inland, Antarctica and the specific terrain of Scott's journey finally disappear altogether as the men venture even deeper into what Ponting in his memoir names "the heart of the Great Alone."[101] For minutes at a time, the camera scans a hand-drawn panorama of a turbulent sky over windswept ground seen from an almost impossible vantage point as Ponting's voiceover carries completely the burden of narrating Scott's efforts the reach the pole, (only to find Amundsen's flag and encampment claiming first discovery) and then Scott's tragic, fatal trek back to the base (Figure 5.4). Dying with his companions from cold and starvation only eleven miles from one of their depots, Scott's once-lively body is represented finally only by his written words. As this story is narrated, a photograph occasionally

Figure 5.4 An etching of an Antarctic landscape in place of photographs or film of Scott's expedition. *90° South: With Scott to the Antarctic* (1933).

offers a generic vision of the terrain, as though we are cutting into a closer scenic detail of the etching. Thus, as this medially schizophrenic film shifts into a historical, narrative mode of human experience, specifically the experience of numbness, snow blindness, and inner turmoil, its representational system transforms Antarctica from a specific, cinematic space into a transcendental resting place for England's fallen heroes. It is as if natural and human history cannot coincide on film. The first is too vast, endless (a key term for Kracauer), and opaque to tell in its totality. The second, reduced to a tragic, heroic narrative, is what Kracauer calls "the uncinematic aura of history," too small and too contained for the medium of film.[102] The final image of the adventure is a hand-rendered sketch of Scott's grave, as if Ponting, knowing Kracauer's reading of photographs of the Rhine, feared that his photograph of this very view might undercut the site's mythic import. Filming this site, it seems, was out of the question.

André Bazin has observed of this and other exploration documentaries that what we do not see on film attests to the authenticity of what remains: "The missing documents are the negative imprints of an expedition," which the protagonists experienced but were too occupied with various obstacles to be able to film. Such documentaries present us with "the premature ruins of a film that was never completed."[103] Kracauer, though he would agree that the documentary is far superior to any staged re-enactment or fictionalization, would also point to the incommensurability of tragedy and cinema, especially with the pathos of Scott's demise. Tragedy "presupposes a finite, ordered cosmos."[104] It is, he writes, quoting Proust, "'a whole with a purpose,' more often than not an ideological purpose," and is "an exclusively mental experience which has no correspondences in camera-reality."[105] The environment of film, by contrast, "is a flow of random events involving both humans and inanimate objects" far beyond human experience and even interest.[106] Whereas tragedy has recourse to the pathetic fallacies of symbolic storms and weather designed by gods or human authors to match the protagonists' feelings, in the cinema, writes Kracauer, now quoting Roger Caillois: "There is no cosmos on the screen. But an earth, trees, the sky, streets and railways: in short, matter." Kracauer concludes that there is an aesthetically determined clash between "the preferences of the medium and the tragic hero's death. His end marks an absolute end: time comes to a stop when he dies. It is evident that this ultimate solution runs counter to the camera's ingrained desire for indefinite rambling."[107] Antarctica's affront to the British hero's death is that the continent continues, indifferent to the history that has played out on its surface. Ponting saves Scott and his model of English masculinity from the insult of the ice's persistence by concluding the film with Scott's ending. In doing so, he also abandons the animated, cinematic image.[108] When fragments give way to tragic narrative in Antarctica, cinema also comes to an end.

We find a similarly incoherent pattern in the remarkable film *South: Ernest Shackleton and the Endurance Expedition,* Frank Hurley's document of Shackleton's astonishing and failed attempt to traverse Antarctica from the Weddell Sea to the Ross Sea via the South Pole. The film begins in 1914 when the *Endurance* sets sail from Buenos Aires. Scenes of daily life revolve almost exclusively around the very photogenic sled dogs until the ship arrives in Antarctic water. Fascinated by the patterns of pack ice and the ship's power to break through it, Hurley continually put himself at great risk to achieve extraordinary views by suspending the camera from a mount on the jib or by perching himself in the crow's nest. In several shots, we can hardly distinguish sky from ice, except that the ship's topmast casts a divine shadow of a cross on the frozen mass below (Figure 5.5). In one especially sensational early-cinema moment, Hurley cranks the camera as the *Endurance* makes it way directly toward him, breaking up the very ice on which he stands. Bringing to mind the modern dangers animated in the Lumière Brothers' *Arrival of a Train at La Ciotat* (1896) and Cecil Hepworth's *How It Feels to Be Run Over* (1900), Hurley, like Ponting before him,

Figure 5.5 The ship's mast casts a divine shadow on the ice below. *South* (1919).

stages attractions for the camera that are no less endangering for having been planned. When the ship becomes trapped in the frozen Weddell Sea more than three hundred miles from land, Hurley films the *Endurance* and the icescape in lateral pans and horizontal tilts. Contemporary critic Fred Camper remarks that these panoramas "look almost like choreographed attempts to depict a scene too awesome to be easily encompassed. [These shots are] less an attempt to provide meaning here than a way of adding visual pleasure to an otherwise monotonous landscape of white."[109] Somewhere between awesome and monotonous, Antarctica, when it can be represented, resists narration. Hurley's own inclinations are to keep with the continent's white indistinctiveness. While he shows us a few of the activities that keep the men productively occupied once they are ice-locked, the crew's other shipboard distractions (the stage plays, the lectures, the singing competitions, all of the ways the men produced a little world in the ship) are absent from this film. Preferring the reign of icy exteriority, Hurley provides no interior (mental or physical) views.

Shortly after the *Endurance*'s hull succumbs to the "attack of the ice" and the crew abandons ship, Hurley is forced to desert his cinematograph, but not before capturing chilling images of the ship being crushed by the mounting ice and the men's efforts to salvage provisions. Once "the real troubles and hardships commenced," a title tells us, the filming comes to an end. The men drift on their frozen encampment, a stretch of the journey we see only through a series of still photographic images (Figure 5.6). Because this is a silent film, moreover, there is no voiceover to animate the account. Intertitles begin to narrate things not shown, and even the intertitles omit many of the most dramatic moments. These include the weeklong voyage to Elephant Island, the drama of one of the crew falling through the ice and nearly to his death, and the ragged state of the men when they finally reach land.[110] A single etching shown for a few seconds stands in for Shackleton's seventeen-day, eight-hundred-mile voyage to South George Island, considered one of the most heroic and oft-narrated maritime adventures in history (Figure 5.7). But Hurley wants us to experience something of the duration of the drama that follows. So once again, as the story moves forward and the most historic events unfold, the image track reverts to etchings, photographs, and filmed scenes taken before the ship sank or rendered long after the men's rescue: scenes of marine animal life, landscapes on the continent and on South George Island.[111] Shackleton undertook this expedition during World War I, whose global conflict is wholly absent from both the continent and the film until an intertitle makes this oblique reference to history: the whale blubber harvested at the South George whaling station is used for munitions. These massive, flayed whale bodies docked in the bay

Figure 5.6 Having abandoned both the ship and the film camera, Shackleton's crew pose for a photograph at their new frozen encampment. *South* (1919).

Figure 5.7 Shackleton's eight-hundred-mile journey to South Georgia Island is captured in this single drawing. *South* (1919).

are suggestive of the carnage such weapons will produce on the other side of the world.[112] Overwhelmingly, the high points of drama and world history are beyond the concreteness of Hurley's camera.

Kracauer helps us to read these texts as films not just about physical reality graspable with the camera; they also attest to the impossibility of narrating this reality and of capturing these natural phenomena without turning away in horror. Failing to record the heroic adventures, discoveries, and resolutely human experiences, these temporally discontinuous films succeed in archiving a heterogeneous ecology of ice, shorelines, men and animals, ice and sky, and apparently empty interiors, and thus provide future historians with the raw materials of an alternate history, even an alternative *natural* history of Antarctica itself. From the vantage of our current moment, Hurley's images, compared with contemporary photographs of the glaciers in South George Island, reveal a pattern of retreating ice and diminished wildlife populations. That is, his film, which set out to tell us about human adventure, has become most useful for natural history.[113] Indeed, these films capture what is largely excluded from such standard accounts as David Day's *Antarctica: A Biography*, which is a history of the continent as human history—the exploration, international diplomacy, and usefulness of Antarctica to the various people and nations that have claimed it as part of their own national experiments. It begins with Cook and ends with the rise of boutique adventure tourism. These films, which are also about adventures and discovery, attest to the bios of the continent itself and to the importance of photography and cinema that record the polar extreme as a physical reality outside of human history. We find a continent whose icy abstractions may be one of its more specific features.

But let us be clear. These are representations of ice, animals, men, and ships. Though both films struggle (and at times fail) to make interesting the monotonous, abstract expanse, several shots by Ponting especially are framed according to genres of Romantic pictorialism. Ponting was drawn to formations such as the now-iconic "ice grotto" that resembled "a veritable Aladdin's Cave of beauty," and the "Castle Berg," which arose out of "the ruins" of a collapsed ice arch, appearing to him "a perfect medieval fortress" (Figure 5.8).[114] Hurley framed images of the *Endurance* miles away and through a coulisse of ice boulders in the foreground, a photograph resembling Caspar David Friedrich's *Das Eismeer* (*The Sea of Ice*, 1823–1825) painted almost half a century after Cook's nonsublime encounter with Antarctica (Figure 5.9). Confronted by an otherworldly nature, Ponting and Hurley impose onto the continent the familiar gravitas of Romantic landscape painting as if to access the realm of the sublime. However, as

Figure 5.8 Ponting's "Castle Berg." *90° South: With Scott to the Antarctic* (1933).

Figure 5.9 *The Endurance* seen from a romantic distance. *South* (1919).

Joseph Leo Koerner explains, Friedrich resisted the scientific renderings of landscape not because he was committed to the capacities of human calculation or imagination, but because he wanted to capture the "obscurity" of the external world and the "radical alterity of nature itself."[115] It may be that the Romantic imaginary finds its photo-finish when humans photograph the Great White South. Despite the similarities of compositions, Ponting's photographs cannot transcend the terrestrial physicality of his subjects.

Writing on the romantic fascination with ice, Eric G. Wilson differentiated between two modes of vision, exoteric and esoteric, that the magnetic poles inspire and that may help us to parse this aesthetic conundrum:

> The exoteric way of seeing is interested in external surfaces, understandable visibilities and social orders. The mode of cognition—shared by orthodox forms of Christianity, political systems and conventional sciences—often views ice as a deathly coldness to be transcended, raw material to be converted into commodity, or static matter to be reduced to law. The esoteric perspective considers internal depths, invisible mysteries and individual experiences. This mode of vision . . . frequently sees icescapes as revelation of an abysmal origin, marriages of opposites, merging of microcosm and macrocosm.[116]

According to this duality, there is no mode of apprehending Antarctica and ice that has recourse to scientific or visionary abstraction. On one hand, the alien nature of Antarctica transforms landscape painting from a genre of art into the hard data of science. Stephen J. Pyne observes that Antarctica serves as a kind of "'ready-made' modernist landscape" in the spirit of Kazimir Malevich's *White on White* (1918), a turn to elemental basics of painting minus the mimetic feints of representation—a shuttling between the antihumanist alterity of materials and transmundane self-reference. Aesthetic modernism, he explains, requires the history of landscape painting and the background of human culture for its extreme refusal of tradition to register as such. Antarctica, already purified and distilled, does modernism one better; it arrived into consciousness already depleted, extreme, acultural, ahistorical, and elemental. Modernism meets its match in the South Pole and, as Pyne reads it, turns on its heel and heads back for the metropolis. "The social context [of Antarctica] was impossible: modern art was done in lofts, not on sledging expeditions."[117] But film and photography present a different set of challenges; they merge or dissolve altogether seemingly distinct esoteric and exoteric abstractions of ice. The problem of differentiating the two, or the task of distinguishing a representation from its object or clearly delineating cinema's formative traditions against its realist possibilities, not only sounds the affront of Antarctica to the desire for representation but also echoes the critiques leveled against Kracauer's conception of reality in *Theory of Film*.

BECOMING EXTRATERRESTRIAL

Miriam Hansen notes in her introduction to Kracauer's book that *Theory of Film* almost immediately became the target of "critical demolition."[118] Soon after its publication, academic film theory exploded any notion that film after Auschwitz was the end of ideology; film before and after war *was* ideology, and Kracauer was dismissed as proffering a naive and outdated theory of cinematic realism. On the other extreme, Pauline Kael declared this book a real cinephilic downer for its pedantry and refusal simply to yield to the pleasure of film. She concludes with this quip: "There are men whose concept of love is so boring and nagging that you decide if that's what love is, you don't want it, you want something else. That's how I feel about Kracauer's 'cinema.'"[119] His cinephilia is not unsophisticated, only monotonous. But one review, in particular, merits sustained attention because it generously critiques the book's reality principle while appreciating the radicality of Kracauer's vision.

Rather predictably, Rudolf Arnheim, art historian, Gestalt psychologist, and film theorist, chafed at Kracauer's overvaluation of cinematic reality as the only proper aesthetic focus of the medium. More than this, he questioned physical reality as being identical to those elements of the world that are available to human perception: "To the best of our understanding we live in a world in which the constellations of basic forces run the gamut from the simplest order to unfathomable complexity." Kracauer's description of cinema thus redeems "not 'physical reality' but a particular view of the world, cherished—to use a handy term—by realistic romanticism."[120] Moreover, if the goal in Kracauer's theory is to reconnect humans with the material world, Arnheim claims that it may not be photographic realism so much as childlike, or even primitive, stylization that is "the prototype of genuine concreteness, or elementary closeness to reality," because it reproduces, at the most basic level, processes by which we translate sensory data into manageable, perceivable forms.[121] Echoing his own arguments in *Film as Art* (1932), Arnheim explains that physical reality in the raw eludes perception and renders objects invisible and abstract. The realistic tendency in photography, as well as in modern Western art (he references the impressionists and Jean Dubuffet), point to a gradual "decline in visibility, complementary to an increasing surrender of the formative capacity of the human mind to the raw material of experience. . . . It is clear that this abandonment of pattern . . . is nothing but the yearning for the unshaped, a return to the raw material of reality."[122] The decrease in visibility—or the decline in the formative tradition in art—occurs when the materials "are no longer a means of representation but as objects for their own sake." Paint as paint. In place of mimetic forms representing the world, art objects are "additions to the material world itself."[123] And this "matter" is akin to the chaotic, elemental environment "before the Creation." Turning away from form, "the artist of a late civilization" takes refuge from reality and "escapes from the duty of man" and the burdens of history.[124] The modernist avant-garde and its fixation on materials does not move us into a spiritual future so much as it returns us to a prehuman past. And when photography and cinema move away from form to fragmentary reality, they likewise do not correct Kracauer's sense of the prevailing abstractness but serve as its supreme examples.

It is useful to clarify that abstraction, in Arnheim's theory, is a distillation of the external world, including organic life, into its most legible and basic form. Like caricatures or stick figures, abstraction is simplified mimesis, which manages to function as representation because human perception is limited and partial and takes in only the most salient features or forms of the external world. Art, then, projects this distilled form onto the world and forms the world itself according to a rational, human need for "meaningful order."[125] This account contrasts with Wilhelm Worringer's psychology of abstraction in his famous 1908 *Abstraction and Empathy* to which Kracauer's *Theory of Film* and early writings on photography merit comparison. For Worringer, abstraction is a response (first found in primitive and premodern art) to the spiritual dread of space, to the "great unrest inspired in man by the phenomena of the outside world."[126] Humans turn to abstraction as a coping mechanism "to seek deliverance from the fortuitousness of humanity as a whole, from the seeming arbitrariness of organic existence in general."[127] Kracauer, as we have seen, encourages spectators to fall headlong into the disarrayed reality (whose features are precisely the fortuitous and contingent) to free them from the false totalities of ideological and scientific abstraction and the seemingly determined present and future they forecast. Worringer pinpoints what he takes to be a transhistorical human anxiety in its encounter with the randomness of nature. Opposed to abstraction is the "urge to empathy" whereby "aesthetic enjoyment is objectified self-enjoyment" expressed in representational art. The empathetic subject does not commune with nature, but projects herself and her feeling into and into the world. The truly aesthetic encounter with life-denying nature is not in the sublime, for Worringer, but in abstraction that "wrests the object of the external world out of its natural context, out of the unending flux of being, . . . to approximate its absolute value."[128] Modernist abstraction, like the abstract geometries of the ancient pyramids, reawakens a sense of the "thing in itself."[129] While Arnheim and Worringer connect modernist art to prehistoric (or, in Arnheim's case, primordial) existence, Worringer values abstractions as the antidote to both romantic self-projection and naturalism's confidence in the relationship between humans and nature, its overall world reverence.[130] And yet Worringer's abstract art fulfills the function of all art: "the maximum bestowal of happiness for the humanity that created it."[131] For Kracauer, the art of cinema casts us out of form and feeling.

Despite these differences, Arnheim concedes that Kracauer compellingly diagnoses the "melancholy in photographic vision." I quote the entire passage from *Theory of Film* that Arnheim excerpts in his review:

> Now melancholy as an inner disposition not only makes elegiac objects seem attractive but carries still another more important implication: it favors self-estrangement, which on its part entails identification with all kind of objects. The dejected individual is likely to see himself in the incidental configurations of his environment, absorbing them with a disinterested intensity no longer determined by his previous preference.[132]

This disinterest, comments Arnheim, is a melancholic surrender to unshaped matter, not a "recovery of man's grip on reality."[133] Yet Kracauer gets something right in his description of the present predicament. We may indeed, writes Arnheim, be in the "last twitches of an exhausted civilization, whose rarified concepts no longer reach the world of the senses. But it is also possible that by cleansing the mind of all shapes, we are approaching the nadir which we must touch in order to rise again . . . so that the scenes of life" may return.[134] Photography's abstraction abets this process.

In Kracauer's account, physical reality is neither so elemental nor chaotic as to be imperceptible, and implicitly he rejects the Gestalt model of mental mapping, its presumption of wholes, and idealist theories of perception, which posit the world known as one whose shape is already mentally formed. Certainly, he rejects a definition of art as that which is productive of human happiness. Art, such that it functions, leads to a clear-eyed attunement to the fragmented world. *Theory of Film* is written with the hope that photography and cinema not only can break habituated ways of seeing (that is Arnheim's claim in *Film as Art*) but also may redeem the physical world from our ideas and feelings about it. As David

Trotter remarks of Kracauer's book: "The direction of the [camera's] gaze is not upwards . . . towards moral intention, but downwards into material existence."[135] We might presume from Trotter's comments that Kracauer's downward, dejected (demoralized?) glance is opposed to and even counter to a moral theory of film. Or we can read this downward orientation as extending to the spectator an outright desubjectivized view of existence, a vision that models a selfless history of the future and promotes estrangement as the basis for postapocalyptic environmental thought. The term for this guarded or ambivalent optimism is *extraterritoriality*.

Gerhard Richter explains of Kracauer's late writing that *extraterritoriality* describes a relationship to a place that can no longer be experienced as home. It captures the fact of "homeless dwelling" in the world, of "dwelling within homelessness itself": "For something to exist in a state of extraterritoriality means to depart from territory as a space and as an idea while still remaining deeply attached to it, that is, attached to it precisely in the act of departing from it." For Richter, Kracauer's fixation on extraterritoriality is a symptom of political and social exile, of not belonging to a place where one lives, of feeling, as Richter writes, "extra," "superfluous," and "outside" of a territory. At the same time, it encapsulates Kracauer's philosophical sense, as Kracauer himself writes, that permanently residing in a "so-called home" is "really unnatural": "Existence as a vagabond is the only true thing."[136] Outside of a territory, an extra to it, Kracauer helps us to unfold a rich notion of territory itself. Again, Richter illuminates the antinomies of "territory," a word that, on one hand, denotes a place that is "settled, circumscribed, defined, articulated and distinguished" as a distinct political or geographical area.[137] On the other hand, territory shares an etymology with *terror* and a *territor* (one who frightens), designating an area "from which people are warned off." Territory at once marks the earth—terra—as a settling place we may call home and designates as terrifying an area that will not be settled. As Richter speculates, territory harbors within it the *unheimlichkeit* of settlement, the idea that "the home that the territory provides cannot be thought apart from terror itself."[138] While *extra*territoriality may be an intensification or excess of these unsettling feelings, in Kracauer's usage it indexes the alienated subject between or even beyond the comforts and terrors that the earth and the human home summon forth. As an optics on the earth that is our habitat, extraterritoriality may even estrange us from any kind of physical or philosophical grounding. In Kracauer's *History*, writes Elena Gualtieri, "photography does not present us with the physical reality which abstract thought prevents us from seeing. Its function is rather that of shaking our belief in the visible, and in the presumption that the visible exhausts the real." Photography becomes a conceptual technology through which humanity may approach an extravisual, extraterritorial, utopic nonspace "between established truths and dogmas."[139] In other words, photography in Kracauer's last writing is an invitation into a virtual, almost imperceptible world far from the anguish of exile.

Kracauer's celebration of cinema in these terms attracts me as a rejoinder, if not correction, to more recent aesthetic and ecocritical theory that moves beyond the fetishization of subjectivity, without abandoning sensual form or even love itself. As the title of his now-classic 2007 book announces, Timothy Morton wants us to explore the generative possibilities of environmental aesthetics in the name of a critical practice he calls an "ecology without nature." Because nature has become, and perhaps as a concept has always been, ideological, abstract, and transcendental, Morton argues that we cannot think of nature or formulate meaningful critiques of our ecological predicament so long as "nature" is still in the mix. Instead, ecocriticism needs to reflect on its own methods, vocabulary, and meaning, and to consider how nature itself is conjured in literary form: "Ideology resides in the attitude we assume toward this fascinating object [nature]. By dissolving the object, we render the ideological fixation inoperative."[140] Because there is no nature without discourse, Morton takes us into the realm of aesthetics and argues for a "gothic" relation to "dark ecology." This gothic "apocalypticism" brings us into contact with a frightening nature that we can neither incorporate nor commodify, and which may be similar to that suspended sublime that is unique to the Antarctic encounter at the end of the world. Dark ecology revolves around "the idea that we want to stay with a dying world" wherein we learn "to love the thingness . . . the mute, objectified quality of the object, its radical nonidentity."[141] Kracauer, a survivor of apocalypse, writing after the apocalypse, would also reject as ideological an apocalyptic embrace of the future. Indeed, far more sanguine in his outlook, Kracauer was trying to arrive at an objective perception, even hope, through the media of film and photography. As he puts it: "Guided by film . . . we approach if at all, ideas no longer on the highway leading through the void but on paths that wind through the thicket of things."[142] Out of this thicket of raw material and cinematically induced sensations, a new (and we might say after Antarctica) cold love for inert, physical reality may emerge—one that even Arnheim admitted had the potential to bring about new, radical thought and therefore strategies of survival in a damaging world erected on an earth that persists beyond us. Thinking like extraterrestrials, we may be able to form nonbinding attachments to hostile places we have never called home, to care for an environment that exists in our absence, and to cultivate "disinterested" identification with an unaccommodating ecosystem undetermined by "previous preference."[143]

As the only continent that has resisted permanent settlement (people who winter over are on a limited tour), with no native population (hundreds have died but only about a dozen babies have been born in Antarctic research stations, none of whom who have grown up on the continent), and with no sovereignty of its own—that is, as a place that has stood apart from and thus has served as a critique of the global project of human worlding—Antarctica is as close to an extraterritory as we are likely to find. For this reason, NASA uses the South Pole for what it calls "analog studies" for astronauts in training. Antarctica is more like Mars than it resembles other places on Earth.[144] Even politically, the continent is suggestive of interstellar diplomacy. Because it involved so many nations making symbolic claims on abstract territory, the Antarctic Treaty established in 1959, writes David Day, "provided a precedence of dealing with sovereignty in outer space."[145] While contentious, the treaty is so far working. This is also the only continent without a history of war and the only destination to which anyone may travel (and live, if possible) without a visa or a passport. Though hardly the place to provide refuge for the homeless, Antarctica may be the last resort for the stateless subject, the only place for people without papers.[146] Its political culture continues to astound. In a recent opinion piece on jihadism, a *New York Times* columnist offhandedly remarked: "Antarctica is the only continent that remains untouched by extremism in the 21st century."[147] Political extremism—and perhaps politics itself—cannot coexist with Antarctica's physical extremes. And thus, I wonder if Antarctica, having for so long eluded visual capture and so productive of numbing experience, is *the* no-place—a utopia on Earth. If so, its melting is not only of the utmost environmental importance but also a matter of political and philosophical urgency.

Today, the Antarctic has yielded to human interest. There are no places or times of year on the continent when filming (digital filming mostly) is prohibitive. Antarctica is fully part of the human world—a territory mapped, named, and mostly known—and it is featured daily in the "breaking news." Once considered a no-man's land "buried in everlasting snow and ice" whose geological history was cordoned off from human nature, Antarctica is now enveloped in the Anthropocene. As I write this sentence, the world has its eye on an iceberg the size of Delaware that has just detached from the Lársen C ice shelf on the east side of the Antarctic Peninsula, requiring that a new map of the continent be created. Glaciologists worry that this calving event will accelerate the rate of the continent's ice flow into the ocean, thereby raising sea levels.[148] Its fast-morphing topography—too fast and vast for cinema—comes to us now through satellite images, remote radar sensors, and digital films often taken from helicopters assessing the effects of human-caused climate change on the ice. Antarctica has become, in a sense, a digital object, a virtual place, and the source of much speculation. In the future, some predict, Antarctica's frozen masses will melt altogether and the continent will join an iceless planet.[149] Its once-exceptional terrain, which has so unsettled human meaning, will become just another part of the world. Without Antarctica to remind us of our own extraterrestrial nature, we will have to return to photography and cinema to glimpse an otherworldly truth and to ponder an earth apart from human meaning.

Conclusion

The Epoch and the Archive

What is the hospitality of cinema in the time of the Anthropocene? In Kracauer's theory, cinema welcomes the viewer to a world made *unheimlich* through the effect of the camera's inhuman optics. The image is for *us*—the human spectators—and yet, in it, the human is potentially just another thing among things, subject to the technology's indifference. Cinema can show us a world without human bodies in it and—still more extreme—it can capture space and time in ways that escape human meaning and feeling altogether. This is the case not just because the camera produces an image mechanically, without the intervention of the human hand.[1] Stanley Cavell writes that cinema "maintains the presentness of the world by accepting our absence from it," and thus film makes our displacement from the world and our denatured state appear to be our "natural condition" through our own actions and technological innovations.[2] By temporally displacing the world, moreover, film "confirms, even explains, our prior estrangement from it."[3] Such that cinema images a world that does not revolve around the human figure, that it has the capacity to reveal an earth without human meaning, and that displacement in film is our *natural* condition, cinema also unsettles our presumed natural right to impose upon the planet's hospitality. If, in the image, humanity enjoys no necessary priority over other animate and inanimate matter, by what right do we humans claim possession of the world and submit the planet to our designs? In Keaton's slapstick environment, in the rental flats of film noir, in the disappearing city of Fengjie, and on the icy shores of Antarctica (to say nothing of the atomic testing range), the world and its nature are as alien as they are alienating. This nature, in most instances a product of human design, does not appear to care for human beings.

Over time, these fabricated cinematic worlds and the human culture they archive may become part of nature as they settle into the geological record. Something of this media archeology comes to us today in Bill Morrison's masterpiece *Dawson City: Frozen Time* (2016), a film composed largely of scenes from semidecomposed nitrate films that were buried in the Yukon Valley's permafrost in 1929 and then excavated in 1978. Host to the gold-digging boom of the late nineteenth century, Dawson City was the "end of the line" for film distribution. Movies arrived to the city's small theaters two or three years after their initial release. In this, the *last* last-run market in North America, films played out the end of their commercial lives. Rather than pay to ship back films that had no value, distributors instructed the theater owners simply to dispose of their goods, all of which eventually found their way into the surrounding earth. Most of the prints were floated down the Yukon River with the rest of the city's trash during the spring thaw, while others were burned (purposefully or accidentally). In 1929, well over five hundred feature films (more than fifteen hundred reels of nitrate film) were crated and placed into the drained Dawson City pool to serve as a landfill when it was paved over to create a permanent base for the city's ice rink. In the intervening decades, the permafrost on which the entire city rests kept many of the reels from totally decomposing and the entire film collection from spontaneously combusting, as nitrate film stock is prone to do. When new construction broke ground in the late 1970s, the backhoe exposed reels of flammable film that were mingled with detritus beneath the ice rink. As a chronotope, "the end of the line" in this film designates both the geographic end of the modern world near the Arctic Circle and the temporal end of cinema's commodity status. At this cinematic graveyard, film does not so much die but, in its devalued form, accumulates as volatile refuse. In 1978, this hazardous material was revalued as a lost cultural heritage and restored, as such. What exactly had been exhumed?

The Dawson City Film Find, as this collection is called, most obviously provides a rich and material record of the world that flickered past Dawson City's movie-goers from 1900 to 1929. Melodramas and westerns, newsreels, travelogues, and occasional science and industrial films, many of which have not been seen since their initial release, provided an escape from the often harsh and desperate conditions of subarctic prospecting. Going to the movies, townspeople glimpsed and in some way participated in the world history (the entertainment, war, and sports) unfolding elsewhere on the planet. The fables of life on the Yukon frontier, in turn, inspired a few Hollywood movies and mesmerized spectators in other community theaters, many of whom joined the gold-mining stampede. This is a history of film and a history of spectatorship that is at once unique to Dawson City and also indicative of Hollywood's "vernacular modernism," as Miriam Hansen has formulated it. The films shown in Dawson City were produced out of the conditions of "mass production, mass consumption, and mass annihilation" and they were distributed internationally.[4] Thematizing the tolls and possibilities of modern experience, Hollywood films (especially, she argues) appealed to global audiences, people who went to the movies in the hopes of escaping, understanding, or confronting in the form of entertainment different but no less shocking forms of modernization, urbanization, and the aspirational cultures of wealth accumulation. The Dawson City Film Find, in other words, indicates what people in Dawson City watched and is likely indicative of the films that circulated and appealed to audiences all over the world from the early teens to the late 1920s.

Drawing on the photographs and home movies from Dawson City's historical society, Morrison also provides a discrete microhistory of the city outside of the movie theater. He documents its many booms and busts since its founding, including the fires that incinerated the entire town annually in its first nine years. Toward the end of the film, Morrison's camera scans an aerial photograph of the Yukon valley transformed by decades of hydroelectric mining and riverbed dredging, processes we see demonstrated in the gold-mining documentaries. This once-pristine hunting ground of the aboriginal Han people, which we spy briefly in photos at the beginning of the film, appears, by the end, to be a veritable moonscape. Local history telescopes a larger story of an excavating, terra-forming humanity: the vernacular Anthropocene. Dawson City's film culture and its resource extraction are both singular (as are all local histories) and exemplary. And we must presume that at the end of other film distribution lines, other caches of film were burned, drowned, or buried at the distributor's request.

What makes Morrison's film rather exceptional, however, is that these two cultural histories are interwoven with natural histories of a different order. In the first instance, Morrison creates montages from the found footage: people walking, kissing, swooning, knocking on doors, strolling down hallways, dancing, gambling, crying, laughing, sleeping, and even watching movies. Taken out of narrative context and brought back to life, these black-and-white silent creatures exhibit serial behavior whose causes, detached from their original story, remain mysterious. Watching these snippets of films from decades past, we apprehend not characters, but people; not costumes, but clothing; not sets, but interiors; and not acting, but being. *Dawson City* turns fiction film into a kind of anthropological database of gestures, emotions, and expressions. It is an archive of the way some people, a species of celluloid life-forms, have moved, lived, emoted, and died.

In second instance, Morrison unearths a natural history of chemical reactions. The Dawson City Film Find is an archive of decay, specifically water damage to celluloid, and the fortuitous aesthetics of a decomposed human world on film. On the edges of many frames the photographic content dissolves into its abstract chemical substrate; this is what film archivists refer to as the "Dawson flutter."[5] As any viewer of Morrison's *Decasia* (2002) might expect, we perceive simultaneously these two properties, or layers of celluloid (mimetic and chemical). But we also apprehend a prophetic tension between the two registers: the intact photographic part of the image appears to struggle against the forces of its undoing and suddenly those decontextualized human gestures become defensive postures. In the film's final montage, human figures are improbably responding to the encroaching water damage in the frame, trying to talk to it, shake hands with it, and escape from it. It is as if these characters already, at the time of filming, sense the fate of their image to be buried or submerged. Their resistance to the image's dissolution is both comic and poignant. The melancholy of many of Morrison's films is that celluloid (nitrate), though it is fragile and self-destructive, decays rapturously and often with foretelling meaning. These images are perhaps all that remain of these once lively beings and their worlds, and they, along with this singular damage, would disappear altogether had they not been disentombed. For film archivists, it is nothing short of a tragedy that so many films have been lost to the elements out of mismanagement and indifference (a title in *Dawson City* declares that 75 percent of all nitrate films have been lost). To save his own work from this fate, Morrison has placed a thirty-five-millimeter copy of *Dawson City: Frozen Time* in the Museum of Modern Art's climate-controlled film vault, where it will be protected from natural elements including unnatural disaster.[6] These are all expressions of a fear and grief that film, art, and the human culture that gives them meaning will eventually disappear.

Indeed, watching this film, we may marvel that any moving picture has survived. Because all nitrate film inevitably decomposes over time and degrades with each viewing, it defies its own status as a permanent record of a performance, a historical event, a passing fad, or moving fiction. That nitrate is also highly flammable, that its combustion has destroyed buildings and small towns and ended flesh-and-blood lives, suggests that in recording and archiving the living world, we not only destroy the image but also threaten to erase the very world captured in it (*Dawson City* recounts numerous film fires, including those that erupted in the city itself). Nitrate celluloid is, in this sense, an anarchic medium that literalizes the paradox of all archives. "The anarchiving destruction," writes Jacques Derrida, "belongs to the process of archivization and produces the very thing it reduces, on occasion to ashes, and beyond."[7] What drives preservation and the creation of the archive is the knowledge and fear of death and an acute sense that the collective culture and its laws must be recorded to persist beyond the event of annihilation. And yet, as Derrida writes, "the movement of [the archive's] inscription is the very possibility of its effacement."[8] In one of his thought pieces, Derrida considers thermonuclear war as the ultimate threat to the archive. This hypothetical event, which would reduce everything to nothing, has had the very real effect of prompting nuclear countries, especially, to proliferate everything—atomic bombs, atomic-proof homes, films, communications, and a host of official and unofficial, secret and open archives—at hypertrophic rates. While nuclear war was the event to be avoided and so far averted, the Cold War, what he called "the fabulous war effort," persists as a profoundly accumulated reality.[9] This is how the archive grows in proportion with (perhaps in excesses of) the forces of its destruction. The more capable human cultures become of total annihilation, the more detailed and durable become their traces. These are the negative dialectics (more durable archives inspire more powerful modes of destruction) that mark an intersection between the archive and the Anthropocene epoch, or the Anthropocene epoch *as* the ultimate human archive inscribed into and onto the planet.

Read through an Anthropocene critique, however, *Dawson City: Frozen Time* intimates how the archive itself is a source for pathos. In the film's brief considerations of a landscape undone by human activity, rivers littered with reels of film, environments made toxic by nitrate fires, land filled with highly flammable stock, and film stock itself manufactured through toxic processes, the film raises the dismal possibility not that humanity will disappear without a trace, but rather that the planet will itself become a human archive without any "natural" remainders. The melancholy of the Anthropocene, in other words, is not human extinction or frailty in the face of inclement weather, rising tides, or even atomic war, but the *impossibility* of eliminating the human and its residuum from the planet. The last image of *Dawson City* emblematizes the human as this chemical trace.

A woman dances with ecstatic abandon while around her the Dawson flutter appears to take part in the merriment. Soon the decay and human figure become one, and water damage looks more like a chemical conflagration. It is not so much that the human has been engulfed by this amorphous nature; the human has *become* it. I take this damaged image of the past as the invitation from cinema to a future. In this (and in most of the images from this film), we may see our world and human selves as already a kind of strange species. Over the deep time of the ages (or epochs), this once-contemporary culture will become in Kracauer's phrasing "peculiar, like an ocean-dwelling octopus."[10] Who knows? Maybe our film culture, or its chemical substances, will in the future appear strange *to* an ocean-dwelling octopus given how many films have surely made their way into the ocean, and presuming these creatures manage to survive us. The invitation of cinema in the time of the Anthropocene may then not be for us, after all. For the future life forms who excavate or penetrate the earth and encounter our traces (including our media culture in some form), we will be the nature upon which they create their worlds and rituals of hospitality. It will be against some version or image of "us" that they, in Srinivas Aravamudan's words, will "spell out their difference and articulate their critique."[11]

Figure 6.1 A figure dances ecstatically until she is engulfed by the water damage in (and to) the image. *Dawson City: Frozen Time* (2017).

NOTES

PRELIMS
1. I thank James McFarland for this translation. The original is published in Brecht, *Werke*, 209.

INTRODUCTION
1. Brecht, *Werke*, 209.
2. Waters et al., "The Anthropocene Is Functionally and Stratigraphically Distinct from the Holocene."
3. The term "Anthropocene" was first coined by the ecologist Eugene Stoermer in the 1980s. It was then proposed as a name for the predecessor to the Holocene epoch by the Dutch atmospheric chemist Paul J. Crutzen in 2000. See McNeill and Engelke, *The Great Acceleration*, 1–6. In 2008, the Anthropocene Working Group of the International Commission on Stratigraphy began the process of vetting the geological evidence that would bring about an official renaming of the current epoch. For a discussion of this process see a lively Comments and Correspondence section of the journal *Nature*: Ellis et al., "Involve Social Scientists in Defining the Anthropocene," 192–193; Zalasiewicz et al., "Anthropocene: Its Stratigraphic Basis," 289.
4. Dipesh Chakrabarty describes how these scales of Anthropocene humanity (as a species, political beings, or indifferent brute force) challenge history and humanistic methods in "The Climate of History."
5. Bruno Latour argues that the Anthropocene confirms once and for all that human agency—the very category of "human subject" and "environmental object"—is a figment of a passing Enlightenment imagination and delusions of human exceptionalism. Latour, "Agency at the Time of the Anthropocene."
6. McKibben, *Eaarth*, 3.
7. Ibid., xii.
8. For a reading of Freud's uncanny as an expression of the death drive, see Royle, *The Uncanny*, 46. Freud, himself, writes that the double was "originally an insurance against the destruction of the ego." Doubling in premodern cultures was a "preservation against extinction." But in the modern psyche the double returns from this surmounted mystical past as "the uncanny harbinger of death." Freud, "The Uncanny," 235.
9. Ibid., 222–223.
10. Gorky, "The Lumière Cinematograph," 25.
11. Ibid., 26.
12. McLuhan, *Understanding Media*.
13. Gorky, "The Lumière Cinematograph," 26.
14. Arendt, *The Human Condition*, 7.

15. Kracauer, "The Calico-World," 281.
16. Ibid.
17. Ibid., 283.
18. Ibid., 281, 287.
19. Ibid., 285–286.
20. Ibid., 281.
21. Shklovsky quoted in Royle, *The Uncanny*, 4.
22. Kracauer, "Calico World," 288.
23. Ibid., 284.
24. Ibid.
25. Ibid., 286.
26. Ibid., 283.
27. As Noa Steimatsky writes, following World War II, the Allies designated Rome's Cincecittá film studio as a temporary refugee camp. Displaced families tried to make use of film props, recently featured in cinematic representations of Italian domesticity, to fabricate an impoverished version of living. See Steimatsky, "The Cincecittá Refugee Camp (1944–1950)."
28. Hayot, *On Literary Worlds*, 44–45.
29. Ibid., 41.
30. Kracauer, "The Calico-World," 283.
31. Hansen, *Cinema and Experience*, 14.
32. Arendt, *The Human Condition*, 1.
33. Ibid., 2–3.
34. Lazier, "Earthrise," 602–603.
35. Arendt, *The Human Condition*, 10.
36. Ibid., 324.
37. Ibid., 52.
38. Oliver, *Earth and World*, 85.
39. Kracauer, "The Calico-World," 284.
40. Steffen, Broadgate, Deutsch, et al., "The Trajectory of the Anthropocene," 3.
41. For a short history of this term, see McNeill and Engelke, *The Great Acceleration*, 213, footnote 4.
42. Steffen et al., "The Trajectory of the Anthropocene," 11.
43. Ibid., 12, 14.
44. Steffen, Crutzen, and McNeill, "The Anthropocene: Are Humans Now Overwhelming the Great Forces of Nature?," 614.
45. Kant, "Perpetual Peace: A Philosophical Sketch."
46. Seyla Benhabib's reading of "Perpetual Peace" and the right of resort in *The Rights of Others*, 40–42.
47. For an extended discussion of the status of the earth/world distinction in Kant's political writings, see Oliver, *Earth and World*, chapter 2. For an analysis of how the Anthropocene radically disrupts Kant's moral philosophy in relation to biological life, see Dipesh Chakrabarty, "Humanities in the Anthropocene."
48. Kant, "Perpetual Peace," 110.
49. Ibid., footnote on 111.
50. Ibid., 114, italics in original.
51. Ibid., 111, italics in original.
52. Ibid., 105.
53. Ibid., 106.
54. Benhabib, *The Rights of Others*, 35–40.

55. Kant quoted in Bernasconi, "Kant's Third Thoughts on Race," 302.
56. Steffen et al., "The Anthropocene: Are Humans Now Overwhelming the Great Forces of Nature?," 616, 618.
57. Steffen et al., emphasize the political but also scientific necessity of differentiating between the responsibility of OECD countries and BRICS (Brazil, Russia, India, China, and South Africa), and the rest of the developing world for human-caused climate change and the effects of the Anthropocene. This is important for the sake of climate justice; it is not a generalized humanity that is causing the earth to change so radically, but the culture of a few large and influential countries. The hope is also that developing nations may avoid reproducing the resource-intensive history of the so-called first world by taking advantage of new technologies. For example, cell phone technology has eliminated the need to create extensive land-line infrastructure. "The Trajectory of the Anthropocene," 13–14. For a history of the OECD and a list of member countries, see the OECD website: http://www.oecd.org.
58. Cheah, *What Is a World?*, 7.
59. "Should International Refugee Law Accommodate Climate Change?"
60. There is much to say on this topic. See "Should International Refugee Law Accommodate Climate Change?"; "The Environment & Climate Change"; McAdam, "Climate Change Displacement and International Law"; Kälin, "Conceptualising Climate-Induced Displacement."
61. "The Environment & Climate Change."
62. Gillis and Popovich, "The U.S. Is the Biggest Carbon Polluter in History."
63. Zalasiewicz, Waters, Williams, et al., "When Did the Anthropocene Begin?" The authors assert: "We propose an appropriate boundary level (for the designation of a new epoch) here to be the time of the world's first nuclear bomb explosion, on July 16th 1945 at Alamogordo, New Mexico" (p. 196).
64. Scranton, *Learning to Die in the Anthropocene*.
65. China is now the world's leading producer of greenhouse gases, but the United States still enjoys the distinction of being the "largest polluter in history." Gillis and Popovich, "The U.S. Is the Biggest Carbon Polluter in History."
66. Aravamudan, "The Catachronism of Climate Change," 8.
67. Ibid., 24.

CHAPTER 1

1. Bullot and Stevens, "Keaton and Snow," 19, 20.
2. Trahair, *The Comedy of Philosophy*, 78. In dialogue with Deleuze's five laws of the action image, Trahair argues convincingly that the Keatonian character does not meet narrative challenges through "self-transcendence" and transformation. Even after rescuing the survivors from the storm, Will has yet to master the basic sailor's knot.
3. Bullot and Stevens, "Keaton and Snow," 23.
4. Bengtson, *Silent Echoes*, 212.
5. "Windstorm Filmed in Keaton Comedy." *Steamboat* press book hereafter.
6. Ibid.
7. Keaton, "Keaton at Venice," 227.
8. Schallert, "'Steamboat Bill' Stormy Fun Special."
9. For examples of slapstick's urban-industrial thesis, see Hansen, "The Mass Production of the Sense," 69; Gunning, "Mechanisms of Laughter," 141; North, *Machine-Age Comedy*, 37.

10. Bilton, "Buster Keaton and the South," 493.
11. Saxon, *Father Mississippi*, 253–276.
12. T. G. Winter letter published in *The Outlook*. Reproduced in Saxon, *Father Mississippi*, 399.
13. For a discussion of Saxon's book and its influence on William Faulkner's environmental thought and poetics, see Parrish, "Faulkner and the Outer Weather of 1927."
14. "After the Flood," 216–217.
15. Hacking, *The Taming of Chance*, 201. See also Mary Ann Doane's discussion of contingency and cinema in *The Emergence of Cinematic Time*, 10, 19.
16. Sloterdijk, *Terror from the Air*. For his discussion of Ypres, see pp. 9–17. The phrase "ecologized war" comes from p. 20.
17. Benjamin, "The Storyteller," 84.
18. Keaton with Samuels, *My Wonderful World of Slapstick*, 20–21.
19. Ibid., 100.
20. Jacobson, *Studios before the System*, 169, 182.
21. Ibid., 171.
22. Ibid., 198.
23. Mark Shiel writes that the classical Hollywood art direction was constrained "quite strictly within the limited, but supposedly infinite, and infinitely variable, space of the soundstage." "Classical Hollywood, 1928–1946," 72. Scott, "Film Sets Grow Larger," quoted in Shiel, 51.
24. Scott, "Film Sets Grow Larger."
25. Hopper, "Studios Theatre Gossip," cited in Shiel, 63.
26. The ice floe sequence in *Way Down East* was inspired by a similar scene from the stage play of "Uncle Tom's Cabin." Edison adapted this play for film in 1903. The shot of his studio-fabricated moving river of ice is included as a special feature on the Kino International DVD release of *Way Down East* (2008).
27. "The Screen," 7.
28. Gish quoted in Oderman, *Lillian Gish*, 93.
29. Ibid., 95.
30. Richard Schickel notes that stunt doubles were used for the second-unit shooting after Griffith and cameraman Billy Bitzer completed principal photography. And a few of the shots with Gish and Barthelmess were filmed in the spring using painted wood for the ice floes. *D.W. Griffith: An American Life*, 433–434.
31. Wagenknecht quoted in Oderman, *Lillian Gish*, 98.
32. For a discussion of the production costs of *Way Down East*, see Schickel, *D.W. Griffith*, 436–438, 444–446. Griffith quoted on 438.
33. "Biggest Money Picture: Sound Film Shy Big Silent Sums," 62. Griffith's *Birth of a Nation* was number one on the list, grossing $10 million in the year of its release. *Variety* muses that this record will not likely be equaled or surpassed.
34. "Snow before Nov. 20 Insured for $25,000," 27.
35. "Nary Snowflake in Mamaroneck," 45.
36. Shiel, "Classical Hollywood," 70. He explains that unscripted shots of "natural rain cloud formations" were included in *Gone with the Wind* because special effects cinematographer Clarence Slifer filmed the skies on the eve of the disastrous Los Angeles rainstorm of 1938.
37. We find a similar series of gags in Keaton's 1921 short *The Playhouse*. In a bedroom, a thuggish man attempts to evict the Keaton character from what we assume is his apartment. When the walls of the room are taken away, we realize

that Keaton's hero is a stagehand. He's not being evicted from his apartment, but reprimanded for sleeping on a set designed to replicate an apartment.
38. Singer, *Melodrama and Modernity*, 152–163. Singer notes that early cinema and the Nickelodeon craze severely curtailed demand for sensational stage melodrama.
39. Keaton, "Keaton at Venice," 227.
40. Miriam Hansen writes that Hollywood cinema's "vernacular modernism" produced a "sensory-reflexive horizon of experience of modernization and modernity" that was legible to audiences all over the world. We could make a similar, though far more specific, argument about Keaton's climatography. "Fallen Women, Rising Stars, New Horizons," 10.
41. Carroll, *Comedy Incarnate*, 11. Carroll argues that Keaton tutors perception through what he calls the "engineer's-eye viewpoint." Because Keaton's techniques exceed the demands of comedy and the hermetic world of the narrative, spectators marvel at the way things (including Keaton's own body) fall into place.
42. Feuer, *The Hollywood Musical*, 4.
43. Feuer, "*Singin' in the Rain*," 450.
44. Trahair, "Ghost in the Machine," 584.
45. Kracauer, *Theory of Film*, 62.
46. Trahair, "Ghost in the Machine," 583.
47. Sloterdijk, *Terror from the Air*, 47.
48. Ibid., 16–18.
49. Ibid., 23.
50. For an elaboration of this term, see Wrathall, *Heidegger and Unconcealment*, 11–34.
51. Sloterdijk, *Terror from the Air*, 50.
52. Ibid., 47.
53. Ibid., 81.
54. Ibid., 81.
55. Dali quoted in ibid., 73.
56. Ibid., 84.
57. Ibid., 60.
58. Ross, *Strange Weather*, 226.
59. Favret, *War at a Distance*, 129.
60. Friedman, *Appropriating the Weather*, 158, 106.
61. Ross, *Strange Weather*, 214–221. Ross discussed how local methods of forecasting were in tension with the US National Weather Service and the emerging global weather culture.
62. King, *The Fun Factory*, 186.
63. Keaton with Samuels, *My Wonderful World of Slapstick*, 97.
64. For Keaton's account of his war experiences, see ibid., 96–104.
65. Miller, *Late Modernism*, 51.
66. Adorno and Horkheimer, quoted in ibid., 51.
67. Poster copy, *Steamboat* press book.
68. "River Junction Passed Away Like Babylon," *Steamboat* press book.
69. "Goldwyn Brought South Seas to Hollywood for 'Hurricane.'" *Hurricane* press book hereafter.
70. "Hurricane over Hollywood," *Hurricane* press book.
71. Nugent, "The Screen: Samuel Goldwyn Turn Nordhoff-Hall 'Hurricane' Loose Across the Screen of the Astor," 31.
72. Ibid.

73. "Hurricane over Hollywood," *Hurricane* press book.
74. Keaton, "Keaton at Venice," 226.
75. Davis, *Ecology of Fear*, 161–165.
76. Ibid., 161.
77. Ibid., 159.
78. "Hurricane over Hollywood," *Hurricane* press book.
79. Naremore, *Acting in the Cinema*, 76–77; see also Trahair, *Comedy of Philosophy*, 90–91.
80. Naremore, *Acting in the Cinema*, 114.
81. Sontag, *Against Interpretation*, 287.
82. Mulvey, "Clumsy Sublime," 3. This is Mulvey's term describing the layered temporality and confusing spatiality of rear-screen projection.
83. Ken Feil argues that the intentional camp and parodic elements in such films as *Twister* (1995) undercut the narrative's attempts at "normative sincerity." The paradox is that the sincerity and not the intentional parody is read by critics as camp. *Dying for a Laugh*, 64–65.
84. "Windstorm Filmed in Keaton Comedy," *Steamboat* press book.
85. Bergson, *Laughter*, 17.
86. Ibid., 21.
87. Carroll, *Comedy Incarnate*, 34.
88. Ibid, 50.
89. Ibid., 63.
90. Keaton, "Keaton at Venice," 224.
91. Doane, *The Emergence of Cinematic Time*, 137.
92. For a discussion of Keaton's exploitation of Los Angeles's varied topography and history of urban development, see Charles Wolfe, "California Slapstick Revisited."
93. Carroll, *Comedy Incarnate*, 49.
94. Lisa Trahair offers a similar reading of this dream sequence in which Keaton's character adapts only to be brutally undercut by the shot change. Reading Keaton through Heidegger's essay "The Question Concerning Technology," Trahair argues that this sequence plays with the tension between diegetic reality and diegetic fiction, as well as a "more serious pondering of the existential crises experienced when a human is reduced to a component part of a technological apparatus he no longer controls." "The Comedy of Technology in the Cinema of Buster Keaton," 583.
95. Bergson, *Laughter*, 26–27.
96. Bilton, "Buster Keaton and the South," 496.
97. Perez, *The Material Ghost*, 103. Emphasis in original.
98. Kenner, "In Memoriam: Buster Keaton," 181, quoted in Perez, 94.
99. Ibid.
100. Berlant, *Cruel Optimism*, 6. Italics original.
101. Ibid., 169. The figure of drowning recurs throughout her discussion of a situation tragedy. See also 178, 180.
102. Ibid., 170.
103. Other critics have noted that Keaton's melodramatic side seems to occur when his characters leave behind urban modernity and venture into the unsettled West and less developed South. See Wolfe, "Western Unsettlement," 299–315.
104. Gellatly, "Steve McQueen."

CHAPTER 2

1. Details of the site not explicit in the film are reported in Miller, "Rescue Crew Finds Grim Toll in Ruins of A-Bombed Town," 2; "Survival Town Buildings Stand Up Well in Test," 2.
2. Hales, *Outside the Gates of Eden*, 150–152.
3. For a more detailed discussion of the test and its myriad technical challenges, see Fehner and Gosling, *Atmospheric Nuclear Weapons Testing*, 135–139.
4. Miller, *Under the Cloud*, 237.
5. Zalasiewicz et al., "When Did the Anthropocene Begin?"
6. Ibid., 196, 201.
7. Ibid., 201.
8. Masco, *Nuclear Borderlands*, 300, 301.
9. Broad, "The Bomb Chroniclers," D1. The Lookout Mountain Air Force Station studio in the Laurel Canyon area of Hollywood, California, is the subject of the documentary *Hollywood's Top Secret Film Studio* (2003). For the official explanation of the studio, see Nevada National Security Site, "Secret Film Studio: Lookout Mountain," National Nuclear Security Administration, 2013. http://nnss.gov/docs/fact_sheets/DOENV_1142.pdf.
10. US Department of Energy, *United States Nuclear Tests*, xv, xviii. Because each test was often composed of a series of detonations, the total number of nuclear *devices* exploded in Nevada is 1,021. "The most bombed place on earth" in reference to the Nevada Test Site, from Topham et al., "Building the Bomb."
11. Fehner and Gosling, *Atmospheric Nuclear Weapons Testing*, 10.
12. Solnit, *Savage Dreams*, 5.
13. Benjamin, "On Some Motifs in Baudelaire," 175.
14. Benjamin, "The Work of Art in the Age of Its Technological Reproducibility," 37.
15. Levin, "Film," 317.
16. Spalding et al., "Age Written in Teeth by Nuclear Tests," 333; Stone, "Cold War's Genetic Fallout."
17. Hersey, *Hiroshima*, 3, 1. Hersey's account was first published in the *New Yorker* in 1946.
18. See Alan Nadel's deft reading of *Hiroshima* and his attention to Hersey's movement between the everyday routine and history. As Nadel argues, Hersey plays the unpredictable nature of the bomb at the moment of its detonation against the known future on which Hersey's "non-fiction novel" relies. Nadel, *Containment Culture*, 53–67.
19. Caruth, *Unclaimed Experience*, 6–7.
20. Saint-Amour, *Tense Future*, 24–25.
21. See, for example, Derrida, "No Apocalypse, Not Now." The special issue is devoted to topic of "nuclear criticism"; Treat, *Writing Ground Zero*; Schwender and Treat, "America's Hiroshima, Hiroshima's America"; Caruth, "Literature and the Enactment of Memory"; Saint-Amour, "Bombing and the Symptom."
22. *Military Participation on Tumbler-Snapper* (1952), produced for US Air Force by the Lookout Mountain Laboratory, may be viewed at archive.org/details/gov.doe.0800011.
23. *Operation Upshot-Knothole* (1953), produced by the Lookout Mountain Laboratory, can be viewed online: archive.org/details/OperationUPSHOT_KNOTHOLE1953.

24. Lippit, *Atomic Light (Shadow Optics)*, 92. On the relationship between art and atomic testing and, for that matter, artists and atomic scientists, see Ponte, "Desert Testing."
25. Bonami, "Painting's Laughter," 21.
26. Fogle, "Spectators at our Own Deaths," 18.
27. de Duve, "Andy Warhol, or The Machine Perfected," 6.
28. Ibid., 11.
29. Foster, "Test Subjects," 35.
30. Koestenbaum, "Any Warhol."
31. de Duve, "Andy Warhol, or The Machine Perfected," 10, 4.
32. Ibid., 14.
33. Ronell, *The Test Drive*, 7, 9.
34. Gusterson, *People of the Bomb*, 151.
35. Ibid., 159–160.
36. Ibid., 157.
37. As part of the troop indoctrination program, entitled Desert Rock, the Marines sent two battalions to participate in Operation Tumbler-Snapper test series. These men were entrenched seven thousand yards from ground zero, a controversially close position. The AEC reluctantly agreed to the closer position proposes by the Marines. For a discussion of the controversy see: Fehner and Gosling, *Atmospheric Nuclear Weapons Testing*, 72–76; Hacker, *Elements of Controversy*, 77–78.
38. Atomic soldiers watched these training films as a matter of indoctrination. For the maneuver, however, troops were divided into two general groups, one that witnessed the detonation at seven thousand yards from ground zero, and a second control group that remained behind at base camp. After the test, both groups filled out questionnaires about the bomb and the low risks posed by radiation. The test question would determine the degree to which witnessing the blast and experiencing its radiation effects firsthand had a measurable difference on soldiers' attitudes toward the bomb and thus their preparedness to carry out a ground attack under its radioactive cloud. *Advisory Committee on Human Radiation Experiments, Final Report*, 460–461.
39. The film can be found at https://archive.org/details/ExerciseDesertRock1951#.
40. This information is based on *Advisory Committee on Human Radiation Experiments, Final Report*. President Clinton created this committee in 1994 to research human test subjects in federally funded radiation research. Chapter 10 "Atomic Veterans" (p. 454–505) offers a detailed history of atomic maneuvers and human-subject testing during atmospheric nuclear detonations. For the "psychology of panic," and the "(emotional vaccination)", see p. 489, fn17.
41. *Advisory Committee of Human Radiation, Final Report*, 463–64.
42. Moreno, "Secret State Experiments and Medical Ethics," 64–66. Moreno notes that the Atomic Energy Commission was especially nervous about weapons development and nuclear preparedness, presuming that the Soviets would have no ethical restrictions on the use of human test subjects. See also *Advisory Committee of Human Radiation, Final Report*, 463, 466–67, 483.
43. The Army proposed to position troops closer to the blast with each test to ascertain "the thresholds of intolerability." The Armed Forces Medical Policy Council objected, noting that the threshold would only be determined when exceeded. *Advisory Committee of Human Radiation, Final Report*, 464–465.

44. Fehner and Gosling *Atmospheric Nuclear Weapons Testing*, 75, 91, 103. Miller, *Under the Cloud*, 159.
45. *Let's Face It* (1954), produced for the US Air Force by the Lookout Mountain Laboratory, youtube.com/watch?v=UwZmzlQfejs.
46. Davis, *Stages of Emergency*, 2.
47. Davis, *Stages of Emergency*, 85. Emphasis original.
48. Buck-Morss, "Aesthetics and Anaesthetics," 8–9.
49. Ibid., 30.
50. Ibid., 33.
51. This film may be seen in full at youtube.com/watch?v=CfQN4sTae3s.
52. Miller, *Under the Cloud*, 301.
53. Willard F. Libby, commissioner of the Atomic Energy Commission, made a similar statement in *U.S. News and World Report*, suggesting that the fallout scare could be a Soviet plot to stymie US weapons development. "The world is radioactive. It always has been and always will be. Its natural radioactivities evidently are not dangerous and we can conclude from this fact that contamination from atomic bombs, small in magnitude or even of the same order of magnitude as these natural radiation, is not likely to be all that dangerous." "The Facts about A-Bomb Fallout," 22.
54. Miller, *Under the Cloud*, 254.
55. Fehner and Gosling, *Atmospheric Nuclear Weapons Testing*, 168–170.
56. Joel Healy was interviewed by his daughter Kelli Healy Salazar for National Public Radio's series "StoryCorps," October 12, 2012. The interview and transcript are available online: http://www.npr.org/2012/10/12/162722650/veteran-risks-in-1950s-bomb-test-a-disgrace.
57. Benjamin, "Work of Art," 30–31.
58. Ibid., 31.
59. Hansen, *Cinema and Experience*, 96.
60. Angell, *Andy Warhol Screen Tests*, 14.
61. Hall Foster makes a similar comparison between Warhol's tests and Benjamin's actor in "Test Subjects," 41.
62. Flately, "Like: Collecting and Collectivity," 94–95.
63. Ibid., 92.
64. Researchers estimate that 2.4 million cancer fatalities have been and will have been caused by atmospheric nuclear testing and elements with very long half-lives. "Because most of the exposure is due to Carbon-14, the majority of deaths will occur over the next few thousand years." International Commission to Investigate the Health and Environmental Effects of Nuclear Weapons Production and Institute for Energy and Environmental Research, *Radioactive Heaven and Earth*, 40.
65. Masco, *Nuclear Borderlands*, 301.
66. This chemical encounter followed by Carey's cellular mutation anticipates Rachel Carson's argument about the nonresiliency of the human body in toxic environments in her 1962 *Silent Spring*.
67. Benjamin "The Destructive Character," 301–302.
68. Wohlfarth, "No-Man's-Land," 60. Ellipsis original.
69. Arendt, "The Conquest of Space," 273–274.
70. Arendt, *The Human Condition*, 322.
71. Colebrook, *Death of the Posthuman*, 13–14. Italics original.
72. *Plowshare* (US Atomic Energy Commission, 1964/65, 28 min.) The date is incorrectly listed at 1961 on various on-line platform. Yet, the film

refers to events in 1964. Available online: https://www.youtube.com/watch?v=Z0F6HQfzjvA.
73. Teller quoted in Kaufman, *Project Plowshare*, 48.
74. *Project Gnome* (Atomic Energy Commission and Lawrence Radiation Laboratory of the University of California, 1961, 28 min.). Available online: https://www.youtube.com/watch?v=DFJ2MyWlXgs.
75. Kuletz, *The Tainted Desert*, 13. Italics original.
76. Vartabedian, "Nevada's Hidden Ocean of Radiation."
77. Teller, "We're Going to Work Miracles," 101.
78. Kaufman, *Project Plowshare*, 92.
79. Quoted in O'Neill, *The Firecracker Boys*, 25.
80. Benjamin, "Work of Art," 35.
81. Miller, *Under the Cloud*, 313.
82. O'Neill, *The Firecracker Boys*, 252–253.
83. For a discussion of this contamination and the rise of the Greenpeace movement, see O'Neill, *The Firecracker Boys*, 274–284.

CHAPTER 3

1. Scranton, *Learning to Die in the Anthropocene*, 16.
2. Ibid., 22.
3. Ibid., 23.
4. Ibid.
5. For a study of climate change disaster cinema, see E. Ann Kaplan, *Climate Trauma*. She analyzes the pretraumatic stress symptomatic of the characters in climate fiction and, by extension, of viewers grappling with the ongoing crisis of environmental collapse. Characters in such films as *Take Shelter* panic to protect their families from the planet's future ruination. Other science fiction films in her study such as *The Road* and *Children of Men* memorialize a past that mirrors our present and offers signs of hope based on the birth or survival of the child. *Film noir*, I will argue, is resolute in offering no hope for the future.
6. McNeill and Engelka, *The Great Acceleration*, 209.
7. Polan, *Power and Paranoia*, 208.
8. Sobchack, "Lounge Time," 166.
9. Guattari, *The Three Ecologies*, 23, 24, 45.
10. Dimendberg, *Film Noir and the Spaces of Modernity*, 10, 164.
11. Ibid., 91.
12. For a history of Bunker Hill in relation to *Kiss Me Deadly*, see Dimendberg, *Film Noir and the Spaces of Modernity*, 151–165. On the history of urban renewal, see Don Parson, *Making a Better World*, 137–162; "Corporate Modernism," in Parson, *Making a Better World*, 156.
13. For a history of nuclear contamination and Native American tribal lands, see Kuletz, *The Tainted Desert*.
14. Fleischer, "*Exiles* on Main Street." This Native American enclave is poetically captured in Scott McKenzie's film *The Exiles* (1961), his master's thesis not commercially released until 2008. His film documents, as one critic puts it, "the doomed spaces" of the Bunker Hill neighborhood, a seedy substitute for the reservation that was itself an already impoverished and unsustainable place.
15. Parson, *Making a Better World*, 145, 147.
16. Ibid., 158.
17. Quoted in ibid., 151.

18. Zarlengo, "Civil Threat."
19. Lapp quoted in Zarlengo, 936.
20. *House in the Middle* (1954) was produced by the National Paint, Varnish, and Lacquer Association with the cooperation of the Federal Civil Defense Administration, https://archive.org/details/Houseint1954.
21. Sobchack, "Lounge Time," 144.
22. Ibid., 155.
23. Biesen, *Blackout,* 3–4.
24. For an in-depth discussion of war shortages, blackouts, and the wartime regime of censorship, see Bieson, "Hollywood in the Aftermath of Pearl Harbor," in *Blackout,* 59–95.
25. Sobchack, "Lounge Time," 166. Italics original.
26. Jacobs, *Detached America,* 7–8.
27. Adorno, *Minima Moralia,* 39.
28. Ibid., 38.
29. Ibid., 116–117.
30. Docherty, *Aesthetic Democracy,* 132–133.
31. Serres, *Malfeasance,* 82.
32. Ibid., 72. Italics original.
33. Borde and Chaumenton, *A Panorama of American Film Noir,* 5, 13. Italics original.
34. Ibid., 160.
35. Simon and Keefe, "The Hollywood Interview: Robert Towne."
36. Edelman, *No Future,* 2.
37. Ibid., 12.
38. Ibid., 31.
39. J. R. McNeill and Peter Engelke write that from 1945 to 2015, the global population tripled from 2.3 billion to 7.2 billion, *The Great Acceleration,* 40–43.
40. National Wildlife Federation Mission and Strategic Plan, https://www.nwf.org/Home/About-Us/Our-Mission.
41. Roosevelt, "Seventh Annual Address to Congress."
42. Sobchack, 162.
43. Dienstag, *Pessimism: Philosophy, Ethic, Spirit,* 31.
44. *The Two Jakes* (1990), the sequel to *Chinatown,* reveals how the irrigated land from the first film is earmarked for suburban subdivisions and oil extraction. But the film is really about the claims of the past—both the diegetic past and the reputation of the previous film—on the present. In his review of *The Two Jakes* (Nicholson, 1990), Owen Gleiberman writes that this sequel to *Chinatown* collapses under the weight and heady revelations of the first film. *The Two Jakes* is "competent and watchable" but "so busy establishing 'parallels' with the first film that it never takes the risks to discover a domain of its own." "The Two Jakes" August 17, 1990. *Entertainment Weekly.* When we consider other noirs in which most of our characters are killed: *Out of the Past, Double Indemnity, The Killers, The Postman Always Rings Twice, Detour,* to name just a few, a sequel is simply impossible.
45. Castoriadis, *The Imaginary Institution of Society,* 207, quoted in Lotz, *The Capitalist Schema,* 75.
46. Sobchak, "Lounge Time," 163.
47. Szalay, *New Deal Modernism,* 225.
48. Ibid., 222.
49. Ibid., 223.

50. Quoted in Szalay, *New Deal Modernism*, 223–224.
51. Ibid., 224.
52. Ibid., 223.
53. Ibid.
54. Dienstag, *Pessimism*, 102.
55. Ibid.
56. Even Busby Berkeley numbers are infused with the heightened rationalization (however empty in meaning) associated with the mass ornament. Noir never rises to this organized decorative level. There are patterns in noir, to be sure, but not a rational system.
57. Kracauer, "Hollywood's Terror Film," 45–46.
58. Dienstag, *Pessimism*, 107
59. Schopenhauer quoted in Dienstag, *Pessimism*, 108.
60. Szalay, *New Deal Modernism*, 222.
61. Cowie, "Film Noir and Women," 130.
62. Ibid., 148.
63. Dienstag, *Pessimism*, 245.
64. Ibid., 256. Italics original.

CHAPTER 4

1. "Welcome to the Anthropocene," *The Economist*.
2. Derrida makes a distinction between the public law of the state and the privacy of the home. Derrida and Dufourmantelle, *Of Hospitality*, 51–55.
3. Derrida, *Adieu to Emmanuel Levinas*, 15–16. Italics original.
4. Yardley, "Chinese Dam Projects Criticized for the Human Costs."
5. The official site has been revised. But its boasting has been quoted in full in the English-language edition of China's *People's Daily*. "Three Gorges Project Sets 10 World Records," http://en.people.cn/200606/09/eng20060609_272430.html.
6. Rolston, "China: Land of Monster Dam, Killer Rivers."
7. See the photo gallery on the Three Gorges Corporation website: http://www.ctgpc.com.
8. Nixon, *Slow Violence and the Environmentalism of the Poor*, 156–157.
9. Sanger and Perlez, "Trump Hands the Chinese a Gift."
10. Waters et al., "The Anthropocene Is Functionally and Stratigraphically Distinct from the Holocene."
11. Richard Gross (NASA Jet Propulsion Laboratory) and Benjamin Fong Chao (NASA Goddard Space Flight Center) calculate that the Three Gorges Dam will lengthen the day by sixty billionths of a second. See "NASA Details Earthquake Effects on the Earth," http://www.jpl.nasa.gov/news/news.php?release=2005-009.
12. Michael Wines reports that in 2012, there were 430 significant landslides attributable to the pressure the Three Gorges Dam's reservoir places on the surrounding landmass. More extreme landslides are expected in the future and thus the Chinese government has begun to relocate even more residents along the dam's new shoreline. "Landslide Risk at Reservoir Cited in China"; Platt, "Chinese Sturgeon Give Up."
13. Sample, "Yangtze River Dolphin Driven to Extinction."
14. Platt, "Chinese Sturgeon Give Up."
15. Vajpeyi, *Deforestation, Environment, and Sustainable Development*, 94.
16. The Internal Displacement Monitoring Center estimates that six million people in China were internally displaced by climate change disasters in 2012 alone. For

a discussion of China's vast "climate migrant" crisis, see Alex Randall, "Climate Change Driving Migration into China's Vulnerable Cities."
17. McNeill and Engelke, *The Great Acceleration*, 168–169. Mao quoted on 169.
18. Ibid., 35; Yeufang and Steil, "China Three Gorges Project Resettlement: Policy, Planning and Implementation," 424–425; Handwerk, "China's Three Gorges Dam by the Numbers."
19. Nixon, *Slow Violence*, 152, 162.
20. Berger, "Ten Dispatches about Place," quoted in Nixon, 161.
21. Jia, "Still Life (Sanxia Haoren) 2006," 66.
22. Chumley, *Creativity Class*, 100. Chumley emphasizes that Jia and Liu Xiaodong are hardly dissident artists. Both are firmly entrenched in China's most visible and government-supported fine arts academy.
23. See his manifesto. Jia, "The Age of Amateur Cinema Will Return."
24. Zhang, "Bearing Witness," 21.
25. Ibid., 16.
26. *Jia Zhangke on Still Life* (Producer Cindi Rowell, New Yorker Films, 2008). Interview with Jia Zhangke on *Still Life* DVD extra (New Yorker Video, 2008). *Jia Zhangke on Still Life* hereafter.
27. For a detailed history of the Three Gorges and the dam's construction, see Cheham, *Before the Deluge*, especially chapters 8–10.
28. *Jia Zhangke on Still Life*. The shape of the monument as a Chinese character is mentioned in McGrath, "The Cinema of Displacement," 43. For the precise dedication of the monument, McGrath cites Ling Zhang's unpublished essay "That Obscure Object of Nostalgia: The Demolition and Reconstruction of Masculine Space in Jia Zhangke's Film *Still Life*." McGrath, 46, footnote 7.
29. *Jia Zhangke on Still Life*.
30. Cheah, "World as Picture and Ruination," 200.
31. For a discussion of the mix of documentary and fictional staging in these two films, see McGrath, "The Cinema of Displacement," 44–45.
32. Wang "Aftershock," 209.
33. Oster, "Scientists Link China's Dam to Earthquake, Renewing Debate"; Kahn, "In China, a Lake's Champion Imperils Himself."
34. For earthquake statistics and information on the man-made reservoir that likely caused it, see "Sichuan Earthquake."
35. Schiavenza, "City in Ruins."
36. When one of the models was no longer able to pose, Liu substituted in a local survivor. Wang, "Aftershock," 207.
37. The aesthetics of immobility and affective passivity are the signature styles of the new official realism, which supplanted the revolutionary romanticism of Mao's era. Liu, like Jia, instructs his models to adopt the stoic expressions associated with portraits commemorating migrant workers upon whose labor China's past and future rests. See Chumley, *The Creativity Class*, 102–103.
38. Wang, "Aftershock," 208.
39. On the connection to scroll painting, see Mello, "Space and Intermediality in Jia Zhang-ke's Still Life."
40. Bryson, "Chardin and the Text of Still Life," 228.
41. Bryson, *Looking at the Overlooked*, 13–14.
42. Bryson, "Chardin," 236.
43. Ibid., 229.
44. Ibid.

45. Ibid., 230.
46. Weisman, *The World without Us*.
47. Bryson, "Chardin," 238.
48. Bryson, *Looking at the Overlooked*, 23–24.
49. Ibid., 24.
50. Ibid., 25.
51. Byrnes, "Specters of Realism," 66.
52. See Bordeleau, "Jia Zhangke's *Still Life*." Bordeleau argues that the title was originally intended to be *jing wu,* the Mandarin equivalent of "Still Life," but referring not to this Western genre, but to Liu's style of "painting from life"—a technique of rendering on-location realism. Eugene Wang's analysis of Liu's painting demonstrates that Liu's realism departs from *en plein air* conventions. I will argue that the still life, even by Jia's own account, describes something more than pictorial style or technique.
53. Jia, "Still Life (Sanxia Haoren) 2006," 66.
54. *Jia Zhangke on Still Life*.
55. Abbas, "Poor Theory and new Chinese Cinema," 6. Unpublished and quoted by permission from the author.
56. Ibid., 10.
57. Ibid., 13.
58. For a discussion of Brecht's engagement with Chinese theater and his occasional misreading of Mei Lan Fang's performance in Brecht's formulation of the Verfremdungseffekte, see Xiaomei, *Occidentalism*, 115–118. Brecht began to influence Chinese communist theater when Huang Tso-ling, deputy head of the People's Art Theater in Shanghai, gave his epic six-hour lecture on epic theater in 1951. Huang, educated in China and England, was eager to find a modernist style of political theater that was attuned to the particularities of Chinese culture. He was delighted to encounter Brecht's writing on the Peking opera. See Hsia, "Bertolt Brecht in China and His Impact on Chinese Drama." The allusion to Brecht's play and implicitly to Brecht's influence on Chinese theater under Mao reminds us that the dam, the play, and the luxury objects are all of piece with a now-post socialism.
59. Lu, "Emerging from Underground and the Periphery," 114.
60. Pheng Cheah, referencing Brecht's play, notes that *Still Life* depicts "the entire spectrum of social corruption, from that of the petty gangster, thugs and cheats Sanming encounters to the large-scale corruption of an emerging business elite and local government administration" (Cheah, "World as Picture Ruination," 197). Ackbar Abbas writes that if we search the film looking for the good people, we risk lingering on a humanist confirmation of goodness (of which there are but a few signs in the film) and missing the film's more interesting "spatial complexities and the duplicities of its documentary style" (Abbas, "Poor Theory," 5).
61. Jia Zhangke, "Still Life," *Jia Zhangke Speaks Out*, 65.
62. Earlier in the film, Sanming walks through a deconstruction site just as a huge wall seems to collapse spontaneously. In the context of this book, it recalls Keaton's house-falling gag from *Steamboat Bill, Jr.*
63. This discussion of *trompe l'oeil* is inspired by Bryson's reading of cubism's still life compositions in *Looking at the Overlooked*, 83–86.
64. Yang's artist statement appears in Shore, *Post-Photography*, 234.

65. The entire series can be viewed online at Hélène Lacharmoise's Galerie DIX9, http://www.galeriedix9.com/en/expositions/presentationarchive/24/uprooted.
66. Shore, *Post-Photography*, 234.
67. Ballard, *The Drowned World*.
68. Uprooted, "Press Release," Hélène Lacharmoise's Galerie DIX9, http://www.galeriedix9.com/en/expositions/presentationarchive/24/uprooted.
69. Boym, *The Future of Nostalgia*, xvi.
70. Ibid., xiv.
71. Ibid., 3.
72. *Jia Zhangke on Still Life*.
73. *Jia Zhangke on Still Life*.
74. Rodowick, *The Virtual Life of Film*, 9.
75. Barthes, *Camera Lucida*, 87, 88–89.
76. Ibid., 96.
77. Cavell, *The World Viewed*, 23.
78. Ibid., 24.
79. Ibid., 40.
80. Ibid., 26.
81. Ibid., 25.
82. Ibid., 159.
83. Ibid., 102.
84. Ibid., 119.
85. Ibid., 95.
86. Rodowick, *The Virtual Life of Film*, 134.
87. Ibid., 174.
88. Ibid., 178.
89. Abbas, "Poor Theory and New Chinese Cinema," 12.
90. Boym, *The Future of Nostalgia*, xviii.
91. Ibid., 49. Italics original.
92. This is the spirit of Boym's remark: "A modern nostalgic can be homesick and sick of home, at once" (ibid., 50).
93. Zielinski, *Deep Time of the Media*, 7, 11.
94. Bachelard, *Water and Dreams*, 12.

CHAPTER 5

1. Dell'Amore, "Why Antarctica Is So Hard on the Body."
2. Walker, *Antarctica*, xv.
3. Day, *Antarctica*, 467.
4. Walker, *Antarctica*, 4.
5. Hall, "Mapping the White Continent."
6. Pollack, *A World without Ice*, 12.
7. See the shots of the *Endurance* taken at night by director Frank Hurley in the film *South: Ernest Shackleton and the Endurance Expedition* (1919). Read Herbert G. Ponting's explanation of flash photography during the Antarctic winter in *The Great White South*, 137.
8. Pyne, *The Ice*, 83.
9. See Roald Amundsen's account in "At the Pole," in *Antarctica: Firsthand Accounts*, 218–224; Day, *Antarctica*, 146–148.
10. Scott, *Scott's Last Expedition*, 424.
11. Green, *Water, Ice & Stone*, 32.

12. Dillard, "An Expedition to the Pole," 60.
13. Pyne, *The Ice*, 101.
14. These dispirited place names are humorously listed in Walker, *Antarctica: An Intimate Portrait*, 16.
15. Nabhan, "The Dangers of Reductionism in Biodiversity Conservation," 479–481.
16. Bernau, "Help for Hotspots," 618, footnote 6.
17. https://www.nature.org (consulted on June 8, 2017). Of course, this image and language are subject to constant change.
18. See this wonderful blog, Ugly Animal Preservation Society, http://uglyanimalsoc.com.
19. Hayot, *The Hypothetical Mandarin*, 5.
20. Richter, *Thought-Images*, 14.
21. Kracauer, *Theory of Film*, 18. Cited as *TOF* hereafter.
22. Hansen, *Cinema and Experience*, 256.
23. See Hansen, "Introduction" to Kracauer's *Theory of Film*, xiii.
24. Schlüpmann, "The Subject of Survival," 112.
25. Kracauer, *TOF*, li.
26. Ibid., 299.
27. Ibid., 299, 300.
28. Ibid., 299.
29. Ibid., 300.
30. Ibid., 18–20.
31. Hansen, *Cinema and Experience*, 256.
32. Kracauer, *TOF*, 14. Ellipses in original.
33. Ibid., 15.
34. Ibid., 29.
35. Bazin, "The Ontology of the Photographic Image," 15.
36. Ibid., 27.
37. Ibid., 55.
38. Baudry, "The Apparatus"; Metz, "The Imaginary Signifier"; Mulvey, "Visual Pleasure and Narrative Cinema." In some respects Kracauer shares with these theorists a sense that Hollywood and closed narrative systems are ideological. But for Kracauer, the photographic and cinematic apparatuses themselves may help us to see outside of ideology. This is a point to which I'll return in the chapter's conclusion.
39. Kracauer, *TOF*, 31.
40. Hansen, "'With Skin and Hair,'" 443. See also Hansen, *Cinema and Experience*, 256–257.
41. Santner, *On Creaturely Life*, 17.
42. Hanssen, *Walter Benjamin's Other History*, 3.
43. Kracauer, "Photography," 47. Cited as *MO* hereafter.
44. Ibid., 48.
45. Ibid.
46. Ibid., 56–57.
47. Ibid.
48. Ibid., 62.
49. Ibid., 56.
50. Ibid., 55.
51. Ibid., 22.
52. Ibid., 56.

53. Ibid., 51.
54. Ibid., 58.
55. Murphy, *German Exploration to the Polar World*, 161–162.
56. Ibid., 5.
57. Lethen, "Refrigerators of Intelligence," 81.
58. Ibid., 86–87.
59. Lethen, *Cool Conduct*, 42–43.
60. Kracauer, *TOF*, 301.
61. Ibid., 302.
62. Ibid., 257.
63. Ibid., li.
64. Von Moltke, *The Curious Humanist*, 155.
65. Kracauer, *TOF*, li.
66. Ibid., 302–303.
67. Ibid., 165.
68. Ibid., li.
69. Ibid., 165.
70. Quoted in Kracauer, *TOF*, 165. Brackets in Kracauer's quotation.
71. Ibid.
72. Ibid., 303.
73. Ibid., 166. For von Moltke, this antihumanism is somewhat compromised at the end of *Theory of Film* when Kracauer discusses briefly Edward Steichen's 1955 *Family of Man* photographic exhibit at MOMA, which suggests Kracauer's participation in Cold War humanist discourse. This late turn is what prompts von Moltke to call Kracauer's humanism "curious" since it is so radically undone by the antihumanist account of film, photography, and spectatorship articulated throughout the rest of the book (pp. 173–185). Indeed, von Moltke concludes that *Theory of Film* "could not be further removed from Steichen's familial humanism" (p. 185).
74. Ibid., 168.
75. Arendt, *The Origins of Totalitarianism*, 362. See also Benjamin Lazier's discussion of this passage in "Earthrise," 602–603.
76. Kracauer, *TOF*, 297.
77. See Eric Hayot's account of modernist form in *On Literary Worlds*, 131–133.
78. Mülder-Bach, "History as Autobiography," 153.
79. Kracauer, *History*, 83. Hereafter cited as *H*.
80. Ibid., 83–85.
81. Ibid., 92.
82. Ibid., 93.
83. Kracauer, *TOF*, 296, li.
84. Kracauer, *H*, 37.
85. Ibid., 33.
86. Kracauer, *TOF*, i. This does not mean that film does not consume raw materials. See Nadia Bozak's important study: *The Cinematic Footprint*.
87. Siskind, "Captain Cook and the Discovery of Antarctica's Modern Specificity."
88. Ibid., 9.
89. Cook, *The Journals*, 412, quoted in Siskind, 13.
90. Ibid., 18.
91. Kracauer, *TOF*, 305.
92. Ibid., 58.

93. Ibid., 304–305.
94. Kant writes: "It follows hence that the sublime is not to be sought in the things of nature, but only in our Ideas." Kant, *The Critique of Judgment*, 109.
95. Thompson, *Scott, Shackleton and Amundsen*, 140.
96. Day, *Antarctica*, 125–127.
97. British literary agent quoted in Day, *Antarctica*, 141.
98. Pyne, *The Ice*, 101.
99. Lynch, "The Worst Location in the World," 302–303. See also the production notes preceding the film on *90° South: With Scott to the Antarctic*.
100. Scott's journey and heroic death are the subjects of the fictionalized Technicolor drama *Scott of the Antarctic* (Charles Frend, 1948) shot on location in Norway and Switzerland. André Bazin famously dismisses this feeble attempt to "imitate the inimitable" through re-enactment in his essay "Cinema and Exploration," 158–159.
101. Ponting, *The Great White South*, 185–186, 189.
102. Kracauer, *TOF*, 82.
103. Bazin, "Cinema and Exploration," 162. See also Rosalind Galt. "'It's So Cold in Alaska.'" This essay concerns Peter Delpeut's *Forbidden Quest* (1993), an experimental film composed of found footage from various polar expeditions. Galt turns to Bazin's essay to theorize the play between the affective allure of the documentary footage, which confronts us with the danger of exploration, on one hand, and our attraction to the fictional story that Delpeut creates by decontextualizing the shots and reassembling them as a fantastic narrative, on the other. As Galt notes, by combining footage from both poles, *Forbidden Quest* also juxtaposes the colonialist narrative of European exploration against the "black slate" of Antarctica (p. 62). As such, among other things, the film demonstrates what's at stake in the archivist's instinct to preserve not just an old film, but also its original political meaning.
104. Kracauer, *TOF*, 101.
105. Ibid., 265.
106. Ibid., 1.
107. Ibid., 266. In *Theory of Film*, Kracauer misattributes this quote to Roland rather than Roger Caillois. See also Hansen, *Cinema and Experience*, 355, note 54.
108. After the hand-drawn rendering of Scott's grave, the film transitions to an engraving of a statue of Scott. The final image is a still photograph of the Antarctic shoreline with the sun low on the horizon.
109. Camper, "Mother Nature's Cold Heart."
110. These events are recounted in Shackleton, *South: A Memoir of the Endurance Voyage*, and are also discussed in the DVD commentary in *South: Ernest Shackleton and the Endurance Expedition* by archivist Luke McKernan (Image Entertainment, 1999).
111. The syndicate sponsoring the film sent Hurley back to South Georgia Island a year later to film additional scenes. See Nichols, "A Survival Tale in the Ice Floes."
112. Shackleton referred to this expedition as "The White Warfare in the South." He and his men were, he claimed, "striving to carry out the ordained task . . . ignorant of the crisis through which the world was passing." Shackleton, *South: A Memoir*, vii.
113. See the use of Hurley's photograph in the Earth Vision Institute's video essay *Extreme Ice Survey: South Georgia Island* (2015). Hurley's photographs from the Shackleton voyage compared with photographs taken today at the same location

confirm that the glacial ice is retreating. See http://earthvisioninstitute.org/share-this/extreme-ice-changes-south-georgia-island-2/.

114. These descriptions are taken from Ponting's voiceover commentary in *90° South* and are also reproduced in *Great White South*, 68, 186.
115. Koerner, *Caspar David Friedrich and the Subject of Landscape*, 226.
116. Wilson, *The Spiritual History of Ice*, 226.
117. Pyne, *The Ice*, 156, 187–189.
118. Kracauer, *TOF*, ix.
119. Kael, "Is There a Cure for Film Criticism?," 292.
120. Arnheim, "Melancholy Unshaped," 292.
121. Ibid., 295.
122. Ibid., 296.
123. Ibid.
124. Ibid., 297.
125. Arnheim, *Film as Art*, 7.
126. Worringer, *Abstraction and Empathy*, 15.
127. Ibid., 24.
128. Ibid., 17.
129. Ibid., 18.
130. Ibid., 46.
131. Ibid., 13.
132. Kracauer, *TOF*, 17, quoted in Arnheim, "Melancholy Unshaped," 295.
133. Arnheim, "Melancholy," 297.
134. Ibid.
135. Trotter, *Cinema and Modernism*, 182.
136. Richter, *Thought-Images*, 108, 112. Kracauer quoted on 112.
137. Ibid., 113.
138. Ibid., 114.
139. Gualiteri, "The Territory of Photography," 89.
140. Morton, *Ecology without Nature*, 20.
141. Ibid., 185–186.
142. Kracauer, *TOF*, 309.
143. Ibid., 17.
144. "Extreme temperatures, harsh winds, and atypical seasons of daylight and darkness are only some of the parallels between Antarctica and the space environment." The isolation in close quarters, moreover, provides the psychologically estranged conditions of life in a space station. See "Antarctica Analog Studies," June 10, 2015, https://www.nasa.gov/hrp/research/analogs/antarctica.
145. Day, *Antarctica*, 493.
146. Ibid., 509. Day notes that this treaty system had led to ecologically damaging tourism in the late 1980s, when the continent became known for the super-rich and adventuring class as the "Antarctic Riviera." Scientists and environmental activists have successfully curbed South Pole tourism. See pp. 505–520.
147. Varagur, "Empowering Women to Break the Jihadi Cycle."
148. Osborne, "Giant Crack in Antarctica's Larsen C Ice Shelf"; Abraham, "Imminent Collapse of a Portion of Larsen C Ice Shelf"; Patel, "A Crack in an Antarctic Ice Shelf"; Viñas, "Antarctic Ice Shelf Sheds Massive Iceberg"; Patel and Gillis, "An Iceberg the Size of Delaware Just Broke Away from Antarctica."
149. "What the World Would Look Like if All the Ice Melted."

CONCLUSION
1. Bazin, "The Ontology of the Photographic Image," 13.
2. Cavell, *The World Viewed*, 23, 41.
3. Ibid., 226.
4. Hansen, "The Mass Production of the Senses," 59.
5. Macaulay, "Explosive Memories."
6. Ibid.
7. Derrida, *Archive Fever*, 94.
8. See Derrida, "No Apocalypse Not Now," 27.
9. Ibid., 23.
10. Kracauer, "Photography," 62.
11. Aravamudan, "The Catachronism of Climate Change," 25.

BIBLIOGRAPHY

Abbas, Ackbar. "Poor Theory and New Chinese Cinema: Jia Zhangke's 'Still Life.'" University of California-Irvine, Critical Theory Institute Public Lecture, December 3, 2008 (unpublished and quoted by permission from the author). Available online: https://www.humanities.uci.edu/critical/pdf/AbbasPoorTheoryStillLife.pdf.

Abraham, John. "Imminent Collapse of a Portion of Larsen C Ice Shelf Hammers Home Reality of Climate Change." *The Guardian*, June 12, 2017.

Adorno, Theodor. *Minima Moralia: Reflections on a Damaged Life*. Translated by E. F. N. Jephcott. London: Verso, 2005.

Advisory Committee on Human Radiation Experiments, Final Report. Washington, DC: US Government Printing Office, 1995.

"After the Flood." *New Republic* 51 (July 20, 1927): 216–217.

Amundsen, Roald. "At the Pole." In *Antarctica: Firsthand Accounts of Exploration and Endurance*, edited by Charles Neider, 197–224. New York: Cooper Square Press, 2000.

Angell, Callie. *Andy Warhol Screen Tests: The Film of Andy Warhol Catalogue Raisonné*. Vol. 1. New York: Abrams and Whitney Museum of American Art, 2006.

Aravamudan, Srinivas. "The Catachronism of Climate Change." *diacritics* 41, no. 3 (2013): 6–30.

Arendt, Hannah. "The Conquest of Space." In *Between Past and Future*, 265–280. New York: Penguin Press, 1968.

———. *The Human Condition*. 2nd ed. Chicago: University of Chicago Press, 1998.

———. *The Origins of Totalitarianism*. New York: Harcourt Books, 1968.

Arnheim, Rudolf. *Film as Art*. Berkeley: University of California Press, 1957.

———. "Melancholy Unshaped." *Journal of Aesthetics and Art Criticism* 21, no. 3 (1963): 291–297.

Bachelard, Gaston. *Water and Dreams, An Essay on the Imagination of Matter*. Translated by Edith R. Farrell. Dallas: Pegasus Foundation, 1983.

Ballard, J. G. *The Drowned World*. New York: Liveright Publishing, 1962.

Barthes, Roland. *Camera Lucida: Reflections on Photography*. Translated by Richard Howard. New York: Hill and Wang, 1981.

Baudry, Jean-Louis. "The Apparatus: Metapsychological Approaches to the Impression of Reality in Cinema." Translated by Jean Andrews and Bernand Augst. *Camera Obscura* 1 (Fall 1976): 39–47.

Bazin, André. "Cinema and Exploration." In *What Is Cinema? Vol. 1*, edited and translated by Hugh Gray, 154–163. Berkeley: University of California Press, 1967.

———. "The Ontology of the Photographic Image." In *What Is Cinema? Vol. 1.*, edited and translated by Hugh Gray, 9–16. Berkeley: University of California Press, 1967.

Bengtson, John. *Silent Echoes: Discovering Early Hollywood through the Films of Buster Keaton.* Santa Monica, CA: Santa Monica Press, 2000.

Benhabib, Seyla. *The Rights of Others: Aliens, Residents and Citizens.* Cambridge: Cambridge University Press, 2004.

Benjamin, Walter. "On Some Motifs in Baudelaire." In *Illuminations: Essay and Reflections*, edited by Hannah Arendt, 155–200. Translated by Harry Zhon. New York: Schocken Books, 1968.

———. "The Destructive Character." In *Reflections: Essay, Aphorisms, Autobiographical Writings*, edited by Peter Demetz, 301–303. Translated by Edmund Jephcott. New York: Schocken Books, 1978.

———. "The Storyteller." In *Illuminations: Essays and Reflections*, edited by Hannah Arendt, 83–109. Translated by Harry Zohn. New York: Schocken Books, 1969.

———. "The Work of Art in the Age of Its Technological Reproducibility (second version)." In *The Work of Art in the Age of Its Technological Reproducibility and Other Writing on Media*, edited by Michael W. Jennings, Brigid Doherty, and Thomas Y. Levin, 19–55. Cambridge, MA: Harvard University Press, 2008.

Berger, John. "Ten Dispatches about Place." In *Hold Everything Dear: Dispatches on Survival and Resistance*, 119–128. New York: Pantheon, 2007.

Bergson, Henri. *Laughter: An Essay on the Meaning of the Comic.* Translated by Cloudesley Brereton and Fred Rothwell. Rockville, MD: Arc Manor, 2008.

Berlant, Lauren. *Cruel Optimism.* Durham, NC: Duke University Press, 2011.

Bernasconi, Robert. "Kant's Third Thoughts on Race." In *Reading Kant's Geography*, edited by Stuard Elden and Eduardo Mendieta, 291–318. Albany: State University of New York Press, 2011.

Bernau, Bradley M. "Help for Hotspots: NGO Participation in the Preservations of the Worldwide Biodiversity." *Indiana Journal of Global Legal Studies* 13, no. 2 (2006): 614–643.

Biesen, Sheri Chinen. *Blackout: World War II and the Origins of Film Noir.* Baltimore: Johns Hopkins University Press, 2005.

"Biggest Money Picture: Sound Film Shy Big Silent Sums." *Variety* (June 21, 1932): 62.

Bilton, Alan. "Buster Keaton and the South: The First Things and the Last." *Journal of American Studies* 40, no. 3 (December 2006): 487–502.

Bonami, Francesco. "Painting's Laughter." In *Andy Warhol/Supernova: Stars, Deaths, and Disasters, 1962-1964*, edited by Douglas Fogle, 20–27. Minneapolis, MN: Walter Art Center, 2006.

Borde, Raymond, and Etienne Chaumenton. *A Panorama of American Film Noir, 1941–1953.* Translated by Paul Hammond. San Francisco: City Lights Books, 2002.

Bordeleau, Erick. "Jia Zhangke's *Still Life*: Destruction as Intercession." *Scapegoat* 3 (July 26, 2023). Accessed July 24, 2017. http://www.scapegoatjournal.org/docs/03/03_Bordeleau_DestructionAsIntercession.pdf.

Boym, Svetlana. *The Future of Nostalgia.* New York: Basic Books, 2001.

Bozak, Nadia. *The Cinematic Footprint: Lights, Camera, Natural Resources.* New Brunswick, NJ: Rutgers University Press, 2012.

Brecht, Bertolt. "Außer diesem Stern." In *Werke: Grosse kommentierte Berliner und Frankfurter Ausgabe.* Vol. 15. (Gedichte 5, 1940–1956). Edited by Werner Hecht, Jan Knopf, Werner Mittenzwei, and Klau-Detlef Müller, 209. Berlin & Weimar: Aufbau-Verlag, and Frankfurt Am Main: Suhrkamp Verlag, 1993.

Broad, William J. "The Bomb Chroniclers." *New York Times*, September 13, 2010.

Bryson, Norman. "Chardin and the Text of Still Life." *Critical Inquiry* 15, no. 2 (Winter 1989): 227–252.

———. *Looking at the Overlooked: Four Essay on Still Life Painting*. London: Reaktion Books, 1990.

Buck-Morss, Susan. "Aesthetics and Anaesthetics: Walter Benjamin's Artwork Essay Reconsidered." *October* 62 (Autumn 1992): 3–41.

Bullot, Erik, and Molly Stevens. "Keaton and Snow." *October* 114 (Autumn 2005): 17–28.

Byrnes, Cory. "Specters of Realism and the Painter's Gaze in Jia Zhangke's 'Still Life.'" *Modern Chinese Literature and Culture* 24, no. 2 (Fall 2012): 52–93.

Camper, Fred. "Mother Nature's Cold Heart." *Chicago Reader*, January 20, 2000. Accessed July 24, 2017. https://www.chicagoreader.com/chicago/mother-natures-cold-heart/Content?oid=901265.

Carroll, Noël. *Comedy Incarnate: Buster Keaton, Physical Humor and Bodily Coping*. Oxford: Wiley-Blackwell, 2009.

Carson, Rachel. *Silent Spring*. 1962. New York: First Mariner Books, 2002.

Caruth, Cathy. *Unclaimed Experience: Trauma, Narrative, and History*. Baltimore: Johns Hopkins University Press, 1996.

Castoriadis, Cornelius. *The Imaginary Institution of Society*. Translated by Kathleen Blamey. Cambridge, MA: MIT Press, 1998.

Cavell, Stanley. *The World Viewed, Enlarged Edition*. Cambridge, MA: Harvard University Press, 1979.

Chakrabarty, Dipesh. "Humanities in the Anthropocene: The Crisis of an Enduring Kantian Fable." *New Literary History* 47, nos. 2 & 3 (Summer 2016): 377–397.

———. "The Climate of History: Four Theses." *Critical Inquiry* 35, no. 2 (Winter 2009): 197–222.

Cheah, Pheng. *What Is a World?: On Postcolonial Literature as World Literature*. Durham, NC: Duke University Press, 2016.

———. "World as Picture and Ruination: On Jia Zhangke's *Still Life* as World Cinema." In *The Oxford Handbook of Chinese Cinemas*, edited by Carlos Rojos and Eileen Cheng-Yin Chow, 190–206. Oxford: Oxford University Press, 2013.

Chetham, Deidre. *Before the Deluge: The Vanishing World of the Yangtze's Three Gorges*. New York: Palgrave MacMillan, 2002.

Chen, Xiaomei. *Occidentalism: A Theory of Counter-Discourse in Post-Mao China*. 2nd ed. New York: Rowman & Littlefield, 2002.

Chumley, Lily. *Creativity Class: Art School and Culture Work in Postsocialist China*. Princeton, NJ: Princeton University Press, 2016.

Colebrook, Claire. *Death of the Posthuman, Essays on Extinction*. Vol. 1. Ann Arbor, MI: Open Humanities Press, 2014.

Cook, James. *The Journals of Captain Cook*. Edited by Philip Edwards. London: Penguin, 1999.

Cowie, Elizabeth. "Film Noir and Women." In *Shades of Noir*, edited by Joan Copjec, 121–165. London: Verso, 1993.

Davis, Mike. *Ecology of Fear: Los Angeles and the Imagination of Disaster*. New York: Vintage Books, 1998.

Davis, Tracy C. *Stages of Emergency: Cold War Nuclear Civil Defense*. Durham, NC: Duke University Press, 2007.

Day, David. *Antarctica, A Biography*. Oxford: Oxford University Press, 2013.

de Duve, Thierry. "Andy Warhol, or The Machine Perfected." Translated by Rosalind Krauss. *October* 48 (1989): 3–14.

Dell'Amore, Christine. "Why Antarctica Is So Hard on the Body—Even for Buzz Aldrin." *National Geographic*, December 1, 2016. http://news.nationalgeographic.com/2016/12/buzz-aldrin-south-pole-antarctica-evacuation-science/.

Derrida, Jacques. *Archive Fever: A Freudian Impression*. Translated by Eric Prenowitz. Chicago: University of Chicago Press, 1996.

———. *Adieu to Emmanuel Levinas*. Translated by Pascale-Anne Brault and Michael Nass. Stanford: Stanford University Press, 1999.

———. "No Apocalypse, Not Now (Full Speed Ahead, Seven Missiles, Seven Missives)." *diacritics* 14, no. 2 (Summer 1984): 20–31.

Derrida, Jacques, and Anne Dufourmantelle. *Of Hospitality*. Translated by Rachel Bowlby. Stanford, CA: Stanford University Press, 2000.

Dienstag, Joshua Foa. *Pessimism: Philosophy, Ethic, Spirit*. Princeton, NJ: Princeton University Press, 2006.

Dillard, Annie. "An Expedition to the Pole." In *Teaching a Stone to Talk: Expeditions and Encounters*, 29–64. New York: Harper, 2008.

Dimendberg, Edward. *Film Noir and the Spaces of Modernity*. Cambridge, MA: Harvard University Press, 2004.

Doane, Mary Ann. *The Emergence of Cinematic Time: Modernity, Contingency, and Archive*. Cambridge, MA: Harvard University Press, 2002.

Docherty, Thomas. *Aesthetic Democracy*. Stanford, CA: Stanford University Press, 2006.

Dussera, Eric. *America Is Elsewhere: The Noir Tradition in the Age of Consumer Culture*. London and New York: Oxford University Press, 2014.

Edelman, Lee. *No Future: Queer Theory and the Death Drive*. Durham, NC: Duke University Press, 2004.

Ellis, Erle, Mark Maslin, Nicole Boivin, and Andrew Bauer. "Involve Social Scientists in Defining the Anthropocene." *Nature* 540 (December 8, 2016): 192–193.

"The Environment & Climate Change." United Nations High Commissioner for Refugees, 2014. http://www.unhcr.org/540854f49.html.

"The Facts about A-bomb Fallout." *U.S. News & World Report*, March 25, 1955.

Favret, Mary A. *War at a Distance: Romanticism and the Making of Modern Wartime*. Princeton, NJ: Princeton University Press, 2010.

Fehner, Terrence R., and F. G. Gosling, *Atmospheric Nuclear Weapons Testing, 1951–1963*. Washington, DC: US Department of Energy, 2006.

Feil, Ken. *Dying for a Laugh: Disaster Movies and the Camp Imagination*. Middleton, CT: Wesleyan University Press, 2005.

Feuer, Jane. "Singin' in the Rain." In *Film Analysis: A Norton Reader*, edited by Jeffrey Geiger and R. L. Rusky, 440–454. New York and London: W. W. Norton, 2005.

———. *The Hollywood Musical*. London: BFI/Macmillan, 1982.

Flately, Jonathan. "Like: Collecting and Collectivity." *October* 132 (Spring 2010): 71–98.

Fleischer, Matthew. "*Exiles* on Main Street: Searching for the Ghosts of Bunker Hill's Native American Past." *LA Weekly*, August 13, 2008.

Fogle, Douglas. "Spectators at our Own Deaths." In *Andy Warhol/Supernova: Stars, Deaths, and Disasters, 1962-1964*, edited by Douglas Fogle, 11–19. Minneapolis, MN: Walter Art Center, 2006.

Foster, Hal. "Test Subjects." *October* 132 (Spring 2010): 30–42.

Freud, Sigmund. "The Uncanny." In *The Standard Edition of the Complete Psychological Works of Sigmund Freud*, Vol. 17, edited by James Strachey and Anna Freud, 219–252. Translated by James Strachey. London: Hogarth Press, 1953–1974.

Friedman, Robert Marc. *Appropriating the Weather: Vilhelm Bjerknes and the Construction of Modern Meteorology*. Ithaca, NY, and London: Cornell University Press, 1989.

Galt, Rosalind. "'It's So Cold in Alaska': Evoking Exploration between Bazin and *The Forbidden Quest*." *Discourse* 28, no. 1 (2006): 53–71.

Gellatly, Andrew. "Steve McQueen." *Frieze Magazine* 46 (May 1999). Accessed December 7, 2015. http://www.frieze.com/issue/review/steve_mcqueen/.

Gillis, Justin, and Nadja Popovich. "The U.S. Is the Biggest Carbon Polluter in History. It Just Walked Away from the Paris Climate Deal." *New York Times*, June 1, 2017.

Gleiberman, Owen. "The Two Jakes." *Entertainment Weekly*, August 17, 1990.

"Goldywn Brought South Seas to Hollywood for 'Hurricane.'" In *The Hurricane* press book (1939). In *Cinema Press Books from the Original Studio Collection*. Woodbury, CT: Research Publications 1988. Microfilm, Wisconsin Center for Film and Theater Research, part two, section B, reel 30.

Gorky, Maxim. "The Lumière Cinematograph." In *The Film Factory: Russian and Soviet Cinema in Document 1896-1939*, edited by Ian Christie and Richard Taylor, 25–26. Translated by Richard Taylor. London: Routledge, 1998.

Green, Bill. *Water, Ice & Stone: Science and Memory on the Antarctic Lakes*. New York: Bellevue Literary Press, 2008.

Gualtieri, Elena. "The Territory of Photography: Between Modernity and Utopia in Kracauer's Thought." *New Formations* 61 (2007): 76–89.

Guattari, Félix. *The Three Ecologies*. Translated by Ian Pindar and Paul Sutton. New York: Continuum, 2008.

Gunning, Tom. "Mechanisms of Laughter: The Devices of Slapstick." In *Slapstick Comedy*, edited by Tom Paulus and Rob King, 137–151. New York and London: Routledge, 2010.

Gusterson, Hugh. *People of the Bomb: Portraits of America's Nuclear Complex*. Minneapolis: University of Minnesota Press, 2004.

Hacking, Ian. *The Taming of Chance*. Cambridge: Cambridge University Press, 1990.

Hales, Peter Bacon. *Outside the Gates of Eden: The Dream of America from Hiroshima to Now*. Chicago: University of Chicago Press, 2014.

Hall, Alan. "Mapping the White Continent." *Scientific American*, November 17, 1995. https://www.scientificamerican.com/article/mapping-the-white-contine-1997-11-17/.

Handwerk, Brian. "China's Three Gorges Dam by the Numbers." *National Geographic News*, June 9, 2006. http://news.nationalgeographic.com/news/2006/06/060609-gorges-dam.html.

Hansen, Miriam. *Cinema and Experience: Siegfried Kracauer, Walter Benjamin, and Theodor W. Adorno*. Berkeley: University of California Press, 2012.

———. "'With Skin and Hair': Kracauer's Theory of Film, Marseille 1940." *Critical Inquiry* 19, no. 3 (1993): 437–469.

———. "Fallen Women, Rising Stars, New Horizons: Shanghai Silent Film as Vernacular Modernism." *Film Quarterly* 54, no. 1 (Autumn 2000): 10–22.

———. "The Mass Production of the Senses: Classical Cinema as Vernacular Modernism." *Modernism/Modernity* 6, no. 2 (1999): 59–77.

Hanssen, Beatrice. *Walter Benjamin's Other History: Of Stone, Animals, Human Beings, and Angels*. Berkeley: University of California Press, 1998.

Hayot, Eric. *On Literary Worlds*. Oxford: Oxford University Press, 2012.

———. *The Hypothetical Mandarin: Sympathy, Modernity, and Chinese Pain*. Oxford: Oxford University Press, 2009.

Healy, Joel. Interview by Kelli Healy Salazar. "StoryCorps." National Public Radio, October 12, 2012. http://www.npr.org/2012/10/12/162722650/veteran-risks-in-1950s-bomb-test-a-disgrace.

Hersey, John. *Hiroshima*. New York: Vintage Books, 1989.

Hopper, Hedda. "Studios Theatre Gossip: Hollywood Sets Would Fool Mother Nature: Scenic Experts Make Land, Sea and Sky Look More Realistic Than Reality." *Los Angeles Times*, November 26, 1939.

Hsia, Adrian. "Bertolt Brecht in China and His Impact on Chinese Drama: A Preliminary Examination." *Comparative Literature Studies* 20, no. 2 (Summer 1983): 231–245.

Hollywood's Top Secret Film Studio. Directed by Peter Kuran. Visual Concepts Entertainment, 2003.

International Commission to Investigate the Health and Environmental Effects of Nuclear Weapons Production and Institute for Energy and Environmental Research. *Radioactive Heaven and Earth*. New York: Apex Press, 1991.

Jacobs, James A. *Detached America: Building Houses in Postwar Suburbia*. Charlottesville: University of Virginia Press, 2015.

Jacobson, Brian R. *Studios before the System: Architecture, Technology, and the Emergence of Cinematic Space*. New York: Columbia University Press, 2015.

Jia, Zhangke. "The Age of Amateur Cinema Will Return." In *One Person's Impression: Complete Guidebook to DV* (Yigeren de yingxiang: DV wanquan shouce), edited by Xianmin Zhang and Yaxuan Zhang. Beijing: China Youth Publishing, 2003. [Available in English online: http://dgeneratefilms.com/critical-essays/jia-zhangke-the-age-of-amateur-cinema-will-return].

———. Interview. "Jia Zhang-ke on Still Life." DVD Extra. (Producer Cindi Rowell, New Yorker Films, 2008). *Still Life* DVD extra (New Yorker Video, 2008).

———. "Still Life (Sanxia Haoren) 2006." In *Jia Zhangke Speaks Out: The Chinese Director's Texts on Film*, 65–66. Translated by Alice Shih. Piscataway, NJ: Transaction Publishers, 2015.

Kahn, Joseph. "In China, a Lake's Champion Imperials Himself." *New York Times* October 17, 2007. http://www.nytimes.com/2007/10/14/world/asia/14china.html?pagewanted=all&_r=0.

Kale, Pauline. "Is There a Cure for Film Criticism?" In *I Lost It at the Movies*, 269–292. Boston: Little Brown, 1965.

Kälin, Walter. "Conceptualising Climate-Induced Displacement." In *Climate Change and Displacement: Multidisciplinary Perspectives*, edited by Jane McAdam, 81–104. Oxford: Hart Publishing, 2010.

Kant, Immanuel. "Perpetual Peace: A Philosophical Sketch." In *Kant: Political Writing*, edited by H. S. Reiss, 99–130. Translated by H. B. Nisbet. Cambridge: Cambridge University Press, 1991.

———. *The Critique of Judgment*. Translated by J. H. Bernard. Amherst, MA: Prometheus Books, 2000.

Kaplan, E. Ann. *Climate Trauma: Foreseeing the Future in Dystopian Film and Fiction*. New Brunswick, NJ: Rutgers University Press, 2016.

Kaufman, Scott. *Project Plowshare: The Peaceful Use of Nuclear Explosives in Cold War America*. Ithaca, NY: Cornell University Press, 2013.

Keaton, Buster. Interview by John Gilett and James Blue. "Keaton at Venice." In *Buster Keaton Interviews*, edited by Kevin W. Sweeney, 219–231. Jackson: University of Mississippi Press, 2007.

Keaton, Buster, with Charles Samuels. *My Wonderful World of Slapstick*. Cambridge, MA: Da Capo, 1982.

Kenner, Hugh. "In Memoriam: Buster Keaton." *National Review,* February, 22 1966.

King, Rob. *The Fun Factory: The Keystone Film Company and the Emergence of Mass Culture*. Berkley: University of California Press, 2009.

Koerner, Joseph Leo. *Caspar David Friedrich and the Subject of Landscape*. 2nd ed. London: Reaktion Book, 2009.

Koestenbaum, Wayne. "Andy Warhol," First Chapter. *New York Times*, September 16, 2001. http://www.nytimes.com/2001/09/16/books/chapters/16-1st-koest.html.

Kracauer, Siegfried. *History: The Last Things before the Last*. Princeton, NJ: Markus Wiener, [1969] 1995.

———. "Hollywood's Terror Film: Do They Reflect an American State of Mind?" In *Siegfried Kracauer's American Writings: Essay on Film and Popular Culture*, edited by Johannes von Moltke and Kristy Rawson, 41–47. Berkeley: University of California Press, 2012.

———. "Photography." In *The Mass Ornament: Weimar Essays*, edited and translated by Thomas Y. Levin, 47–63. Cambridge, MA: Harvard University Press, 1995.

———. "The Calico-World: UFA City in Naubablesberg." In *The Mass Ornament: Weimar Essays*, edited and translated by Thomas Y. Levin, 281–288. Cambridge, MA: Harvard University Press, 1995.

———. *Theory of Film: The Redemption of Physical Reality*. Princeton, NJ: Princeton University Press, 1997.

Kuletz, Valeria L. *The Tainted Desert: Environmental and Social Ruin in the American West*. London: Routledge, 1998.

Latour, Bruno. "Agency at the Time of the Anthropocene." *New Literary History* 45, no. 1 (Winter 2014): 1–18.

Lazier, Benjamin. "Earthrise; or, The Globalization of the World Picture." *American Historical Review* 116, no. 3 (2011): 602–630.

Lethen, Helmut. *Cool Conduct: The Culture of Distance in Weimar Germany*. Translated by Don Reneau. Berkeley: University of California Press, 2002.

———. "Refrigerators of Intelligence." Translated by Gail Wise and Thomas Ketron. *qui parle* 5, no. 2 (1992): 73–101.

Levin, Thomas J. "Film." In *The Work of Art in the Age of Its Technological Reproducibility and Other Writing on Media*, edited by Michael W. Jennings, Brigid Doherty, and Thomas Y. Levin, 19–55. Cambridge, MA: Harvard University Press, 2008.

Lippit, Akira Mizuta. *Atomic Light (Shadow Optics)*. Minneapolis: University of Minnesota Press, 2005.

Lotz, Christian. *The Capitalist Schema: Time, Money, and the Culture of Abstraction*. Lanham, MA: Lexington Books, 2014.

Lu, Sheldon H. "Emerging from Underground and the Periphery: Chinese Independent Cinema at the Turn of the Twenty-First Century." In *Cinema at the Periphery*, edited by Dine Iordanova, David Martin-Jones, and Belen Vidal, 104–118. Detroit: Wayne State University Press, 2010.

Lynch, Dennis. "The Worst Location in the World: Herbert G. Ponting in the Antarctic, 1910-1912." *Film History* 3, no. 3 (1989): 291–306.

Macaulay, Scott. "Explosive Memories: Five Questions for *Dawson City: Frozen Time* Director Bill Morrison." Filmmaker Magazine, June 8, 2017. http://filmmakermagazine.com/102598-explosive-memories-five-questions-for-dawson-city-frozen-time-director-bill-morrison/#.WXjMptPyuMI.

Marzec, Robert P. *Militarizing the Environment: Climate Change the Security State*. Minneapolis: University of Minnesota Press, 2015.

Masco, Joseph. *Nuclear Borderlands: The Manhattan Project in Post-Cold War New Mexico*. Princeton, NJ: Princeton University Press, 2006.

McAdam, Jane. "Climate Change Displacement and International Law: Complementary Protection Standards." In *Legal and Protection Policy Research Series*. Geneva: United Nations High Commissioner for Refugees, 2011. Accessed July 27, 2017. http://www.unhcr.org/4dff16e99.pdf.

McGrath, Jason. "The Cinema of Displacement: The Three Gorges Dam in Feature Film and Video." In *Displacement: The Three Gorges Dam and Contemporary Chinese Art,* edited by Wu Hong, 33–46. Chicago: Smart Museum of Art, University of Chicago, 2008.

McKernan, Luke. "DVD Commentary." *South: Ernest Shackleton and the Endurance Expedition*. DVD. Director: Frank Hurley. Chatsworth, CA: Image Entertainment, 1999.

McKibben, Bill. *Eaarth: Making a Life on a Rough New Planet*. New York: St. Martin's Griffin, 2011.

McLuhan, Marshall. *Understanding Media: The Extensions of Man*. Cambridge, MA: MIT Press, 1994.

McNeill, J. R., and Peter Engelka. *The Great Acceleration: An Environmental History of the Anthropocene*. Oxford, MA: Belknap Press, 2014.

Mello, Cecília. "Space and Intermediality in Jia Zhang-ke's Still Life." *Aniki* 1, no. 2 (2014): 274–291.

Metz, Christian. *The Imaginary Signifier: Psychoanalysis and Cinema*. Translated by Celia Britton. Bloomington: Indiana University Press, 1982.

Miller, Richard L. *Under the Cloud, the Decades of Nuclear Testing*. New York: Free Press, 1986.

Miller, Robert C. "Rescue Crew Finds Grim Tool in Ruins of A-bombed Town." *Washington Post,* May 7, 1955.

Miller, Tyrus. *Late Modernism: Politics, Fiction, and the Arts between the World Wars*. Berkeley: University of California Press, 1999.

Moreno, Jonathan. "Secret State Experiments and Medical Ethics." In *Expanding Horizons in Bioethics,* edited by A. W. Galston and C. Z. Pepperds, 58–70. Berlin: Springer, 2005.

Morton, Timothy. *Ecology without Nature: Rethinking Environmental Aesthetics*. Cambridge, MA: Harvard University Press, 2007.

Mülder-Bach, Inke. "History as Autobiography: *The Last Things before the Last*." Translated by Gail Finney. *New German Critique* 54 (1991): 139–157.

Mulvey, Laura. "Clumsy Sublime." *Film Quarterly* 60, no. 3 (Spring 2007): 3.

———. "Visual Pleasure and Narrative Cinema." *Screen* 16, no. 2 (1975): 6–18.

Murphy, David Thompson. *German Exploration to the Polar World: A History, 1870–1940*. Lincoln: University of Nebraska Press, 2002.

Nabhan, Gary Paul. "The Dangers of Reductionism in Biodiversity Conservation." *Conservation Biology* 9, no. 3 (1995): 479–481.

Nadel, Alan. *Containment Culture: American Narratives, Postmodernism, and the Atomic Age*. Durham, NC: Duke University Press, 1995.

Naremore, James. *Acting in the Cinema*. Berkeley: University of California Press, 1988.

"Nary Snowflake in Mamaroneck: Griffith's 'Two Orphans' Lacking It, His Policy for $25,000 Becomes Due." *The Insurance Press* 45 (F. Webster: New York, 1921): 4. New York Public Library, digitized November 6, 2009.

Nevada National Security Site. "Secret Film Studio: Lookout Mountain." National Nuclear Security Administration, 2013. http://nnss.gov/docs/fact_sheets/DOENV_1142.pdf.

Nichols, Peter M. "A Survival Tale in the Ice Floes." *New York Times,* April 23, 1999.

Nixon, Rob. *Slow Violence and the Environmentalism of the Poor.* Cambridge, MA: Harvard University Press, 2011.

North, Michael. *Machine-Age Comedy.* New York: Oxford University Press, 2007.

Nugent, Frank S. "The Screen: Samuel Goldwyn Turn Nordhoff-Hall 'Hurricane' Loose Across the Screen of the Astor." *New York Times,* November 10, 1937.

Oderman, Stuart. *Lillian Gish: A Life on Stage and Screen.* Jefferson: McFarland & Company, 2000.

Oliver, Kelly. *Earth and World: Philosophy after the Apollo Missions.* New York: Columbia University Press, 2015.

O'Neill, Dan. *The Firecracker Boys.* New York: St. Martin's Press, 1994.

Osborne, Hannah. "Giant Crack in Antarctica's Larsen C Ice Shelf Grew 11 Miles in Just Six Days." *Newsweek,* June 1, 2017.

Oster, Gautam Naik Shai. "Scientists Link China's Dam to Earthquake, Renewing Debate." *Wall Street Journal,* February 6, 2009. http://www.wsj.com/articles/SB123391567210056475.

Parrish, Susan Scott. "Faulkner and the Outer Weather of 1927." *American Literary History* 24, no. 1 (Spring 2012): 34–58.

Parson, Don. *Making a Better World: Public Housing, the Red Scare, and the Direction of Modern Los Angeles.* Minneapolis: University of Minnesota Press, 2005.

Patel, Jugal K. "A Crack in an Antarctic Ice Shelf Is 8 Miles from Creating an Iceberg the Size of Delaware." *New York Times,* June 9, 2017.

Patel, Jugal K., and Justin Gillis. "An Iceberg the Size of Delaware Just Broke Away from Antarctica." *New York Times,* July 12, 2017. https://www.nytimes.com/interactive/2017/06/09/climate/antarctica-rift-update.html?emc=eta1&_r=0.

Perez, Gilberto. *The Material Ghost: Film and Their Medium.* Baltimore: Johns Hopkins University Press, 1998.

Platt, John R. "Chinese Sturgeon Give Up, Stop Breeding in Polluted Yangtze River." *Scientific American* "Extinction Countdown Blog," September 14, 2014. http://blogs.scientificamerican.com/extinction-countdown/chinese-sturgeon-give-up-stop-breeding-in-polluted-yangtze-river/.

Polan, Dana. *Power and Paranoia: History, Narrative, and the American Cinema, 1940–1950.* New York: Columbia University Press, 1986.

Pollack, Henry. *A World without Ice.* New York: Avery, 2010.

Ponte, Alessandra. "Desert Testing." In *The House of Light and Entropy,* 97–134. London: Architectural Association, London, 2012.

Ponting, Herbert G. *The Great White South: Traveling with Robert G. Scott's Doomed South Pole Expedition.* New York: Cooper Square Press, 2001.

"Production Notes." In *90° South: With Scott to the Antarctic.* DVD. Image Entertainment, 1991.

Pyne, Stephen J. *The Ice: A Journey to Antarctica.* Iowa City: University of Iowa Press, 1986.

Randall, Alex. "Climate Change Driving Migration into China's Vulnerable Cities." *Chinadialogue,* June 10, 2013. https://www.chinadialogue.net/article/show/single/en/6113-Climate-change-driving-migration-into-China-s-vulnerable-cities.

Richter, Gerhard. *Thought-Images: Frankfurt School Writers' Reflection from Damaged Life.* Stanford, CA: Stanford University Press, 2007.

Rodowick, D. N. *The Virtual Life of Film*. Cambridge, MA: Harvard University Press, 2007.

Rolston, Holmes. "China: Land of Monster Dam, Killer Rivers." *The Coloradoan*, August 19, 2015. http://www.coloradoan.com/story/life/2015/08/19/three-gorges-dam-streches-miles-across-chinas-yangtze-river/31996981/.

Ronell, Avital. *The Test Drive*. Chicago: University of Illinois Press, 2005.

Roosevelt, Theodore. "Seventh Annual Address to Congress, Dec. 3, 1907." Excerpted on the National Public Television project, "Archives of the West." http://www.pbs.org/weta/thewest/resources/archives/eight/trconserv.htm.

Ross, Andrew. *Strange Weather: Culture, Science, and Technology in the Age of Limits*. London and New York: Verso, 1991.

Royle, Nicholas. *The Uncanny*. New York: Routledge, 2003.

Saint-Amour, Paul K. "Bombing and the Symptom: Traumatic Earliness and the Nuclear Uncanny." *diacrticis* 30, no. 4 (Winter 2000): 59–82.

———. *Tense Future: Modernism, Total War, Encyclopedic Form*. Oxford: Oxford University Press, 2015.

Sample, Ian. "Yangtze River Dolphin Driven to Extinction." *The Guardian*, August 8, 2007.

Sanger, David E., and Jane Perlez, "Trump Hands the Chinese a Gift: The Chance for Global Leadership." *New York Times*, June 1, 2017. https://www.nytimes.com/2017/06/01/us/politics/climate-accord-trump-china-global-leadership.html?_r=0.

Santner, Eric K. *On Creaturely Life: Rilke, Benjamin, Sebald*. Chicago: University of Chicago Press, 2006.

Saxon, Lyle. *Father Mississippi*. New York and London: The Century Co., 1927.

Schallert, Edwin. "'Steamboat Bill' Stormy Fun Special." *Los Angeles Times*, June 8, 1928.

Schiavenza, Matt. "City in Ruins: The Legacy of Sichuan's Big Earthquake." *The Atlantic*, May 14, 2013. http://www.theatlantic.com/china/archive/2013/05/city-in-ruins-the-legacy-of-sichuans-big-earthquake/275838/.

Schickel, Richard. *D.W. Griffith: An American Life*. New York: Simon and Schuster, 1984.

Schlüpmann, Heide. "The Subject of Survival: On Kracauer's *Theory of Film*." Translated by Jeremy Gaines. *New German Critique* 54 (1991): 111–126.

Schwender, Peter, and John Wittier Treat. "America's Hiroshima, Hiroshima's America." *boundary 2* 21, no. 1 (1994): 233–253.

Scott, John L. "Film Sets Grow Larger." *Los Angeles Times*, September 1, 1929.

Scott, Robert F. *Scott's Last Expedition: The Personal Journal of Captain R.F. Scott, R.N., C.V.O, on His Journey to the South Pole*. New York: Doss, Mean, 1929.

Scranton, Roy. *Learning to Die in the Anthropocene: Reflections on the End of a Civilization*. San Francisco: City Lights Books, 2015.

"The Screen." *New York Times*, September 4, 1920. Proquest Historical Newspapers.

Shackleton, Ernest. *South: A Memoir of the Endurance Voyage*. New York: Carroll & Graff, 1998.

Shiel, Mark. "Classical Hollywood, 1928-1946." In *Art Direction & Production Design*, edited by Lucy Fischer, 48–72. New Brunswick, NJ: Rutgers University Press, 2015.

Shore, Robert. *Post-Photography: The Artist with a Camera*. London: Laurence King Publishing, 2014.

"Should International Refugee Law Accommodate Climate Change?" UN News, July 3, 2014. http://www.un.org/apps/news/story.asp?NewsID=48201#.VfBUPSRhpiG.

"Sichuan Earthquake." *New York Times*, May 6, 2009. http://topics.nytimes.com/top/news/science/topics/earthquakes/sichuan_province_china/index.html.

Simon, Alex, and Terry Keefe. "The Hollywood Interview: Robert Towne." n.d. http://thehollywoodinterview.blogspot.com/2009/10/robert-towne-hollywood-interview.html.

Singer, Ben. *Melodrama and Modernity: Early Sensational Cinema and Its Contexts*. New York: Columbia University Press, 2001.

Siskind, Mariano. "Captain Cook and the Discovery of Antarctica's Modern Specificity: Towards a Critique of Globalization." *Comparative Literature Studies* 24, no. 1 (2005): 1–23.

Sloterdijk, Peter. *Terror from the Air*. Translated by Amy Patton and Steve Corcoran. Los Angeles: Semiotext(e), 2009.

"Snow before Nov. 20 Insured for $25,000: Eighteen Companies Take Unique Griffith Risk on Films of 'The Two Orphans.'" *New York Times*, October 30, 1921.

Sobchack, Vivian. "Lounge Time: Postwar Crisis and the Chronotope of Film Noir." In *Reconfiguring American Film Genres: Theory and History*, edited by Nick Brown, 129–170. Berkeley: University of California Press, 1998.

Solnit, Rebecca. *Savage Dreams: A Journey into the Hidden Wars of the American West*. Berkeley: University of California Press, 1994, 2014.

Sontag, Susan. *Against Interpretation and Other Essays*. New York: Farrar, Straus and Giroux, 1996.

Spalding, Kirsty L., Bruce A. Buchholz, Lars-Eric Bergman, and Jonas Frisén. "Age Written in Teeth by Nuclear Tests." *Nature* 437 (September 15, 2005): 333–334.

Steffen, Will, Paul J. Crutzen, and John R. McNiel. "The Anthropocene: Are Humans Now Overwhelming the Great Forces of Nature." *AMBIO: A Journal of the Human Environment* 36, no. 8 (2007): 614–621.

Steffen, Will, Wendy Broadgate, Lisa Deutsch, Owen Gaffney, and Cornelia Ludwig. "The Trajectory of the Anthropocene: The Great Acceleration." *Anthropocene Review* (2015): 1–18.

Steimatsky, Noa. "The Cincecittá Refugee Camp (1944-1950)." *October* 128 (Spring 2009): 23–30.

Stone, Richard. "Cold War's Genetic Fallout." *Science*, February 7, 2002. http://www.sciencemag.org/news/2002/02/cold-wars-genetic-fallout.

"Survival Town Buildings Stand Up Well in Test." *Los Angeles Times*, May 6, 1955.

Szalay, Michael. *New Deal Modernism: American Literature and the Invention of the Welfare State*. Durham, NC: Duke University Press, 2000.

Teller, Edward. "We're Going to Work Miracles." *Popular Mechanics* 113, no. 3 (March 1960): 97–101.

"Three Gorges Project Sets 10 World Records." *People's Daily*. http://en.people.cn/200606/09/eng20060609_272430.html.

Thompson, David. *Scott, Shackleton and Amundsen: Ambition and Tragedy in the Antarctic*. New York: Thunder's Mouth Press, 2002.

Topham, Laurence, Alok Jha, and Will Franklin. "Building the Bomb." *The Guardian*, September 22, 2015. https://www.theguardian.com/us-news/ng-interactive/2015/sep/21/building-the-atom-bomb-the-full-story-of-the-nevada-test-site.

Trahair, Lisa. "Ghost in the Machine: The Comedy of Technology in the Cinema of Buster Keaton." *South Atlantic Quarterly* 101, no. 3 (Summer 2002): 573–588.

———. *The Comedy of Philosophy: Sense and Nonsense in Early Cinematic Slapstick*. Albany: State University of New York Press, 2007.

Treat, John Whittier. *Writing Ground Zero: Japanese Literature and the Atomic Bomb.* Chicago: University of Chicago Press, 1993.

Trotter, David. *Cinema and Modernism.* Oxford: Blackwell, 2007.

US Department of Energy, National Nuclear Security Administration Nevada Field Office. *United States Nuclear Tests: July 1945 through September 1992.* Oak Ridge: US Department of Energy, 1994. http://nnsa.energy.gov/sites/default/files/nnsa/inlinefiles/doe%20nv%202000e.pdf

Vajpeyi, Dhirendra K. *Deforestation, Environment, and Sustainable Development: A Comparative Analysis.* Westport, CT: Praeger, 2001.

Varagur, Krithika. "Empowering Women to Break the Jihadi Cycle." *New York Times,* June 20, 2017.

Vartabedian, Ralph. "Nevada's Hidden Ocean of Radiation." *Los Angeles Times,* November 13, 2009. http://articles.latimes.com/2009/nov/13/nation/na-radiation-nevada13.

Viñas, Maria-Jose. "Antarctic Ice Shelf Sheds Massive Iceberg." *Earth Observatory,* July 13, 2017. https://earthobservatory.nasa.gov/IOTD/view.php?id=90557.

Von Moltke, Johannes. *The Curious Humanist: Siegfried Kracauer in America.* Berkeley: University of California Press, 2016.

Walker, Gabrielle. *Antarctica: An Intimate Portrait of a Mysterious Continent.* New York: Houston Mifflin Harcourt, 2013.

Wang, Eugene. "Aftershock: Eugene Wang on the Recent Work of Liu Xiaodong." *Artforum International* 50, no. 6 (February 2012): 204–211.

Waters, Colin N., Jan Zalasiewicz, Colin Summerhayes, Anthony D. Barnosky, Clément Poirier, Agnieszka Galuszka, Alejandro Cearreta, Matt Edgeworth, Erle C. Ellis, Michael Ellis, Catherine Jeandel, Reinhold Leinfelder, J.R. McNeill, Daniel De Richter, Will Steffen, James Syvitski, Davor Vidas, Michael Wagreich, Mark Williams, An Zhisheng, Jacques Grinevald, Eric Odada, Naomi Oreskes, Alexander P. Wolfe. "The Anthropocene Is Functionally and Stratigraphically Distinct from the Holocene." *Science* 351, no. 6269 (February 8, 2016): 1–10.

Weisman, Alan. *The World without Us.* New York: St. Martin's Press, 2007.

"Welcome to the Anthropocene." *The Economist,* May 26, 2011. http://www.economist.com/node/18744401.

"What the World Would Look Like if All the Ice Melted." *National Geographic Magazine,* September 2013. https://www.nationalgeographic.com/magazine/2013/09/rising-seas-ice-melt-new-shoreline-maps/.

Wilson, Eric G. *The Spiritual History of Ice: Romanticism, Science and the Imagination.* New York: Palgrave MacMillan, 2003.

"Windstorm Filmed in Keaton Comedy." In *Steamboat Bill, Jr.* press book (1928). In *Cinema Press Books from the Original Studio Collection.* Woodbury, CT: Research Publications, 1988. Microform, Wisconsin Center for Film and Theater Research, part two, section B, reel 35.

Wines, Michael. "Landslide Risk at Reservoir Cited in China." *New York Times,* April 18, 2012. http://www.nytimes.com/2012/04/19/world/asia/landslide-peril-near-chinese-reservoir-grows-official-says.html?_r=0.

Wohlfarth, Irving. "No-Man's-Land: On Walter Benjamin's 'Destructive Character.'" *Diacritics* 8, no. 2 (Summer 1978): 47–65.

Wolfe, Charles. "California Slapstick Revisited." In *Slapstick Comedy,* edited by Tom Paulus and Rob King, 169–189. London and New York: Routledge for the AFI Film Readers Series, 2010.

———. "Western Unsettlement: Transcontinental Journey, Comic Plotting and Keaton's *Go West*." *New Review of Film and Television Studies* 5, no. 1 (December 2007): 299–315.

Worringer, Wilhelm. *Abstraction and Empathy*. Translated by Michael Bullock. Chicago: Elephant, [1908] 1997.

Wrathall, Mark A. *Heidegger and Unconcealment: Truth, Language and History*. Cambridge: Cambridge University Press, 2011.

Yardley, Jim. "Chinese Dam Projects Criticized for the Human Costs." *New York Times*, November 19, 2007. http://www.nytimes.com/2007/11/19/world/asia/19dam.html?fta=y&_r=0.

Yeufang, Duan, and Shawn Steil. "China Three Gorges Project Resettlement: Policy, Planning and Implementation." *Journal of Refugee Studies* 16, no. 4 (2003): 422–443.

Zalasiewicz, Jan, Colin Waters, and Martin J. Head. "Anthropocene: Its Stratigraphic Basis." *Nature* 541 (January 19, 2017): 289.

Zalasiewicz, Jan, Colin N. Waters, Mark Williams, Anthony D. Barnosky, Alejandro Cearreta, Paul Crutzen, Erle Ellis, Michael A. Ellis, Ian J. Fairchild, Jacques Grinevald, Peter K. Haff, Irka Hajdas, Reinhold Leinfelder, John McNeill, Eric O. Odada, Clément Poirier, Daniel Richter, Will Steffen, Colin Summerhayes, James P.M. Syvitski, Davor Vidas, Michael Wagreich, Scott L. Wing, Alexander P. Wolfe, An Zhisheng, Naomi Oreskes. "When Did the Anthropocene Begin? A Mid-Twentieth Century Boundary Level Is Stratigraphically Optimal." *Quaternary International* 383 (2015): 196–203.

Zarlengo, Kristina. "Civil Threat, the Suburban Citadel, and Atomic Age American Woman." *Signs* 24, no. 4 (Summer 1999): 933–936.

Zhen, Zhang. "Bearing Witness: Chinese Urban Cinema in the Era of 'Transformation.'" In *The Urban Generation: Chinese Cinema and Society at the Turn of the Twenty-First Century*, edited by Zhang Zhen, 1–45. Durham, NC: Duke University Press, 2007.

Zielinski, Siegfried. *Deep Time of the Media: Toward and Archeology of Hearing and Seeing by Technical Means*. Cambridge, MA: MIT University Press, [2002] 2008.

INDEX

Abbas, Ackbar, 146, 158, 222n60
abstract art, as distillation of external world, 195–196
Abstraction and Empathy (Worringer), 195–196
acting, film vs. stage, 83–84
actuarial subjectivity, as mental ecology of film noir, 117–121; insurance narratives, 117–120; and pessimism, 119–120
Adorno, Theodor, 108–109
aesthetics; and apocalypticism, 198; catastrophic aesthetic of Buster Keaton, 25; of natural world, 3; and on-location filmmaking, 7–8; simulationist aesthetics and early filmmaking, 6–7
Alaska, Ogotoruk Creek nuclear waste site, 95–96
Aldrich, Robert, 100–101
alienation; cinematic portrayals of, 15; in work of Buster Keaton, 55, 56–58
aliens, appearance of in *Still Life*, 138–139, 139f
ambition, in film noir, 125–126
Amundsen, Roald, 164, 183
analog media, in Anthropocene era, 18, 155–156, 159
Anderson, Thom, 101
Angell, Callie, 84
Antarctica; aesthetics of filming, 18, 19–20; Antarctic Treaty of 1959, 199, 227n146; in Anthropocene era, 199–200; and awareness of natural history, 175–176; climate and isolation of, 162–166, 185–186, 227n144; depiction of void, 165–166; effects of climate change, 199–200, 226–227n113; as exception to globalization, 181–182; exploitation of natural resources, 183–184, 189, 191; and extraterritoriality, 199–200; filmmaking in, 163–164, 167–168; first cinematic representations of, 182–184, 191; flash photo of *The Endurance* in winter, 164f; McMurdo Station, 162; as modernist landscape, 193; photo from plane, 165f; place names in, 166; response to environmental changes in, 166–167; romantic fascination with, 193; *South: Ernest Shackleton and Endurance Expedition*, 183, 188–191, 188f, 190f, 192f; *90° South: With Scott to the Antarctic*, 183, 184–187, 185f, 186f, 192f; tragedy and cinema in, 187–188
Antarctica: A Biography, 191
Anthropocene era; affinity with cinema, 4–5; Antarctica in, 199–200; archives in, 205–206; article in *The Economist* announcing, 129–131; beginnings in nuclear age, 63–64, 68, 81, 211n63; beginnings in 1950s, 10–11; definition of, 2; hospitality in, 12–15, 15–20, 130–131, 201–202; introduction to cinema in, 15–20; as "no analog" world, 154, 155f; and on-location filmmaking, 8–9; origins in end of

Anthropocene era (*cont.*)
    Enlightenment, 14, 209*n*5; origins of term, 209*n*3; and space travel, 9–10; and Three Gorges Dam, China, 132; unpredictability in, 19
Aravamudan, Srinivas, 19, 206
Arbuckle, Fatty, 45
archeology, and geological engineering, 147
archives, in Anthropocene era, 205–206
arctic, romantic fascination with, 193
Arendt, Hannah; anthropogenic environment, 4; earth/world distinction, 10–11; effects of atomic age, 90; *The Human Condition*, 9–10; totalitarianism and fictional worlds, 179
Arnheim, Rudolph, 194–195, 196
artificial world; early film sets, 5–7, 15–17; significance in film and environment, 5–12
artistry, and climatic weaponry, 41–42
Art of Worldly Wisdom (Weber), 176
Asphalt Jungle: The City under the City, 107–108, 108*f*, 109, 116
asynchronization, and comic sequences, 50
atmoterrorism; introduction of, 40–45; as localized phenomenon, 44
Atomic Bomb (Warhol), 72–73
Atomic Energy Commission; and medical ethics, 216*n*42; *Operation Upshot-Knothole*, 70; *Plowshare*, 91; Project Plowshare, 17–18, 63–64, 217–218*n*72; recognition of radiation hazard, 217*n*53; Tumbler-Snapper tests, 68
Atomic Tests in Nevada, 80–81
"Außer diesem Stern," Bertolt Brecht, 1–2
automatism, and comic sequences, 52–53

Bachelard, Gaston, 161
Barthelmess, Richard, 30–31
Barthes, Roland, 156
Bazin, André, 154, 171, 172, 187, 226*n*100
Beichuan, China, 140–141
Biesen, Sheri Chinen, 107

Benjamin, Walter; cinema's polytechnic training, 66; film *vs.* stage acting, 83–84; nature and natural history, 173; reality and art, 95; "The Destructive Character," 89; "tiny, fragile human body," 79–80
Bennet, Joan, 123
Berger, John, 135
Bergman, Ingrid, 49
Berlant, Lauren, 56
Bernau, Bradley, 166
Bickford, Charles, 114
Bilton, Alan, 26
Bitzer, Billy, 31, 212*n*30
Black Square, 41–42
Boat, The, 26, 56–57, 57*f*
Bonami, Francesco, 72
Bond, Rudy, 117
Borde, Raymond, 110, 111
Bordeleau, 222*n*52
Boym, Svetlana, 153, 159, 223*n*92
Brecht, Bertolt, 1–2, 147, 222*n*58
Brute Force, 114–115
Bryson, Norman, 142–143
Buchanan, Ann, 84, 85*f*
Buck-Morss, Susan, 79–80
Bullot, Eric, 25
Bunker Hill neighborhood of Los Angeles, as setting for film noir, 101–102, 102–103, 103*f*, 218*n*14
Byrd, Richard E., 164–165
Byrnes, Corey, 145

Caillois, Roger, 187
Camper, Fred, 189
Carroll, Noël, 50, 52, 213*n*41
Caruso, Anthony, 107
Caruth, Cathy, 67
cash, portrayal of in film noir, 116–117
Castoriadis, Cornelius, 116
catastrophic aesthetic of Buster Keaton, 25
Cavell, Stanley, 156, 157–158, 201
celluloid, end of era, 18
Chakrabarty, Dipesh, 209*n*4
Chaplin, Charles, 47–48
Chaumenton, Etienne, 110, 111
Cheah, Pheng, 14, 139, 222*n*60
children, as motivation for change, 112, 113

Chinatown, 111–112, 219*n*44
Chinese sturgeon, endangered status of, 134
chlorine gas attacks, of World War I, 40–45
cinema; and abstractions of natural world, 169–170, 176–177, 178; after World War II, 170, 178–179; Antarctica, first representations of, 182–184, 191; Antarctica as landscape, 185–186, 193–194; in Anthropocene era, 4–5, 15–20; decline of formative tradition in, 194–195; eeriness of early cinema, 3–4; and extraterritoriality, 198–200; film acting *vs.* stage acting, 83–84; and filming in nuclear age, 17; films unearthed in Dawson City Film Find, 202–204; film theory of 1970s, 172; and ideal pursuit of history, 179–180; and passivity, 156–158; simulationist aesthetics and early filmmaking, 6–7; and tragedy, 187
cinematography, and Anthropocene era, 154, 155–161
cities; efforts to decentralize in nuclear age, 102; as portrayed in film noir, 99, 100–102
City of Fear, 125–126, 125f
Civil Defense films; *Atomic Tests in Nevada*, 80–81; *Duck and Cover*, 66–67; *House in the Middle*, 103–104, 104f, 105f; *Let's Face It*, 78; *Operation Cue*, 59–62, 88
climate; Buster Keaton's depiction of, 23–25, 24f, 25f; Buster Keaton's engineering of, 26; filming in natural weather, 16, 212*n*36; and film studio relocation, 28–29; manufactured in wartime, 40–45; as simulated on early film sets, 7, 15–17
climate change; and Anthropocene era, 2, 11, 14, 211*n*57, 211*n*65; article in *The Economist* on, 129–131; climate change disaster cinema, 218*n*5; climate change refugees, 15, 220–221*n*16; and disaster narratives, 97–98; displacement caused by, 220–221*n*16; effect on geo-politics, 11; effects in Antarctica, 166, 199–200, 226–227*n*113; geoengineering intended to address, 134; release of methane into atmosphere, 97; restoration following, 130
"Climate of History, The," (Chakrabarty), 209*n*4
climate science, militarization of, 27–28
Climate Trauma (Kaplan), 218*n*5
Clinton, William Jefferson, 216*n*40
Colebrook, Claire, 90–91
comedy; asynchronization and, 50; environmental comedy, 45–53; fortuitousness of slapstick comedy, 40; maladaptation and comic sequences, 52–53; slapstick comedy and cinematic world-making, 44–45; *vs.* "camp," 49, 214*n*83
commerce; importance to peace, 12–13; and origins of Anthropocene era, 14
Cook, James, 162–163, 181, 182
Cooper, Maxine, 106
cosmocracy, and ecology of film noir, 110
Cowie, Elizabeth, 123
Crutzen, Paul J., 11, 209*n*3
Cummins, Peggy, 112

Dali, Salvador, 41–42
Dall, John, 112
dams; construction of in China, 134–135; phenomenon of megadams, 133–134; *see also* Three Gorges Dam, China
Daudet, Alphonse, 53
Davis, Mike, 48
Davis, Tracy C., 78
Dawson City: Frozen Time, 202–204, 205–206
Dawson City Film Find, 202–204
Day, David, 191, 199
Deadpan, 57–58
death drive, as portrayed in film noir, 123–124
Decasia, 204
Delpeut, Peter, 226*n*103
Derrida, Jacques; essay on nuclear criticism, 67; planetary hospitality, 130; practice of archiving, 205; public law of the state *vs.* privacy of the home, 220*n*2
Desert Rock program, 216*n*37

Index [245]

"Destructive Character, The" (Benjamin), 89
Detour, 121–122
Dienstag, Joshua Foa, 115, 120, 122, 124, 125
digital cinematography, and Anthropocene era, 154, 155–161
Dillard, Annie, 165
Dimendberg, Edward, 100, 218n12
disaster narratives, and preparation for climate change, 97–98
"Disaster" series, Andy Warhol, 72
displacement; caused by dam construction, 133–136, 138–139, 139f; depicted in *Still Life,* 135–136; and nostalgia, 153
Docherty, Thomas, 109
dolphin, Yangtze river, 134
Dong, 139
Double Indemnity, 118, 119, 120, 122
drama, "failed seriousness" in, 49
Drygalski, Erich von, 175
Duck and Cover, 66–67
Dunaway, Faye, 111
Duve, Thierry de, 72, 73

Earth; atomic age, impact of, 89–90; atomic age, potential destructiveness of, 63–64; earth/world distinction, 10–11; effects of human habitation on, 2–3
earthquake, Sichuan, China, 2008, 140–141
ecology; and ecocriticism, 198; ecologies of war, 40–45
Economist, The, article on climate change, 129–131
Edelman, Lee, 99, 112
Edwards, Vince, 125–126, 125f
Endurance, The; final voyage of, 188–189, 188f; flash photography of, 164f; seen from a romantic distance, 192f
Engelke, Peter, 98
Enlightenment; Antarctica and political philosophy of, 181–182; and Anthropocene era, 14; and notions of hospitality, 12–14
environment; effects of industrialization in *Our Hospitality,* 54; and efforts to preserve Antarctica, 166–167; environmental homelessness, 56–58, 57f

environmental comedy, 45–53; of Buster Keaton, 28, 29–30
environmental design; of Buster Keaton, 34–38, 36f, 37f; in musicals, 38–40
environmental displacement; caused by dam construction, 135–136; depicted in *Still Life,* 18–19, 135–136; and nostalgia, 153
"Essay on the Imagination of Matter, An" (Bachelard), 161
estrangement, and photography, 170–172
eviction narratives; cinematic portrayals of, 15; environmental homelessness, 56–58, 57f; in *One Week,* 55; in *The Boat,* 56–57; in *Way Down East,* 30; *see also* homelessness
Exercise Desert Rock, 76–77, 78
Exiles, The, 218n14
extinction of species, in Yangtze river, 134
extraterritoriality, origins and implications of, 197–200
Extreme Ice Survey: South Georgia Island, 226–227n113

Faust (Murnau), 7
Favret, Mary, 43
Feil, Ken, 214n83
Feuer, Jane, 38–39
Film as Art (Arnheim), 194–195
filmmaking; aesthetics of on-location, 7–8; in Antarctica, 163–164, 167–168, 182–184, 191; introduction of soundstages, 29–30; migration of companies to Los Angeles, 28–29; worldliness of, 5–12
film noir; characteristics of genre, 98–99; characters and worldview of, 99; as extinction narrative, 99–100; human ambition in, 125–126; introduction of, 18; sequels to, 219n44; terror noir, 121–126
film noir, environmental ecology of, 100–110; *Asphalt Jungle: The City under the City,* 108f; property ownership, 110; temporary housing, 106–107, 108–109; urban landscape of, 99, 100–102, 102–103, 103f, 104

[246] *Index*

film noir, mental ecology of, 117–121; insurance narratives, 117–120; and pessimism, 119–120

film noir, social ecology of, 110–117; *Brute Force*, 114–115; cash, portrayal and use of, 116–117; children as motivation for change, 112, 113; *Chinatown*, 111–112; geological engineering, 111; *Gun Crazy*, 112–113, 113*f*; *The Killers*, 115–116; *Nightfall*, 117; and pessimism, 115; sense of malaise, 110–111; spatial dislocation and temporal confusion, 115–116

film noir, terror noir, 121–126; death drive in, 123–124; human ambition in, 125–126; passivity in, 122–123; pessimism of, 122, 124–125

films; and Dawson City Film Find, 202–204; film sets, artificial world and use of, 5–7, 15–17; film theory of 1970s, 172; preservation of, 204, 205–206

Flatley, Jonathan, 85

floods, as result of geological engineering, 26–27

Forbidden Quest, 226*n*103

Ford, John, 46–47

Foster, Hal, 72

Freud, Sigmund; aesthetics of natural world, 3; uncanniness, 209*n*8

Friedman, Robert Marc, 44

Friedrich, Caspar David, 191, 193

Galt, Rosalind, 226*n*103

Garfield, John, 118

General, The, 40

geological engineering; and archeology, 147; and atomic age, 17–18; in *Chinatown*, 111; and connection to natural disasters, 26–27; and hospitality in nuclear age, 91–95, 94*f*; intended to address climate change, 134

geo-military strategy, 43–44

geo-politics; climate change refugees, 15, 220–221*n*16; effect of climate change on, 11

Germany; chill of modernity in Weimar era, 176; interest in polar exploration, 175

Gish, Lillian, 30–31, 31*f*, 32*f*

Gleiberman, Owen, 219*n*44

globalization; Antarctica as exception to, 181–182; and model of global weather system, 43, 213*n*61

Goldwyn, Samuel, 47

Gone with the Wind, 212*n*36

Gorky, Maxim, 3–4

Great Acceleration; defined, 11; and Enlightenment, 14; and nuclearism, 63; and sustainability of natural world, 114

Great Leap Forward, China, 134–135

Great Mississippi Flood of 1927, 26–27

Green, Bill, 165*f*

Greenpeace, founding of, 96

Griffith, D. W.; filming in natural weather, 16, 212*n*30; and Hollywood norms, 28–34, 31*f*; *Way Down East*, 32*f*, 212*n*30; weather and *Orphans of the Storm*, 33–34, 43

Gualtieri, Elena, 197

Guattari, Félix, 99

Guermantes Way, The (Proust), 170–171

Gun Crazy, 112–113, 113*f*

Gusterson, Hugh, 73–74

Hagen, Jean, 108

Hales, Peter Bacon, 62–63

Haller, Albert von, 153

Hansen, Miriam; on critical reaction to Kracauer, 194–195; reflexive ecology, 38; on Siegfried Kracauer, 8, 168, 172, 213*n*40; "vernacular modernism," 203; on Walter Benjamin, 84

Hanssen, Beatrice, 173

Hayden, Sterling, 107

Hayot, Eric, 8, 167

Healy, Joel, 83, 217*n*56

Heidegger, Martin, 41, 43

Hersey, John, 67, 215*n*18

Hiroshima, Japan, nuclear attack on, 67, 69, 72, 102

Hiroshima (Hersey), 215*n*18

history, ideal pursuit of, 179–181

History: The Last Things before the Last (Kracauer), 179–180

Hitchcock, Alfred, 49

Holden, William, 124

"Hollywood Sets Would Fool Mother Nature" (Hopper), 29

Hollywood's Top Secret Film Studio, 215n9
Holocene era; article in *The Economist* announcing end of, 129–131; climate change and end of, 14
homelessness; environmental homelessness, 56–58; and shelter in film studios, 210n27; *see also* eviction narratives
Hopper, Hedda, 29
hospitality; in Anthropocene era, 12–15, 15–20, 201–202; in Buster Keaton's work, 53–55; of deconstructed cities, 150–151, 151f; Enlightenment notions of, 12–14; and film noir, 18; and geological engineering, 19; inhospitality of weather, 28, 53–55; of nuclear age, 91–96; planetary hospitality and climate change, 129–131
House in the Middle, 103–104, 104f, 105f
Huang Tso-ling, 222n58
Human Condition, The (Arendt), 9–10
human enterprise, and connection to natural disasters, 26–27
humanity, effects of human habitation on Earth, 2–3
Hurley, Frank, 164f, 188–189, 191
Hurricane, The, 46–47
Huston, John, 107–108, 108f

immobility, aesthetics of, 221n37
incest, crime of in *Chinatown,* 111
Incredible Shrinking Man, The, 86–89, 88f
Industrial Dispersion Policy, 102
industrialization, in *Our Hospitality,* 54
inhumanism, of atomic age, 83–91, 85f, 88f
insurance narratives, in film noir, 117–120

Jacobson, Brian R., 29
Jaffe, Sam, 109
Jia Zhangke; and digital cinematography, 154, 158–159; *Dong,* 139–140; and environmental displacement, 18–19; realism of, 221n37; *Still Life,* 130–131, 131–139, 143–144, 145–146

Kael, Pauline, 194
Kai Xian, China, 151–152, 153, 160

Kant, Immanuel, 12–14, 54–55
Kaplan, E. Ann, 218n5
Keaton, Buster; autobiographical elements in work, 28; character transformation, 211n2; comedy of technology in, 214n94; depiction of weather and climate, 23–24, 25f; engineering of climate in, 26; environmental comedy of, 42–43, 45–46, 47; environmental design of, 29–30, 34–38; homelessness in *The Boat,* 56–57, 57f; and hospitality, 53–55; and melodrama, 214n103; *One Week,* 55; "perfect contingencies" in, 40; *The Playhouse,* 210–213n37; studio sets, 16, 17; tutoring of perception, 213n41; use of localized weather, 44–45
Keith, Brian, 117
Kelly, Gene, 39–40
Keystone Studios, 45
Killers, The, 115–116, 123
King, Rob, 44–45
Kiss Me Deadly, 100–102, 102–103, 103f, 104, 106f
Koerner, Joseph Leo, 193
Kostenbaum, Wayne, 72
Kracauer, Siegfried; appeal to nature and natural world, 173, 176–177, 181; cinema after World War II, 179; cinema and tragedy, 187; Cold War humanist discourse, 225n73; on estranging effects of photography, 171–172, 174–175; and extraterritoriality, 197–200; fortuitousness of slapstick comedy, 40; *History: The Last Things before the Last,* 179–180; ideology and closed narrative systems, 224n38; model of filmmaking and spectatorship, 167–168; "Photography," 173–175; photography, mechanical representation of, 176; postapocalyptic film, 19; simulationist aesthetics of early film sets, 5–6, 7, 8; terror noir, 121; *Theory of Film: The Redemption of Physical Reality,* 168–170, 172–173, 177–178, 179, 194–200; theory of film and theory of history, 20
Kuletz, Valerie L., 92–93

Lancaster, Burt, 114, 116
landscape; Antarctica as modernist landscape, 193; radioactive contaminants, 93, 95–96; remaking of in nuclear age, 92–95, 94f; and survival in *Our Hospitality*, 53–54; urban landscape of film noir, 99, 100–103, 103f, 104, 106–107, 108f
Lang, Fritz, 7, 123–124
Lapp, Ralph, 102
Laszlo, Ernest, 101
Latour, Bruno, 209n5
Lazier, Benjamin, 9
Lethen, Helmut, 175–176
Let's Face It, 78
Levin, Thomas Y., 66, 174–175
Libby, Willard F., 217n53
Liu Xiaodong; and ecology of Three Gorges Dam, 131, 140; paintings by, 18, 19; realism of, 221n37, 222n52; as subject of Jia's *Dong*, 139
Li Zhubing, 136
Lookout Mountain Studios, 64–65, 215n9
Los Angeles, California; Bunker Hill neighborhood as setting for film noir, 101–102, 102–103, 103f, 218n14
Los Angeles Plays Itself, 101
"lounge time," chronotope, 107
Lu, Sheldon H., 147

maladaptation, and comic sequences, 52–53
malaise, sense of in film noir, 110–111
Malevich, Kazimir, 41–42, 193
Ma Lizhen, 148
Maltese Falcon, 122–123
Mao Zedong, 134–135
Masco, Joseph, 64, 86
McKenzie, Scott, 218n14
McKibben, Bill, 2–3
McMurdo Station, Antarctica, 162
McNeill, John R., 11, 98
McQueen, Steve, 57–58
Meeker, Ralph, 101
megadams; phenomenon of, 133–134; and planetary dislocation, 138–139, 139f
meteorology, as martial science, 43–44
Metropolis, 7

microclimates, on early film sets, 7, 15–17
military; militarization of weather, 43–44; uses of climate science, 27–28
Military Participation on Tumbler-Snapper, 68–70, 70f, 71–72, 74–75, 75f, 76–78, 76f, 77f
Miller, Tyrus, 45–46
Moltke, Johannes von, 177, 178–179, 225n73
Morrison, Bill, 202, 203, 204
Morton, Timothy, 198
Mülder-Bach, Inka, 179
Mulvey, Laura, 49
Murder, My Sweet, 123
Murphy, David Thomas, 175
musicals, use of found environments in, 38–39
mutation, and inhumanism of atomic age, 85–89

Nadel, Alan, 215n18
Nagasaki, Japan, nuclear attack on, 69, 102
Naremore, James, 48–49
narratives; and destruction in Buster Keaton, 25; disaster narratives and climate change, 97–98; film noir as extinction narrative, 99–100; insurance narratives in film noir, 117–120
Native American populations, relocation to urban centers, 101–102, 218n14
natural disasters; human enterprise as cause, 26–27; violence of, 27
natural history; defining, 173; and fascination with Antarctica, 175–176; and postapocalyptic theory of film and history, 180–181
natural resources, of Antarctica, 183–184, 189, 191
nature and natural world; aesthetics of, 3–4; cinema and abstractions of, 169–170; and ecocriticism, 198; filmmaker as explorer, 177–178; natural forces, unpredictability of, 50–53, 51f; outside of human world, 168; photography and presentation of, 183; and work of Siegfried Kracauer, 173, 181

Navigator, The, 42–43
Nevada Atomic Testing Site; cinematic records of atomic testing, 68; films produced at, 63; materials contaminating, 93; and nuclear unpredictability, 81; number of devices exploded, 215n10; as outdoor laboratory and film studio, 17
Nicholson, Jack, 111
Nightfall, 117
Nixon, Rob, 133, 135
nostalgia, and environmental displacement, 153
nuclear age; and Anthropocene era, 17, 64, 68, 81, 211n63; arts of training and testing, 71–81; atomic inhumanism, 83–91; cinematic record of, 63–64, 66–71, 70f, 71f, 74–77, 75f, 77f; contamination of landscape, 93, 101; efforts to decentralize cities, 102; hospitality of, 91–96; Lookout Mountain Studios, 64–65; nuclear unpredictability, 81–83; *Operation Cue*, 59–63, 60f, 62f; Operation Plowshare, 17–18, 91–95, 94f, 217–218n72; presence in everyday life, 66–71; Project Plowshare, 17–18, 63–64, 217–218n72; radiation hazards, medical recognition of, 82, 95, 216n43, 217n64; radiation hazards, psychological preparation for, 77–78, 216n38, 217n53; Survival City, Nevada, 59–63, 60f, 62f; Tumbler-Snapper test, 68–70, 70f
nuclear age, arts of training and testing, 71–81; *Atomic Tests in Nevada*, 80–81; *Exercise Desert Rock*, 76–77; *How to Survive a Nuclear War*, 75; *Military Participation on Tumbler-Snapper*, 68–70, 71–72, 74–75, 75f, 76–78, 76f, 77f; nuclear war, psychological anesthetics for, 78–81, 103–104, 104f, 105f, 216n38, 217n53; *Operation Upshot-Knothole*, 70–71, 71f, 78; radiation hazards, psychological preparation for, 77–78, 216n38, 217n53; Warhol, Andy, 72–73
Nugent, Frank, 47
Nuremberg Code, for medical experimentation, 77–78

Ogotoruk Creek, Alaska, nuclear waste site, 95–96
Oliver, Kelly, 10
One Week, 26, 55
Operation Cue, 59–63, 60f, 62f
Operation Plumbbob: Military Effects Studies, 82–83
Operation Plumbbob, nuclear tests, 81–82, 83
Operation Tumbler-Snapper, 216n37
Operation Upshot-Knothole, 70–71, 71f, 78
Orphans of the Storm, 33–34, 43
Our Hospitality, 26, 53–55
Out of Beichuan, 141–142, 141f
Out of the Past, 112

painting; Antarctica as modernist landscape, 193; Beichuan, China, 141f, 142; decline of formative tradition in, 194–195; scenes of Three Gorges Dam, China, 140–141; still life, characteristics of, 144–146; still life, history of, 142–143
Parson, Don, 102
passivity; and cinema, 156–158; in film noir, 122–123
peace, importance of commerce and trade to, 12–13
Peck, Gregory, 49
Perez, Gilberto, 55
"Perpetual Peace" (Kant), 12–14, 54–55
pessimism, of film noir, 115, 119–120, 122, 124–125
photography; and analog *vs.* digital arts, 155–156; Antarctica as landscape, 193–194; decline of formative tradition in, 194–195; estranging effects of, 170–172, 174–175; and extraterritoriality, 197–200; and ideal pursuit of history, 179–180; as mechanical representation of reality, 176; and presentations of natural world, 183; *Uprooted* series, 151–161, 152f, 160f
"Photography," (Kracauer), 173–174
Playhouse, The, 212–213n37
Plowshare, 17–18, 91–95, 94f, 217–218n72
Polan, Dana, 98

[250] Index

Polanski, Roman, 111
Pollack, Henry, 163
Ponting, Herbert G., 183, 184–185, 185–186, 187–188, 191
Postman Always Rings Twice, The, 118
present-tenseness, as social ecology of film noir, 110–117; *Brute Force,* 114–115; cash, portrayal and use of, 116–117; children as motivation for change, 112, 113; *Chinatown,* 111–112; geological engineering, 111; *Gun Crazy,* 112–113, 113f; *The Killers,* 115–116; *Nightfall,* 117; and pessimism, 115; sense of malaise, 110–111; spatial dislocation and temporal confusion, 115–116
preservation, and film archives, 204, 205–206
Project Gnome, 92
Project Plowshare, 17–18, 63–64, 217–218n72
Proust, Marcel, 170–171
Pyne, Stephen J., 163, 165–166, 193

radiation hazards, psychological preparation for, 77–78, 216n38, 217n53
Redgrave, Michael, 123
reflexive ecology, in work of Buster Keaton, 38
refugees; climate change refugees, 15, 220–221n16; developmental refugees, 135–136
"Refuge for the Homeless," (Adorno), 108–109
Reynolds, Debbie, 39–40
Richter, Gerhard, 168, 197
Rodgers, Gaby, 104
Rodowick, D. N., 155–156, 158
Romanticism, and polar regions, 193
Ronnell, Avital, 73
Roosevelt, Theodore, 113–114
Rucker, Joseph, 164

Saint-Amour, Paul K., 67
Salazar, Kelli Healy, 217n56
Sanming Han, 131
Santner, Eric L., 173
Sanxia Haoren; see *Still Life*
Saxon, Lyle, 27
Schickel, Richard, 212n30

Schlüpmann, Heidi, 169
Schopenhauer, Arthur, 122
Scott, Robert F., 164, 183, 185–186, 187–188, 226n100
Scott of the Antarctic, 226n100
Scranton, Roy, 18, 97
Scudder, Thayer, 135
Secret beyond the Door, 123–124
Sedan, nuclear cratering test, 92, 94, 95
Sedgwick, Edie, 86f
Serres, Michel, 110
Seven Chances, 26, 50–53, 51f
Shackleton, Ernest, 188–189
Sherlock Jr., 52
Shiel, Mark, 212n23
Shklovsky, Victor, 6–7
Shoulder Arms, 47–48
Sichuan province, China, 2008 earthquake, 140–141
simulationist aesthetic, and early filmmaking, 6–7
Singin' in the Rain, 39–40
Siodmak, 115–116
Siskind, Mariano, 181–182
slapstick comedy; and cinematic world-making, 44–45; fortuitousness of, 40
Sloterdijk, Peter, 27–28, 40–45
Sobchack, Vivian, 99, 106, 107, 114
Solnit, Rebecca, 66
Sontag, Susan, 49
soundstages, introduction of, 29–30
South: Ernest Shackleton and Endurance Expedition, 164f, 183, 188–191, 188f, 190f, 192f
90° South: With Scott to the Antarctic, 183, 184–187, 185f, 186f, 192f
space travel, and man-made worlds, 9–10
Spellbound, 49
Spillane, Mickey, 100–101
St. George, Utah, as witness to atomic testing, 80–81
Steamboat Bill, Jr.; autobiographical elements in, 28; comic weather, 50; depiction of climate and weather in, 23–24f, 25f; engineering of cyclone in, 26; as environmental comedy, 45–46; and environmental design, 16–17, 34–38, 36f, 37f; local weather in, 44–45; precariousness and restaging in *Deadpan,* 57–58

Index [251]

Steffen, Will, 11, 14
Steimatsky, Noa, 210n27
Stevens, Molly, 25
Still Life; and deconstruction of city, 148–150, 149f; digital cinematography of, 154; and ecology of Three Gorges Dam, 130–131; and environmental displacement, 18–19, 135–136; and hospitality amid deconstruction, 150–151, 151f; and plot of Bertolt Brecht play, 147; production and composition of, 131–139, 132f, 137f, 139–140, 139f; and still life scenes, 143–146, 144f, 145f, 146–147, 155f
still life painting; characteristics of, 144–146; history of, 142–143
Stoermer, Eugene, 209n3
storms, attunement to human emotions, 33–34
Stuart, Randy, 88f
sturgeon, in Yangtze river, 134
Sturken, Martia, 50
Sunset Boulevard, 124
Survival City, Nevada, 59–63, 60f, 62f, 80–81
Szalay, Michael, 118, 119

Tartarin Sur Les Alpes, 53
Teller, Edward, 91, 92, 93, 95
tenancy, as environmental ecology of film noir, 100–110, 108f; property ownership, 110; temporary housing, 106–107, 108–109; urban landscape, 99, 100–102, 102–103, 103f, 104
territory, and extraterritoriality, 197
terror noir, 121–126; death drive in, 123–124; human ambition in, 125–126; passivity in, 122–123
Theory of Film: The Redemption of Physical Reality (Kracauer); antireferential treatment of nature, 168–170; and becoming extraterrestrial, 194–200; cinema after World War II, 179; filmmaker as explorer, 177–178; redemption through alienation, 172–173
Three Gorges Dam, China; and accompanying deconstruction, 132–134, 148–150, 149f; art and ecology of, 130–131; effects of geological engineering, 220n11, 220n12; effects on environment, 18–19; as megadam, 133–134; and photographic record of Kai Xian village, 151–161; scenes painted, 140–141; *Still Life* film depicting effects of, 131–139, 132f
Three Gorges Displaced Population, 140
tornadoes, in American folklore, 48
totalitarianism, and fictional worlds, 179
Tourneur, Jacques, 117
Towne, Robert, 111
trade, and origins of Anthropocene era, 14
tragedy, and cinema, 187
Trahair, Lisa, 40, 211n2, 214n94
Trotter, David, 196–197
Truman, Harry S., 102
Tumbler-Snapper nuclear test, 68–70, 70f; see also Military Participation on Tumbler-Snapper
Turner, Lana, 118
Twister, 214n83
Two Jakes, The, 219n44

unconcealment, Heidegger's notion of, 41, 43
Uprooted photography series, 151–161, 152f, 160f
urban landscape, of film noir; *Asphalt Jungle: The City under the City*, 108f, 109; Bunker Hill neighborhood of Los Angeles, 100–102; disappearing habitats, 99, 102–103; property ownership, 110; temporary housing, 106–107, 108–109; and untidy living, 103f, 104

von Moltke, Johannes, 177, 178–179, 225n73

Wagenknecht, Edward, 32
Wang, Eugene, 140, 141–142
Wang Hongwei, 147
war, manufactured climates in, 40–45
Warhol, Andy; "Disaster" series, 72–73; screen tests series, 65–66, 84–86, 85f, 86f

Way Down East; attunement of weather to human emotions, 33–34; ice floe sequence in, 31*f*, 212*n*26; Mamaroneck blizzard, 32*f*; scenic realism of, 30–32
weaponry, climatic weaponry, 41–42
weather; attunement to human emotions, 33–34, 43; California megastorm of 1926, 48; comic weather, 50; and environmental comedy, 45–53; as force of divine justice, 46–47; and hospitality, 53–55; humorless *vs.* comedic, 48–49; inhospitality of, 28; melodramatic weather, 49; militarization of, 43; simulation of in *Steamboat Bill, Jr.*, 35–38, 36*f*, 37*f*; and survival in *Our Hospitality,* 53–54; use of localized, 44, 212*n*36
Weather Channel, success of, 50
Weber, Max, 176
Weisman, Alan, 143, 163
White on White, 193
Williams, Grant, 87, 88*f*

Wilson, Eric G., 193
Wines, Michael, 220*n*12
With Byrd at the South Pole: The Story of Little America, 164, 165*f*
Wohlfarth, Irving, 89
World War I, manufactured climates of, 40–45
World War II, cinema after, 170, 178–179
World Without Us, The, 143, 163
Woronov, Mary, 86*f*
Worringer, Wilhelm, 195–196

Yangtze River, effect of damming on native species, 134
Yang Yi, photography by, 18, 19, 131, 151–161, 152*f*, 160*f*
Yukon Valley, Dawson City Film Find in, 202–204

Zalasiewicz, Jan, 17, 64
Zhang Zhen, 137
Zhao Tao, 135
Zielinski, Siegfried, 159

Printed in the USA/Agawam, MA
December 13, 2018

692928.012